The Making of Teachers in the Age of Migration

Also Available from Bloomsbury

Migration Narratives, *Stanton Wortham, Briana Nichols, Katherine Clonan-Roy and Catherine Rhodes*
Teacher Agency, *Mark Priestley, Gert Biesta and Sarah Robinson*
Education, Migration and Development, *edited by Amy North and Elaine Chase*
Educating for Durable Solutions, *Christine Monaghan*
Borderless Higher Education for Refugees, *edited by Wenona Giles and Lorrie Miller*
Issues and Challenges of Immigration in Early Childhood in the USA, *Wilma Robles-Melendez and Wayne Driscoll*
The Promise and Practice of University Teacher Education, *Alexandra C. Gunn, Mary F. Hill, David A.G. Berg and Mavis Haigh*
Identities and Education, *edited by Eleftherios Klerides and Stephen Carney*
Internationalization of Higher Education for Development, *Susanne Ress*
Academics' International Teaching Journeys, *edited by Anesa Hosein, Namrata Rao, Chloe Shu-Hua Yeh and Ian M. Kinchin*

The Making of Teachers in the Age of Migration

Critical Perspectives on the Politics of Education for Refugees, Immigrants and Minorities

Edited by
Sabine Krause, Michelle Proyer
and Gertraud Kremsner

BLOOMSBURY ACADEMIC
LONDON • NEW YORK • OXFORD • NEW DELHI • SYDNEY

BLOOMSBURY ACADEMIC
Bloomsbury Publishing Plc
50 Bedford Square, London, WC1B 3DP, UK
1385 Broadway, New York, NY 10018, USA
29 Earlsfort Terrace, Dublin 2, Ireland

BLOOMSBURY, BLOOMSBURY ACADEMIC and the Diana logo are trademarks of
Bloomsbury Publishing Plc

First published in Great Britain 2023
This paperback edition published 2024

Copyright © Sabine Krause, Michelle Proyer and Gertraud Kremsner and contributors, 2023

Sabine Krause, Michelle Proyer and Gertraud Kremsner and contributors have asserted their right under the Copyright, Designs and Patents Act, 1988, to be identified as Author of this work.

For legal purposes the Acknowledgements on p. xiv constitute an extension of this copyright page.

Cover design: Grace Ridge
Cover image © Sellwell / Getty Images

Open Access was graciously co-funded by the Faculty of Educational Sciences and the Department of Education at the University of Innsbruck, Austria, the Institute of Pedagogy, Department of School Education/General Didactics at the University of Koblenz, Germany and beeflip.at.

This work is published open access subject to a Creative Commons Attribution-NonCommercial-NoDerivatives 4.0 International licence (CC BY-NC-ND 4.0, https://creativecommons.org/licenses/by-nc-nd/4.0/). You may re-use, distribute, and reproduce this work in any medium for non-commercial purposes, provided you give attribution to the copyright holder and the publisher and provide a link to the Creative Commons licence.

Bloomsbury Publishing Plc does not have any control over, or responsibility for, any third-party websites referred to or in this book. All internet addresses given in this book were correct at the time of going to press. The author and publisher regret any inconvenience caused if addresses have changed or sites have ceased to exist, but can accept no responsibility for any such changes.

A catalogue record for this book is available from the British Library.

A catalog record for this book is available from the Library of Congress.

ISBN: HB: 978-1-3502-4415-3
PB: 978-1-3502-4419-1
ePDF: 978-1-3502-4416-0
eBook: 978-1-3502-4417-7

Typeset by Deanta Global Publishing Services, Chennai, India

To find out more about our authors and books visit www.bloomsbury.com and sign up for our newsletters.

Contents

List of Tables	vii
List of Contributors	viii
Acknowledgements	xiv

Thinning the Thickets – an Introduction *Michelle Proyer, Sabine Krause and Gertraud Kremsner* 1

Part I Theoretical Approaches to the Making of a Teacher

1 On Being a Teacher: How to Respond to the Global Construction of Teachers and Their Teaching? *Gert Biesta* 15

2 Being Prepared for Diverse Classrooms: Boundaries of Professional Devices and the Dangers of Inclusive Teaching *Ayşe Yolcu* 32

3 Mobility and Education *Susanne Ress* 49

4 Shared (Hi)stories of (Invisible) Living in the In-Between?: Experiences of and Perspectives on Being, Becoming and Remaining a Teacher in Austria *Tina Obermayr and Marie-Claire Sowinetz* 67

Part II International Perspectives on (Local) Politics of Education

5 Pedagogy and Research Cooperations in the Neoliberal Politics of Speed: Reflections for Critical Pedagogical Professionalization in Migration Societies *Nadja Thoma* 85

6 Unravelling the Nuanced Experiences of Multilingual Internationally Educated Teachers in Bridging Programmes: A Focus on Language *Clea Schmidt, Henrike Terhart, Rory Mc Daid and Michelle Proyer* 102

7 Career Jumpers on Their Way to Teacher Professionalism – Challenges and Opportunities Based on Different Working Backgrounds *Miriam Voigt and Inka Engel* 119

8	The Colleague-Outsider Conundrum: The Case of Zimbabwean Migrant Teachers in South African Classrooms *Kudzayi Savious Tarisayi*	133
9	Heroic Teachers? Understanding the Choices and Strategies of Teachers in a Context in Flux *Ritesh Shah*	149

Part III Critical Reframing in an Age of Migration

10	Migrant Teachers Filling the Gap: Required but Not Revered *Sadhana Manik*	169
11	The Subtle Work of Whiteness in Canadian Teacher Education *Lilach Marom*	185
12	A Two-Tiered System of Teacher Preparation *Kerry Kretchmar*	203
13	Teacher Migration and Education in the (Post)colonial Context: Lessons from the Global South *Phillip D. Th. Knobloch*	220
14	Reframing the Teacher in an Age of Migration: Concluding Thoughts *Sabine Krause, Michelle Proyer and Gertraud Kremsner*	239

Index   253

Tables

0.1	Detailed Overview of the Book's Contributions	7
3.1	Conceptualizations of Mobility and Immobility	53
6.1	Overview Methodology of the Primary Research Studies as a Basis for the Transnational Secondary Study	107
14.1	Valued Citizens of the Twenty-First century	244

Contributors

Gert Biesta is Professor of Public Education at the Centre for Public Education and Pedagogy, Maynooth University, Ireland, and Professor of Educational Theory and Pedagogy at Moray House School of Education and Sport, University of Edinburgh, UK. His research focuses on philosophical perspectives on educational issues with a vast body of publications on schools/schooling, education, subjectivation, recent international developments in education and the nexus of education and democracy. He is – among others – co-editor of the *British Educational Research Journal* and co-editor of the book series *Theorizing Education* (with Stefano Oliverio). For further information, visit https://www.gertbiesta.com/.

Inka Engel is a postdoctoral researcher and works as a science manager in the transfer team at the University of Koblenz, Germany. She studied teaching and education and taught at various schools and universities. She completed her master's degree in school management and quality development in Kiel. She did her PhD in the field of teacher training at the University of Koblenz, Germany. She continues and works in the field of school research, transfer and currently focuses on holocaust communication.

Philip D. Th. Knobloch is a temporary academic councillor at the Institute for General and Vocational Education at the Technical University of Dortmund, Germany. He currently substitutes the professorship of general education with a focus on historical education research. His field of work includes General, Historical, Comparative and Intercultural Education. His research interests include decolonial, consumer aesthetic and global citizenship education.

Sabine Krause is Professor of General Education Science at the University of Innsbruck, Austria. In her research, she investigates philosophical questions of education and Bildung, pedagogical relationships and the relationship between theory and practice. Her publications include 'Doing participatory stories research: detoxing narratives' (together with Gertraud Kremsner, Michelle Proyer and Raphael Zahnd) and 'Doing theory entlang disziplinärer Grenzen:

Arbeiten mit Fotografien (Doing theory along disciplinary boundaries using photography)'. Sabine's recent research focuses on photography and visual narratives in education and educational borderlands.

Gertraud Kremsner is Professor for Heterogeneity and Inclusion at the University of Koblenz, Germany. Her main focus lies in analysing hegemonial structures in educational settings and originally takes off from dis/ability studies (in education) with particular focus on inclusive research (with persons with learning difficulties). Her work emanates from a broad interpretation of inclusion with constant consideration of intersections. Together with Michelle Proyer and Sabine Krause, she is involved in the program 'Educational Basics for Displaced Teachers' at the University of Vienna, Austria.

Kerry Kretchmar, PhD, is Associate Professor of Education at Carroll University in Waukesha, Wisconsin, United States. Her research examines the impact of market-based reforms on teacher preparation and teaching. Her work has been published in journals such as *Educational Policy*, *Urban Education*, *The Urban Review* and the *Journal of Education for Teaching*.

Sadhana Manik is Associate Professor in Geography in the School of Education at the University of KwaZulu-Natal (UKZN), South Africa. Her research interests include international teacher mobility and migration, student access, support and success in higher education and school geography. She has published extensively and served as an editor in her research niche areas. She is the coordinator of the Global South for SANORD's Teacher Education Project, a special interest group of the global universities network, SANORD. She is the project leader for two international higher education collaborations between UKZN, South Africa and Western Norway University of Applied Sciences (HVL), Norway. She was awarded 'excellence in teaching' by UKZN in 2018, featured in the 'top 30 most published researcher' list in the College of Humanities at UKZN in 2019 and took awards in 2021 for her international education collaborations and community engagement.

Lilach Marom is Assistant Professor at Simon Fraser University, British Columbia, Canada. Her research focuses on questions of diversity, equity and social justice in education and aims to highlight structural and institutional barriers to the diversification of education and the teaching profession. Lilach has worked as an educator in multiple locations and countries (Israel, the United

States and Canada) with culturally and racially diverse populations. Her research has appeared in publications such as *Review of Education, Pedagogy, and Cultural Studies* (2017), *Teaching and Teacher Education* (2019/2020), *Race Ethnicity and Education* (2019), *Critical Studies in Education* (2019) and *Globalisation, Societies and Education* (2021). Lilach's current project explores the experiences of international students in Canadian higher education.

Rory Mc Daid is Director of Research at the Marino Institute of Education, Dublin, Ireland. At the Marino Institute of Education he is the coordinator of the Migrant Teacher Project for Immigrant Internationally Educated Teachers. His research interests include teacher diversity, the education of refugee and asylum-seeking children, recognition of first languages in schools, qualitative research methodologies, minority ethnic and minority language parental involvement in schools and cultural mediation in schools.

Tina Obermayr was a research assistant in the Erasmus+ Project 'R/EQUAL – Requalification of (recently) immigrated and refugee teachers in Europe', University of Vienna, Centre for Teacher Education, Vienna, Austria. Currently, she is a university assistant/prae doc also at the University of Vienna, Centre for Teacher Education, Vienna, Austria. Her research mainly focuses on philosophical and theoretical issues around inclusive education; in detail, it connects the research areas of phenomenology and inclusive education. In her doctoral project, she does research on the topics of vulnerability and (chronic) pain.

Michelle Proyer is Associate Professor of Inclusive Education at the Centre for Teacher Education and Department of Education at the University of Vienna, Austria. Her research and teaching focuses on inclusive education in and out-of-school contexts, teacher education and instruction studies. Her research projects and publications aim at exploring the intersection of disability and other dimensions of diversity, such as culture and forced migration.

Susanne Ress is a postdoctoral researcher and Program Coordinator of the International Master of Educational Quality (IMPEQ) at the Chair of Foundations in Education at the Otto-Friedrich University of Bamberg, Germany. Her research brings together theories from critical development studies, comparative and international education, critical Black and ethnic studies, and post-foundational approaches to education, examining educational responses to global challenges from a majority world perspective. Her research on Africa-Brazil relations in higher education has been published in *Comparative Education Review* (2018), *Compare* (2020), and as monograph titled *Internationalization of Higher Education for Development: Blackness and Postcolonial Solidarity in Africa-Brazil Relations* (2019). Her current research focuses on teacher education, global learning, sustainability and decolonial and more-than-human perspectives in education.

Clea Schmidt is Professor of Curriculum, Teaching and Learning at the University of Manitoba, Canada. Her research interests include diversifying the teaching force in transnational settings, education in culturally and linguistically diverse contexts, intersectionality in education and critical qualitative research.

Ritesh Shah is Senior Lecturer of Comparative and International Education at the University of Auckland, New Zealand. Most of his research occurs in international settings where changes in political, economic or social regimes driven by crises and/or conflict have led to calls for significant reform to a nation's education system. In the past decade, Ritesh has conducted research and consultancy work in Latin America, Southeast Asia, Oceania and the Middle East. He has published on this work in a range of journals and books and also contributed to global policymaking of organizations such as the World Bank and USAID. Ritesh is currently leading a transnational research project on opportunities and challenges to better embed non-formal and informal education programmes into the national education systems of Jordan, Uganda, Nigeria, Lebanon and Pakistan.

Marie-Claire Sowinetz has been working for UNHCR, the UN Refugee Agency, in press and public information since 2012. One of her focus areas is education and youth work and the development of educational materials on flight and trauma. She studied journalism and communication studies as well as romance studies at the University of Vienna, Austria, and the Université Nice Sophia Antipolis, France.

Kudzayi Savious Tarisayi is Lecturer in the Department of Curriculum Studies at Stellenbosch University, South Africa. His research focuses on international teacher migration and contemporary issues in education. His work highlights the challenges faced by migrant teachers in Afrophobic spaces in South Africa.

Kudzayi has worked as an educator in Zimbabwe and South Africa. His research has appeared in publications such as *Education as Change* (2017/2019), *Alternation* (2018/2020), *COGENT* (2020) and *Journal of International Migration and Integration* (2021). Kudzayi's current project explores the experiences of Zimbabwean migrant teachers in South Africa.

Henrike Terhart is Researcher and Lecturer at the Department of Education and Social Sciences, University of Cologne, Germany. Academic head of the bridging programme 'LehrkräftePLUS' Cologne for internationally educated teachers, supported with financial means of the Ministry of Culture and Science of the German State of North Rhine-Westphalia. Research interests include education and migration, school development and teacher professionalisation in transnational perspective and methodologies of qualitative social research.

Nadja Thoma is a postdoctoral researcher in the Department of Education at the University of Vienna, Austria, and a senior researcher at the Institute of Applied Linguistics at EURAC Research, Bolzano/Bozen, Italy. Her research connects critical theories of education and sociolinguistics and focuses on education and teacher professionalization in the context of migration and social inequality. She works with methodologies and methods of interpretative social research, such as ethnography and biographical research. Currently, she is leading a project on multilingualism and language education in South Tyrolean kindergartens and a project on educational biographies of university students in Montenegro.

Miriam Voigt is a postdoctoral researcher and works as a science manager at the University of Koblenz, Germany. Prior to her current position, she worked at the Munich Chamber of Commerce and Industry and as a human resources manager in a company. She did her PhD at the University of Kassel, Germany, on the topic of school development research. Her current research focuses on methods of knowledge transfer, on teacher and intrapreneurship education and citizen science.

Ayşe Yolcu is a researcher at the Department of Mathematics and Science Education, Hacettepe University, Turkey. Her work mainly focuses on the examination of how human differences are historically and discursively configured in mathematics education and teacher education. She has been teaching mathematics education courses for prospective teachers at Hacettepe

University, Turkey, following the completion of her PhD at University of Wisconsin-Madison, United States. Her research has appeared in publications such as *Teachers and Teaching* (2021) and *ZDM-Mathematics Education* (2019). Yolcu's current project explores the formation of citizens and their differentiations in mathematics education reforms.

Acknowledgements

This volume began with an invitation from Bloomsbury to edit a book on current issues and trends in international perspectives on inclusive education. Against the background of our research in the field of culture and education, teacher education, inclusive education and especially as teachers in a certificate course for refugee teachers, the invitation from Bloomsbury was too tempting. We believe that teacher education needs to adapt to migratory movements in this time and age, just as it does no harm for schools to internationalize their teachers. Previous research has also shown that internationalization is often only driven in certain directions and that access to the school system varies greatly for international teachers.

It was thus clear that the emerging book would have to take up and elaborate on very different, globally distributed perspectives on internationally trained teachers. Perceptions of the teaching profession are too often a closely knit and immobile imagery that remains guided by nation states' traditional approaches to knowledge transfer. We advocate for innovative approaches to what makes a teacher in a global age, guided by ideas beyond national borders and perceptions and renouncing neoliberal ideals.

We would like to express our sincere thanks to all the contributors to this volume, who continued to believe in the project even during a pandemic and provided a wide range of contributions. These have sometimes diverged from the initial abstracts over the period of the book's creation but contribute more than ever to a necessary academic discourse.

Michael Rasell was a critical reader for introduction and conclusion – thank you a lot! Minella Kurtovic-Netto took on the mammoth task of formally checking the incoming manuscripts, pointing out ambiguities and preparing the contributions for the publisher. Lena Gleirscher prepared the book's index and organized all the little but time-consuming things coming up with publishing a book. Many thanks for this!

Finally, we would like to thank Mark Richardson, Evangeline Stanford and Anna Elliss from Bloomsbury, who patiently accompanied and supported the book from the first idea to the finished script. Last but not least, we would like to express our sincere gratitude to the reviewers who enabled a refinement of the initial idea of the book and helped shape its focus.

Thinning the Thickets – an Introduction

Michelle Proyer, Sabine Krause and Gertraud Kremsner

This edited volume stems from our interest in what seems to be a rather simple-sounding question: What makes a teacher? At first glance, the project to answer this general question with a book seems naive, especially since there are already many publications on teacher education. However, against the backdrop of increasing and diversified global migration movements, the question needs to be revisited concerning the observation that those moving are being received and treated increasingly differently, as we can currently observe with different treatment of displaced Ukrainians. Simultaneously, and as a result of migration processes, the pupil body is becoming more diverse, and there is also (unnoticed) potential for more diversity among teachers. These aspects imply that migration is the book's central topic, but Migratory Studies are not the main ones fuelling the interest of the book. Our main focus is rather the question of what challenges emerge when we look at teachers in times of migration?

In times of ever-growing social dynamics, professionals feel a constant need to reorientate, upgrade their skills or leave their profession due to migration or flight. With the contributions in this book, the authors aim to challenge hegemonically induced hindrances and barriers to the teacher profession at all school levels. The challenges addressed here lie in institutional and structural barriers that affect employment opportunities due to the prevalence of certain perceptions of teachers (their background, habitus, appearance) and their (pedagogical) ideas and work from an education studies perspective. Hence the book's blunt title, its assemblage of strong voices from different parts of the world and its high hopes to indicate direct links to possible adjustments – by understanding complex interrelations and seemingly paradoxical strategies of including non-trained nationals while excluding trained non-nationals. These mechanisms of inclusion and exclusion in times of migration seem outdated – but point to a task of schools that goes beyond the empowerment of individual learners: that is the task of educating citizens of the nation state. The underlying assumption here is that only nationally trained teachers, with desired habitus, presumed Indigenous or localized knowledge and competence at that, are up to this task of stabilizing the nation state. In this respect, education is always closely interwoven with political issues. In an 'age of migration', we argue, characterized by social and cultural movements across (national) boundaries with migration becoming a common ground, the question of clear belonging to a social or cultural group or even to a nation state has become secondary.

In the following, we recall the general tasks of teachers; we embed these tasks along with internationalization of the teaching profession; and we subsequently outline a current (un)making of the teacher that we face.

Assumptions about Teachers and Teaching

The basic idea of what makes a teacher can be traced through history and across all cultures: A teacher is not only a knowledgeable person, or a person in possession of knowledge. From a traditional perspective, what makes teachers so special is that they pass on knowledge to other people, usually younger ones, in an organized way. The aim is to give those who are not yet knowledgeable the opportunity to acquire the knowledge or competencies they need to live in the community. Teaching and learning are interactive activities that revolve around an object and take place in a specific situation. It is the teachers who, given the situation and the object, strive to make the objective teachable and learnable. Against the background of their own knowledge and experiences within society, they encourage learners to acquire knowledge and skills that help them to become part of society and thus take part in joint activities (Schleiermacher 2000). Teachers, like all educators, assume responsibility for the world and the pupils through their ordering of knowledge and selection of teaching materials. As Hannah Arendt put it: 'educators here stand in relation to the young as representatives of a world for which they must assume responsibility although they themselves did not make it . . . Vis-a-vis the child it is as though [the teacher] were a representative of all adult inhabitants, pointing out the details and saying to the child: This is our world' (Arendt [1961] 2006: 189). It is a challenge to grasp the world as such and to make it accessible to others: 'This is a world characterized by rapid change, radical uncertainty and sometimes rabid competition, but it is also one that can be secured by ties of family, love, identity and belonging' (Friesen 2017: 7).

If we are lucky, teachers will step away from what Freire (1973) called the 'banking model of education', which works by 'filling' pupils' heads with knowledge, and which seems increasingly common again, with talk of competencies trumping all other qualities. Freire advocated for teachers to keep an open mind about the issues raised in situated learning processes, to focus on the co-creation of knowledge and to view themselves not only as teachers but also as learners, who learn from their (diverse) pupils. However, educational considerations now begin where teaching and learning for an unknown and uncertain future need the creation of formalized teaching/learning settings that help to unravel complexities and prepare for possible futures. This is particularly the case in highly specialized and diverse societies, including migration societies. The brief reminder of the fundamental relationship between teacher, learner and subject raises some essential questions in diverse societies: Who is selected and judged as knowledgeable, knowledgeable in the correct contexts or – more precisely – as teachers? Who are the learners who acquire knowledge? What knowledge is worth passing on?

Concerning the fundamental relation between teacher, learner and subject, what is most challenging for teachers is diversity and rapid change, even if this can be said to be part of 'life itself'. Teachers must constantly adapt to new conditions of life and teaching and have ever-expanding knowledge and experience. With increasing societal and cultural diversity, what is to be taught and learned also becomes question-worthy. If we think of teachers as mediators between learners, subjects and fast-changing societal expectations, the work of teaching personnel must shift in times of changing diversity. To take up Hannah Arendt again: for which world do teachers take responsibility, for which world do they want to prepare? What is schooling for in these times, and which professional skills are needed? Moreover, finally, the question: what standards should students and teachers meet? What norms are imposed on them?

If we conceive the pedagogical in this way, even school can no longer be considered as a place for imparting the 'right' (localized) knowledge and specific competencies for action. The uncertainty makes teaching a profession that relies on self-reflection around the positioning that teachers find themselves in, rethinking the relation to diverse pupils (or colleagues at school or students in teacher education) and reimagining possible (unknown) futures. Sharon Todd (2012) makes visible the impossibility of knowing what will be right and useful in the future, thus placing the ethical negotiation of the future at the centre of education again. This brings us back to the question of what makes a teacher: Thus far, a teacher has limited but ever-expanding knowledge; they alone cannot determine the learner's knowledge but must involve the learner in a co-construction; the future is undetermined and cannot be predicted by policy papers, meaning that educational situativity must always be reflected in pedagogical action and responsible teaching for assumed developments in a given context.

With these considerations, we laid some fundamentals for the 'making of a teacher', primarily aimed at teachers' activities and performance even when the pedagogical situation in the classroom will only play a marginal role in this book. Rather, the book focuses on teachers themselves, their performed and expected interactions, the assumption and adoption of a desired habitus and the effects of external structural challenges and dynamics. Teachers thus find themselves caught between pedagogical, societal and political demands that contribute to a 'making of teachers' at different levels. In their contributions, the authors will nevertheless keep in mind that the relationship between teachers and learners and the tasks teachers undertake do not finally define who teachers are.

Internationalization of the Teaching Sphere

With major shifts in the education sector but close to no flexibility or innovation – at least not noteworthy or sustainable – in relation to educational policies, we are left with a striking and perplexing paradox: While teaching remains the formalized privilege of nationally trained professionals, most parts of the world have seen an increase in communities with learner diversity and migratory experiences and/or generational diverse memories. While internationalization is considered an asset and the advantage of diverse collaborative structures has been acknowledged or at least heard of, the teaching profession remains unimpressed, growing more hostile or complicated regarding non-locally trained professionals. Here, traditions continue to lead education/educational settings while their actuality is already called into question by everyday experience. Meanwhile, specific abilities, such as language competencies in prestigious languages at highly advanced levels (in the best case, native speakers), are desirable and might be exempted from strict regulations, for example, British or American teachers teaching English. Needs vary according to what a localized learning context deems worthy and necessary. It also touches upon localized competence schemes or internationalized tests, suggesting what counts as desirable.

This absurdity is further fuelled by an ever-growing lack of teaching professionals in some areas of the world (see, e.g. García and Weiss 2019 for recent trends in the United States). Measures are being taken to remedy the shortage, known for a long time. Strategies are manifold, with varying degrees of dystopian elements, with some researchers even suggesting exchanging teachers for artificially intelligent devices (Bosede et al. 2018). Also, the innovative potential in teacher education and/or recruiting measures seems variable or non-existent. Additionally, measures taken are often designed for the short term and focused on specific groups, for example, meeting a lack of male teachers or a lack of STEM teachers. This has led to another group becoming accepted among professionally trained teachers: lateral entrants. These are professionals in other (mostly technical) disciplines who lack educational training, knowledge, instructional experience and theoretical competence. Short-term programmes – so-called crash courses – enable them to serve as temporary solutions to the structural challenges of providing sufficient professionals. These fast tracks must not only be criticized for their 'quick and dirty' and therefore (overly) basic training but also because they produce 'second-rate teachers' who are likely to be employed in marginalized schools (e.g. in lower-income communities and/or communities of colour) which will only serve to reproduce marginality, as Kerry Kretchmar analyses in her chapter of this book.

Against this backdrop, the solution seems quite simple: teachers with a (forced) migration background could (and should?) be employed in the school systems of their destination countries because they did not leave their profession – nor, in most cases, their passion – behind. Nevertheless, they are denied entry into these school systems as recognized professional teachers until they meet further – and all too often unattainable – requirements. International findings point to a lack of acknowledgement and insuperable barriers to bridging these two seemingly compatible circumstances. Thus, while classrooms are becoming internationalized and learning and teaching issues are also being explored in international research settings, the group of teachers remains largely homogeneous, following notions of a desirable teaching body.

Local (national) traditions and styles of reasoning become apparent with the arrival of more teachers who have received training elsewhere (also referred to as 'internationally educated or trained teachers' – see our concluding thoughts in chapter 14). The denial of access to the school system and thus discrimination against these teachers open up discussions about the necessities of teacher education; necessary virtues for teachers and/or reasons for them being necessary; and the role that nationality, identity, race, gender and belonging play in this regard, and the reasons behind the denial of entry. The debates about who can access positions in the school system take place on different levels and with different objectives. They include policymakers, teacher educators, schools and school teachers, administrative personnel and – of course – the international teachers themselves. As styles of reasoning change with the rising internationalization of academia, researchers are becoming more aware of national traditions and limitations (Popkewitz, Wu and Martins 2015; Heidrich et al. 2021). However, the gap between academia and the school system seems to be wider than ever in the field of international professionals: a theory and practice gap deluxe.

(Un)making the Teacher in an Age of Migration

Now that we outlined the basic features of pedagogical processes and raised the question of who is predominantly employed as a teacher, it is now necessary to look at the excluded persons at the margins. We thus turn to the '(un)making of teachers in an age of migration'. We invited a number of prestigious researchers from different corners of the world to answer this book's initial question. Despite challenges of communication and availabilities due to the Covid-19 pandemic, we were overwhelmed with interest in our project and a will to contribute to this book.

The book's contributions fall into three groups: summarized under the title 'Theoretical Approaches to the Making of a Teacher', theoretical explorations of recurring themes such as the relationship between teachers and learners, mobility, diversity and arriving in a foreign school system. The second part of the book ('International Perspectives on (Local) Policies of Education') gathers contributions from different geographical areas and specific recurring themes and challenges throughout the book. Finally, the third part, titled 'Critical Reframing in an Age of Migration', brings together contributions that make visible local hegemonies and global ones.

The following table gives an overview of the book's arrangement with three parts and foci of the chapters. It serves as navigation through geographical representation and variety and illustrates the contribution's diversity. It outlines not only the voices, materials and methodological stances represented but also topics touched upon that go way beyond education and migration and include, among others, violence and abuse, questions of belonging, teacher and personal identity, teacher shortage and national nuances, national teacher education programs and systems and qualification acknowledgement schemes.

Part I of the book, entitled 'Theoretical Approaches to the Making of a Teacher', brings together four very different approaches to the demands placed on teachers.

Table 0.1 Detailed Overview of the Book's Contributions

	Approach	Author's Region and Continent	Voices
Part I: Theoretical Approaches to the Making of a Teacher			
Biesta	Theoretical; continental philosophy and educational theory	Ireland and Scotland; Europe	Governmental (policy papers); philosophy of education
Yolcu	Discursive analysis of policy texts; societies of control; governmentality	Turkey; Asia	Governmental (policy papers), to create 'inclusive' classrooms in Turkey
Ress	Reflections on former research; critical Black and ethnic/postcolonial lens	Germany; Europe	African students in Brazil (indirectly)
Obermayr and Sowinetz	Semi-structured interviews and qualitative content Analysis with main focus on teachers' narratives	Austria; Europe	Narratives of displaced teachers living in Austria
Part II: International Perspectives on (Local) Politics of Education			
Thoma	Ethnographic approach; small-story narratives; educational theory	Austria; Europe	Small-story narratives from teachers and social workers of refugee students in Austria
Schmidt et al.	Secondary qualitative analysis/empirical synopsis of research; translingual activism	Austria, Germany, Ireland; Europe and Canada; North America	Internationally educated teachers (IETs) in different bridging programmes in Europe and Canada
Voigt and Engel	Mapping; teacher education lens	Germany; Europe	Teacher education for career jumpers and lateral entry teachers in Germany
Tarisayi	Qualitative multisite study using interviews; belonging	South Africa; Africa	Zimbabwean migrant teachers in South African classrooms
Shah	Semi-structured interviews (most significant change technique) in external evaluation studies; strategic relational Approach	New Zealand; Oceania	Turkish and Jordanian teachers working with Syrian refugee children and volunteer or temporary Syrian refugee teachers in Jordan and Turkey

(Continued)

Table 0.1 (Continued)

	Approach	Author's Region and Continent	Voices
Part III: Critical Reframing in an Age of Migration			
Manik	Two case studies across fifteen years of empirical research; professional identity and belonging	South Africa; Africa	South African migrant teachers in the UK and the United Arab Emirates
Marom	In-depth, semi-structured interviews; critical race theory	Canada; North America	Racialized/minoritized teacher candidates: Indigenous, East Asian Canadian, South Asian Canadian
Kretchmar	Theoretical; critical reflection on neoliberal policies regarding teacher education	United States; North America	Governmental (policy papers) on fast-track programs
Knobloch	Theoretical; cultural studies approach, decolonial theory	Germany; Europe	Decolonizing voices: historical (Argentina) and recent (Germany)

If one is to think about what hegemony can be in pedagogical settings and during teacher training, one must also think about the work for which teachers are being prepared, that is, what they are supposed to do in educational institutions. In his chapter, Gert Biesta gives two answers to this question: firstly, the now almost overpowering answer of so-called 'evidence-based education', which reduces the teacher to a factor in educational processes. Secondly, based on an idea of pedagogy that can be traced back to the Enlightenment, he offers a different understanding of interactive educational settings and how teachers are required to perform pedagogical art in such settings. This fundamental relationship is already challenged in Ayşe Yolcu's contribution, where she looks specifically at how the (increasing) diversity in the classroom shapes the relationships between teachers and learners. Culturally diverse classrooms require teachers to deal with a diversity of learners. However, reading Yolcu's contribution, this too quickly becomes a management issue to be solved with reflection and thus a responsibility placed on individual teachers. Here, the hegemonic idea of self-governance is imposed on teachers, subjecting teaching processes to this performative doing.

The seemingly common understanding of 'being a teacher' is also shaken if teachers come from different contexts of thought and enter a school system with different ideas of teaching and learning and different theoretical justifications.

Susanne Ress refers to this in her contribution, where she looks at mobility and the change of frames of reference that comes with it. As she shows, distinct forms of and diverse valuations of mobility have emerged against historically different backgrounds. While it is not yet always a valued asset, she proposes that sharing stories about moving might help make it more of a norm for many people. Finally, the 'making' of a teacher refers to the question of which school system the teacher was 'made' for? Which normative (national) references should teachers refer to in their work, and for which society do they educate? What are the challenges when leaving one frame of reference and going to another? In their chapter, Tina Obermayr and Marie-Claire Sowinetz take up the experiences of refugee teachers who, as 'internationally trained teachers' in Austria, suddenly have to orient themselves in a completely new way in their understanding as teachers and within the institution.

This book aims to help develop a more precise and more nuanced picture of questions related to (the hindrance of) transnational knowledge transfer by including representations and topics from various geographical areas (varied both in terms of contributors' backgrounds and also with regards to the locations of research activities) and topics spanning teaching strategies, teacher identities and systematic discrimination in relation to localized practices, also in a comparative perspective. Thus, Part II of this book focuses on 'International Perspectives on (Local) Politics of Education'.

Nadja Thoma's contribution explores the sense-making processes of teachers in neoliberal migration societies. Using findings from a project with refugee children in Austria, the author elaborates on how specific nuances of imbalances in power relations are reified and maintained by the fast-forward teaching approaches that teachers apply due to outside pressures. Her chapter gives insights into the dilemmas that teachers might face daily if their personal motivation differs from the need to adjust to ever-growing stressors and how time constraints might further affect teacher–researcher relationships. These dynamics affect research and point to the need to further assess how research needs to be redesigned to capture the complexity of the teaching profession and teaching as such in ever-changing migration societies (see chapter 14). A collective of four authors – Clea Schmidt, Henrike Terhart, Rory McDaid and Michelle Proyer – also draws on the concept of neoliberalism and intertwines it with postcolonial efforts by taking a comparative route to expose discriminatory language practices. They do so by analysing recertification measures for internationally trained teachers in Canada, Germany, Ireland and Austria. Applying the idea of *translingual activism*, the authors take a stance for certification programs to apply and promote non-linguistic approaches. From recertification to little or no certification, Miriam Voigt and Inka Engel depict current strategies in Germany to tackle teacher shortages and a growing number of students. In introducing us to current procedures of incorporating *career jumpers* and those seeking *lateral entry* into teaching, the authors create a detailed overview, also referring to recent developments around Covid-19. They also address the challenges that an untrained or only basically trained workforce might face or bring to the table.

Part II proceeds with Kudzayi Savious Tarisayi's contribution. The author dives into the dynamics between Zimbabwean and South African teachers to exemplify how non-local teachers can face hostility and discrimination. Targeting school spaces as specific locations, he elaborates on the concepts of belonging and teacher collegiality and how the latter might go awry and even turn into violence. Adding a micro, or more personality- or relationship-focused perspective, Ritesh Shah's contribution thematizes the lack of reference to teachers' identities in relation to teachers' readiness to work in crisis-ridden contexts or with students with precarious living conditions. Using the examples of Turkey and Jordan and contrasting the roles of formally qualified or well-established teachers, respectively, against the situation of volunteer and untrained teachers, he sheds light on the narratives of frontline actors. He thereby bridges transnational perspectives by juxtaposing the supposed realities of teaching with the understandings of those who actually teach.

Part III focuses on different approaches to a 'Critical Reframing in an Age of Migration'. Authors ask how the teaching persona is constructed through frameworks within and beyond national and/or educational borders. First – and based on fifteen years of empirical research – Sadhana Manik analyses troubling classroom experiences of South African migrant teachers in two countries in the Global North: the UK and the United Arab Emirates (UAE). She concludes that these teachers experience deskilling, devaluing and exploitation abroad. Given that their experience is critical to their professional integration, their sense of belonging to a global teaching fraternity and teacher retention, she argues for equal treatment in their work environment and protection of their rights to prevent them from being devalued professionally.

While Manik looks at teachers going abroad for work, Lilach Marom focuses on people studying to become teachers in British Columbia/Canada. Based on interviews with racialized teacher candidates, she argues that teacher education programs still promote White Normativity, even though they praise diversity at a discursive level. Her findings show the massive gap between the rhetoric of diversity in these programs and participants' experiences and how institutionalized whiteness is transmitted through subtle, racial microaggressions. Racialized teacher candidates have to pay both an emotional and professional toll when confronting whiteness in teacher education.

Kerry Kretchmar analyses the two-tiered teacher preparation system in the United States by fundamentally criticizing non-university fast-track programs that have grown over the past twenty-five years due to a neoliberal shift in perceptions about what constitutes effective teaching and to whom that effectiveness applies. However, fast-track teachers frequently teach in low-income schools that primarily serve students of colour. In contrast, schools in the middle-class and wealthy communities continue to be staffed by teachers prepared through university-based programs. Simultaneously, some of these fast-track programs spread internationally and approach teacher preparation and educational policy as borderless and unified around the same narrow, managerial vision of teaching and learning.

Based on historical references, Phillip Knobloch highlights lessons from the Global South, particularly Argentina. By taking a closer look at the distinction between Western and non-Western countries (referring to both Stuart Hall and Walter Mignolo), he examines the discussions in Argentina in the nineteenth century. The young state encouraged immigration and hoped to develop an identity as an independent nation through education. The author raises the question of who is educating and who is supposed to educate whom. He then analyses how concepts of the West and the non-West shape our thinking and actions in contemporary teacher education.

In the concluding chapter 14, the editors bring together themes such as an overview of approaches and voices in the book and associated challenges, framing current discussions around recognition processes and pointing to current boundaries in education. Critically re-evaluating the guiding questions of the book, we highlight its limitations and outline possible further research areas and agendas.

References

Arendt, H., ed. (2006), 'The Crisis in Education', in *Between Past and Future*, 185–208, New York: Penguin.

Bosede, I. E. and A. D. Cheok (2018), 'Why Not Robot Teachers: Artificial Intelligence for Addressing Teacher Shortage', *Applied Artificial Intelligence*, 32 (4): 345–60. doi: 10.1080/08839514.2018.1464286.

Freire, P. (1973), *Pädagogik der Unterdrückten. Bildung als Praxis der Freiheit*, Reinbek bei Hamburg: Rowohlt.

Friesen, N. (2017), *Mindful Practice & Hope for the Future: Schleiermacher's Human Education*. Available online: https://www.normfriesen.info/wp-content/uploads/2017/10/PPR-on-Schleiermacher-6.pdf (accessed 31 October 2021).

García, E. and E. Weiss (2019), 'The Teacher Shortage is Real, Large and Growing, and Worse Than we Thought. The first report in "The Perfect Storm in the Teacher Labor Market" series', Economic Policy Institute, 26 March. Available online: https://www.epi.org/publication/the-teacher-shortage-is-real-large-and-growing-and-worse-than-we-thought-the-first-report-in-the-perfect-storm-in-the-teacher-labor-market-series/ (accessed 31 October 2021).

Heidrich, L., Y. Karakaşoğlu, P. Mecheril and S. Shure, eds (2021), *Regimes of Belonging – Schools – Migrations. Teaching in (trans)national Constellations*, Preprint, Universität Bremen. doi:10.26092/elib/486.

Popkewitz, T. S., Y. Wu and C. S. Martins (2015), 'Practical Knowledge and School Reform: The Impracticality of Local Knowledge in Strategies of Change', in D. Tröhler and T. Lenz (eds), *Trajectories in the Development of Modern School Systems*, 20–34, London and New York: Routledge.

Schleiermacher, F. D. E. (2000), *Texte zur Pädagogik: Kommentierte Studienausgabe: Band 2*, Frankfurt: Suhrkamp.

Todd, S. (2012), 'Going to the Heart of the Matter', in G. J. J. Biesta (eds), *Making Sense of Education*, 79–84, Dordrecht: Springer.

Part I

Theoretical Approaches to the Making of a Teacher

On Being a Teacher

How to Respond to the Global Construction of Teachers and Their Teaching?

Gert Biesta

1. Introduction: National Cultures of Education and Global Constructions of Teaching

Teachers who migrate to a different country will soon realize that different nations and regions have significantly different educational structures and cultures. Differences in educational structures are relatively easy to perceive, both with regard to how education itself is organized and with regard to all the regulations that surround education. Gaining a good understanding of differences in educational cultures may take longer, as these differences are often located at the level of taken-for-granted assumptions which, because they are considered to be normal, are neither questioned nor explicitly articulated. While migrating teachers may therefore need to do quite a lot of work to adjust to a new environment, the taken-for-granted assumptions that inform *their* ways of being and doing can also help in making visible what is taken for granted and goes unquestioned in the settings in which they arrive.

While migrating teachers will, on the one hand, encounter new and different local practices, they may, at the very same time, meet traces and in some cases even explicit manifestations of what we might term a 'global construction' of teachers and their teaching – a construction that is intimately connected to a global education measurement 'industry' (Biesta 2015) which has significantly impacted on educational policy and practice, including policy and practice concerning teachers and their education, in many countries around the world. Migrating teachers may thus encounter a rather odd mix of educational cultures and structures that are *both* local, regional and national and influenced by global trends that, in a sense, hover above local practices and systems. This situation raises many questions. The question I wish to take up in this chapter is what kind of frame of reference migrating teaching might utilize to navigate these complexities and contradictions.

2. Another Review of Teacher Education

At the time of writing this chapter, the Australian federal government had just launched a review of teacher education or, as some of my colleagues in Australia referred to it, *another* review of teacher education.[1] The launch document bears all the hallmarks of a discourse about teachers, teaching and schools that has emerged over the past decades and has managed to become near-hegemonic in education policy and, through this, is having a significant impact on education practice.

The headlines sound quite familiar. We read that Federal Education Minister Alan Tudge has launched the review into initial teaching education as 'a key element of the government's ambition to lift Australian school standards'. The review is being conducted against the background of 'a new target to return Australia to the top group of education nations globally by 2030, noting that our school standards have steadily slipped over the last two decades'. The review is seen as 'the most critical element towards lifting standards, noting that the quality of teaching is the most important in-school factor influencing student achievement'. The review will address two questions: 'How to attract and select high-quality candidates into the teaching profession, and how to prepare them to become effective teachers?' And all this is contextualized by a semi-factual observation that 'since 2006, the number of top students choosing to study education has declined by a third, and many teachers are still graduating from their courses insufficiently prepared to teach in a classroom'.

It is instructive to read a bit more: 'Minister Tudge said Australia's teachers are some of the most dedicated and hard-working in the world and the review would help grow and support the workforce.' 'Particularly over the last year, we have seen how important our teachers are to Australian kids and we want to provide them with the best platform to produce better student outcomes', Minister Tudge said. 'We used to consistently be in the top group of education nations and I am confident we can get there again. The recommendations of this review will help ensure we attract high-quality, motivated candidates into teaching and develop them into teachers with the skills our students need. We want the finest students choosing to be teachers and we also want to make it easier for accomplished mid- and late-career individuals to transition into the profession, bringing their extensive skills and knowledge into our school classrooms.' And finally: 'The review builds on the reforms the government has already made to improve ITE, including assessing and accrediting ITE courses and testing graduates' literacy and numeracy before they can enter a classroom to teach.'

The terms of reference for the review are clear and concise. The opening sentence simply states that 'teachers and school leaders are the largest in-school influence on student outcomes'. And it then lists ten questions under two headings which, for the sake of transparency, I will quote in full as well:

PART A – Attracting and selecting high-quality candidates into the teaching profession

1. How can we further encourage high-performing and highly motivated school leavers to enter ITE and choose teaching as a career?
2. What changes to admissions and degree requirements, including recognition of prior experience, would better attract and support suitable mid- and late-career professionals from other fields transition into the profession and become quality teachers?
3. How can we increase ITE completion rates so that quality ITE students graduate and pursue careers as quality teachers?
4. What more can be done to address issues with workforce supply in some subject areas (particularly mathematics) and schools?
5. How can we attract a more diverse cohort into ITE so that teachers better mirror the diversity in school students and society?

PART B – Preparing ITE students to be effective teachers

6. What more can we do to ensure that ITE curriculum is evidence based and all future teachers are equipped to implement evidence-based teaching practices?
7. What more can ITE providers and employers do to ensure ITE students are getting the practical experience they need before they start their teaching careers?
8. How can Teaching Performance Assessment arrangements be strengthened to ensure graduate teachers are well-prepared for the classroom?

9. How can leading teachers, principals and schools play a greater role in supporting the development of ITE students?
10. Can ITE providers play a stronger role in ongoing professional development and support of teachers

3. The Global Construction of Teaching and Teachers: Quality, Standards and Effectiveness

I have provided a fair amount of detail about the Australian government's announcement, not because it contains much that is special or unique but precisely because it contains so much that has become all too familiar. It is, in a sense, remarkable that the Australian government sees a need for another review, as the same questions have been asked over and over again in many countries. What interests me for the purpose of this chapter, however, is first and foremost how teaching and the role of teachers in teaching is being depicted – and one could also say: constructed – in policy texts like this one. Three things stand out.

The first is the frequent use of the word 'quality', such as in references to 'high-quality candidates', 'high-quality, motivated candidates' and 'quality ITE students', and echoed in notions such as 'finest students' and 'high-performing and highly motivated school leavers', on the assumption that teacher education will turn this select group into 'quality teachers'. What is odd is that the frequent reference to finding or attracting the 'right' students to teacher education displays a fairly low belief in the power of teacher education itself. It seems that the problem is already constructed as a supply problem – teacher education simply cannot get the 'right' students – rather than as the question how anyone interested in becoming a teacher could receive the most appropriate education. And what of course is also problematic about the frequent use of the word 'quality' is that it actually says very little. No one is against quality, but the real question is what counts as quality and who has a say in it.

This relates to a second characteristic, which is the particular depiction of the 'point' of education. The point of education is strongly conceived in terms of 'student achievement' and 'outcomes', and to the extent to which any reference is made to educational subject matter, we can only see references to 'literacy and numeracy' and to 'mathematics'. Apart from that, it remains very unclear what kind of 'outcomes' are supposed to be pursued or what kind of 'achievement' would be considered valuable, by whom and for what reasons.

What is also remarkable is that the overall policy ambition does not seem to be about providing children and young people with worthwhile education. Rather, the main 'framing' of the discussion is about lifting Australian school standards so that Australia may return 'to the top group of education nations globally by 2030'. What this top group is, how it is being defined, what matters in this top group and how this ambition may be helpful for children and young people in Australia are absent from the document. It seems as if ultimately the point of the whole educational 'enterprise' is not what schools can do for children and young people but what children and young people can do for the performance of Australia in international league tables (Apple 2000).

If this is already beginning to make a career in teaching less attractive – many students go into teaching because they want to make a difference in the lives of their pupils, not because they want to boost the performance of their country in a league table – the third characteristic I wish to mention concerns the way in which teachers and their teaching are depicted. This is predominantly framed by the headline that 'teachers and school leaders are the largest in-school influence on student outcomes' which already seems to reduce the complex work of teaching to that of being 'an influence' on student outcomes (other literature even refers to the teacher as a 'factor' – see e.g. King-Rice 2003). Moreover, this influence is depicted in a thoroughly mechanistic way, that is, as a matter of the *production* of 'student outcomes', as if teaching were work on a kind of educational assembly line.

It is not remarkable, therefore, that the professionalism sought for is entirely captured in terms of *effectiveness*. Effectiveness denotes the degree to which a particular process is able to produce a particular outcome. Yet just suggesting that teaching should be effective and that teachers should be effective is not just empty – the question that needs to be asked first is effective for *what* – but is also insufficient and ultimately problematic. The point that is overlooked in the claim that teaching should be effective vis-à-vis the production of certain outcomes is that such effectiveness can be achieved in all kinds of ways, including ones that are educationally deeply problematic. Would it be permissible to pay students for their achievements, if that turns out to be effective? Would it be permissible to bribe them? To actually give them the right answers to the test so that they will achieve a perfect score?

All this comes together in the remarkable phrase that teachers ultimately just need 'to implement evidence-based teaching practices'. There is no need, in other words, for teachers to be inventive or thoughtful. If they just implement what the evidence allegedly says, or they just do as they are told, everything should be alright – which begins to raise the question why one would actually need such 'high-quality' candidates if this is all that their work in schools is going to be about.

4. Technicism, Good Intentions and a Slippery Slope

As mentioned, I am not singling out this example from Australia because it is unique but because it is so familiar. One question this raises is why this particular 'construction' of teachers and teaching has managed to become so omnipresent.

At a general level there is the appeal of technicism, that is, of the idea that complex problems can be addressed through technological means that seek to reduce complexity and bring an array of different variables under control. There are many stories about the apparent success of medicine and agriculture where, through a combination of research and development, humankind has managed to increase control. Although we do know that the advance of technology in these fields also creates serious ethical problems, the appeal of technicism remains strong, also with regard to education. This belief is also fuelled by researchers who promise that with more research, with more of the 'right' research, and also with more money for (their) research, they will eventually be able to deliver the so-called 'evidence base' that will put education on a secure path of progress (albeit that it is never entirely sure what this path will look like, where it will lead to, what the financial and human costs for getting there are and when this promised land will actually arrive).

In addition to the general appeal of technicism, there is also a more specific educational dynamic that has contributed to the rise of the idea that educational matters are fundamentally technical matters. It has to do with a particular chain of events which, elsewhere, I have characterized as a 'slippery slope' (Biesta 2019). This chain started with a clear social justice argument, captured in the suggestion that every child and young person, irrespective of *who* they are, *where* they are or where they are *from*, should have access to good education. This laudable ambition then raised the question how we can ensure that education is everywhere of sufficient quality which, in turn, raised the question how we can *judge* the quality of education. One decisive step was taken when the question of *judgement* became translated into the question how we can *measure* the quality of education. A second decisive step was taken when the question of measuring the quality of education turned into the question how we can measure the quality of educational *outcomes* (see e.g. Spady 1994; and for an 'early' critique Jansen 1998).

The question which outcomes *should* be measured soon turned into the question which outcomes *can* be measured, and so the good intentions of the social justice argument eventually turned into the current 'age of measurement' (Biesta 2010), in which the key question is whether we are (still) measuring what is being valued or whether we have reached a situation where many just value what is being measured and take the latter as a valid indicator of the quality of education. And all this has been heavily 'supported' by the rise of GEMI, the 'global education measurement industry' (Biesta 2015; Hopmann 2008).

These developments have resulted in a degrading of teachers, transforming them from thinking, judging and acting professionals into 'factors' in the production of learning outcomes. They have contributed to the rise of a culture of performativity, where *indicators* of quality become redefined as *definitions* of quality so that, for example, the position on a league table becomes a strategic target in itself. And what is perhaps most worrying is how all this has contributed to an inner erosion of education itself, making the actors in education increasingly *cynical* about what really matters as long as performance indicators are met – a development documented in chilling detail by Dianne Ravitch (Ravitch 2011).

5. Regaining Teacher Agency: Why Language Matters

It is, of course, quite a claim to suggest that the construction of teachers and their teaching I have presented here amounts to a *mis*representation. I am aware that there are policymakers and researchers who believe that this is actually an accurate and desirable presentation of teachers and their teaching. I am also aware that for a significant number of teachers this is simply their reality: it is not just the context in which they work but also the discourse 'through' which they work. There are, however, also many teachers who are deeply concerned about this state of affairs, including those who are making a case for a 'flip' of the system, one where teachers are not there to execute commands from 'higher up' but are central agents in the educational endeavour (see e.g. Evers and Kneyber 2015; Netolicky, Andrews and Paterson 2018; Soskil 2021).

These observations have to do with the theme of teacher agency. In the research I conducted with colleagues on this topic about teachers in Scotland (Priestley, Biesta and Robinson 2015), we found a number of things that are relevant for the question how teachers might navigate the complexities of their settings and what helps and hinders them in achieving a degree of agency. To refer to agency as something that is *achieved* highlights our insight that agency is not so much an individual possession – some kind of power teachers may or may not have – but rather emerges out of the interplay of individual capacity and the cultures and structures within which teachers work.

In our research we found, for example, that whereas policy puts a strong emphasis on individual capacity and rhetorically did position teachers as 'curriculum makers', this was not backed up by a change in accountability structures. As a result, many teachers felt that whereas they were seen as competent agents at the 'front door' of the school, their scope for professional judgement was significantly curtailed through the structures that arrived through the 'back door'. We also found that culture is by far the most difficult thing to change in the educational 'set-up'. Cultures are persistent because they emerge from ways of doing, thinking and speaking that often remain implicit and are engrained in the routines and even the rituals of everyday practice.

One finding that is particularly relevant for this chapter concerns the role of language and, more specifically, the discursive resources teachers have to make sense of what they are doing and what they are encountering. This has to do with beliefs and values but even more so with the ways in which teachers *talk* about education and (their) teaching. We found significant differences, which we partly characterized in terms of the impact of teachers' experiences over time. The way in which beginning teachers are able to talk about and make sense of what they are doing is different from the way in which more experienced teachers talk, and one could say that over time the talk becomes more nuanced and multilayered simply because teachers have been around for longer. Yet we also saw a 'generational effect' in that the ways in which teachers talked about education and their teaching were clearly linked to the particular time in which they had been educated and 'grown up' as teachers.

The key difference here is whether teachers have ways of talking about education that allow them *to have a perspective on* the situation they find themselves in or whether their talk simply coincides with the present 'common sense'. In the latter case, it is not only difficult to envisage a different state of affairs; it is even difficult to imagine that things *can be* different, let alone to consider that things *ought* to be different. Of course, there is always a further need for judgement about what may be a desirable state of affairs, but everything begins with the ability to have a critical distance to the current situation and the 'common sense' constructed around it.

In the remainder of this chapter I will outline a language to talk about teaching and the work of the teacher that is at least significantly different from the 'global construction'. I am not claiming that this way to talk about education is the one and only way to do it, but by providing a different 'account' of teaching it becomes possible to put the current global hegemony in a perspective from which judgement about desirable futures for teachers and their teaching becomes possible.

6. Teaching: Intentional, Relational and Purposeful

I wish to take my starting point in the observation that teaching is a relational, intentional and purposeful activity (Biesta and Stengel 2016). Firstly, teaching is not something one can do on one's own but implies a relationship between teachers and (their) students. Secondly, teaching does not happen by accident; those who teach, or try to teach, do so deliberately. And thirdly, teaching is done with a sense of purpose, which means that it is done for a reason. Teachers have good reasons for what they teach and how they teach, and these reasons have something to do with what they hope that their activities will bring about on the side of their students, albeit that it remains open whether or not this will happen as the 'success' of teaching is not just reliant on what teachers do but also on what students do with what they are being taught.

Over the past decades, the prevalent answer to the question what teaching is *for* has become 'learning'. This is, however, a rather impoverished idea of what teaching should aim for and actually also a rather unhelpful idea. This is not just because learning can happen anywhere, also without teaching. It is also because learning can go in any direction, and therefore just to say that teaching should bring about learning or that teachers should 'facilitate' learning says actually very little. The point of education rather is that students learning *something*, that they learn it *for a reason* and that they learn it *from someone*. Education, in other words, always raises questions of content, purpose and relationships. And it is here that teaching comes in, because whereas students can learn all kind of things from being in educational settings – including how to cheat or how to pass an exam with minimal effort – the work of the teacher is to direct the attention of students to particular subject matter, particular themes, particular issues and particular tasks and, most importantly, to do so with particular reasons and purposes in mind. Teaching, in other words, is always conducted with an orientation.

Elsewhere (e.g. Biesta 2009, 2010, 2020) I have suggested that there are actually three purposes (or as I prefer: domains of purpose) that are always at stake when education takes place. One important reason why we engage in education is to make knowledge and skills available to our students. We can refer to this as knowledge acquisition, but it is perhaps better to say that one important purpose of education is *qualification*, that is, providing students with knowledge, skills, attitudes and dispositions that make it possible for them to do something. This 'doing' can either be quite specific, such as becoming qualified for a particular job or profession; but it can also be understood more broadly, such as the way in which schools seek to equip children and young people for their life in complex modern societies.

Some argue that qualification is the sole purpose, because they are worried that anything else gets education into difficult normative questions. This may sound reasonable, but the problem is that since education is unable to provide children and young people with all existing knowledge and skills, there is inevitable selection. In everything we do we thus present our students with a particular 'selection' of the world or, more positively formulated, with a particular *representation* of the world. The ways in which we do this inevitably influence our students in some way. Normative questions are therefore inescapable, even if education were confined to of knowledge and skills.

In the literature the presentation of different representations of the world is known as *socialization*. Some highlight the ways in which this goes on behind the backs of our students – the idea of the hidden curriculum. Yet we can also see socialization as an important second purpose of education, where we try to provide our students with orientation in the world, that is, with a sense of direction. Education as socialization is about providing our students with an orientation into existing cultures, traditions and practices, with the invitation that they locate themselves within them.

7. The Student, Object or Subject?

Discussions about socialization, particularly strong(er) and (more) directive approaches, raise an important further question, which has been part of the modern educational conversation at least since the Enlightenment. The question here is whether education can and should approach students as 'objects' that need to be(come) qualified and socialized – which seems to be the dominant 'undertone' of the global construction of teaching – or whether education always needs to ensure that children and young people can become subjects of their own life.

There are different ways in which we can refer to this third domain. I tend to refer to it with the word *subjectification*, which is perhaps a rather odd word in English and a more common word in other languages. It refers to the ambition that students end up as subjects of their own life and not as objects of educational 'interventions'. It therefore stands in sharp contrast to education that aims for objectification, that is, education which is only interested in controlling students and their acting, thinking and judgement. Of course we cannot force our students to be subjects of their own life, but we can 'remind' our students of this possibility to exist as subject of their own life. And we can provide them with opportunities to encounter and practice with the complexities of what this means (see Biesta 2020, for more detail).

Dietrich Benner has suggested the phrase *Aufforderung zur Selbsttätigkeit* as a way to capture the educational work in this domain (Benner 2015). This can be translated as 'summoning to self-action', although the 'summoning' may sound a bit strict and a word like 'encouragement' might be more helpful. This should not be understood as the encouragement to be *oneself*, and also not the encouragement just to become active. It is perhaps best to see this as the injunction to be *a* self, that is, to try to be a subject of one's own life, with all the complexities and responsibilities that come with it.

Also helpful here is Benner's distinction between affirmative and non-affirmative education (Benner 2015: 146–55). Whereas qualification and socialization are, to a large degree, affirmative, in that they start from certain ideas about what education should achieve and where children and young people should end up, the domain of subjectification is precisely the opposite of this, because here it is not for educators to tell children and young people how they should be and become but rather to provide opportunities for them to figure out for themselves how to live their own lives in the best way possible. That is why the educational work in this domain has to be non-affirmative and has to proceed with caution.

I wish to suggest that qualification, socialization and subjectification are not only three *legitimate* purposes of education; in a sense they are also three *inevitable* purposes. In all instances of education there is always something for teachers to offer to students and for students to acquire to their benefit. Because qualification always represents (aspects of) the world in a particular way, there is always also socialization going on. And all this also has an impact on the student as subject, to begin with because becoming more knowledgeable or skilled (qualification) and gaining orientation in a particular domain or field (socialization) provides students with increased possibilities for thinking, judgement and action.

The fact that these three domains of purpose are inevitable, first of all, suggests that the three domains are always entangled with each other; they cannot exist separately, because every act of qualification is also an act of socialization and also impacts on the student's subject-ness, positively or negatively. It suggests, secondly, that in the design and enactment of education teachers should always consider what they seek to achieve in relation to each of these domains. Thirdly, although the three domains are always 'in play' in education, it does not mean that they can exist in perfect harmony. There are always potential tensions between, say, what one seeks to achieve in the domain of qualification and what is possible in the other domains. There can be synergy – understanding subject matter well also provides a degree of orientation and contributes to one's agency – but there can also be conflicts – for example, when a too strong push on the domain of qualification undermines students' agency.

The challenge for teachers, therefore, is not just to think and act in a three-dimensional way, that is, with an eye on the three domains of educational purpose. The challenge is also to try to secure a meaningful balance and think carefully about the costs of emphasizing one domain to the detriment of the other domains. This, as I will argue in the next section, is one important reason why teaching needs to be understood as an art and why teachers need artistry rather than techniques. Yet the main point here is that a proper sense of the complexities of educational purpose is absolutely crucial in order to be able to respond to – and actually resist – technicist reductions of the work of teachers.

8. On the Artistry of Teaching

One key message emerging from the discussion so far is that teaching cannot and should not be enacted as a form of control, that is, as a kind of intervention that, under 'ideal' circumstances and based upon the best 'evidence', should be aimed at producing pre-specified learning outcomes. This is not to suggest that everything should be open, which is the mistake of those who denounce teaching in favour of learning. But it is to challenge the view that education is ultimately a causal system (an ontological claim) and that, once we have perfect knowledge about the mechanics of the system (an epistemological claim), teaching can become a matter of administering those interventions that produce the desired outcomes (a praxeological claim) – 'implementing evidence-based teaching practices', as it was called in the Australian document. The whole point of teaching is precisely *not* the production of outcomes but a matter of educating human beings so that they are able to act in more knowledgeable and more thoughtful ways, have a sense of direction and orientation and, through this, take it upon themselves to be subjects of their own lives.

If this is not a matter of implementing evidence-based practices, how then should we understand the work of teachers? These questions relate back to a rather old discussion which has been framed, correctly in my view, as the question whether teaching should be understood as a 'science' or as an 'art'. A most helpful engagement with this question can already be found in the work of Aristotle, for which the difference between 'science' and 'art' is not a matter of different kinds of knowledge but actually begins with a proper understanding of the reality we are acting 'in' and 'upon' in practical fields such as education.

With regard to this Aristotle makes a helpful distinction between the theoretical life (the *bios theoretikos*) and the practical life (the *bios praktikos*). The theoretical life is concerned with 'the necessary and the eternal' (Aristotle 1980: 140), that is, with those aspects of reality that do not change, such as the movement of the planets or the stars in the sky. Aristotle's main insight, however, is that most of what our lives are about takes place in the domain of the *variable* (for this term see Aristotle 1980: 42), that is, the domain of change. This is the world in which we act and where our actions have consequences but where there is no guarantee that our actions will always have *the same* consequences. It is the domain of possibility, not of certainty. Knowledge in this domain is about the relationships between our actions and the possible consequences of our actions. This is so for our interaction with the material world (technology), with the living world (plants and animals) and our actions in the social domain. While we can gain much knowledge about possible relationships between actions and consequences in these domains, there is never a guarantee that when we act in the same way in the future, the same consequences will follow. And precisely there lies the difference between 'science' and 'art'.

What is also interesting is that Aristotle makes a further distinction between two 'modes' of acting in the domain of the variable and two related forms of judgement. *Poiesis* or 'making action' is about the making of things – such as, for example, a saddle or a ship – although I prefer to think of it more broadly as action that brings something into existence. We might also call it 'productive action' as it is about bringing into existence what did not exist before. The kind of knowledge we need for *poiesis* is *techne:* 'knowledge of how to make things' (Aristotle 1980: 141). *Techne* is about finding the means that will bring about what one seeks to bring about. *Techne* encompasses knowledge about the materials we work with and about the techniques we can apply to work with those materials. Yet making something, such as a saddle, is never simply about following a recipe. It requires judgements about the application of our previous knowledge and experience to *this* piece of leather, for a saddle to fit *this* particular horse and for *this* particular person riding the horse. So we make judgements about application, production and effectiveness in our attempts to bring something into existence. The best English word for *techne* is probably craftsmanship, although, in a slightly narrower translation, we can also think of it as consisting of practical knowledge and practical judgement.

The domain of the variable is, however, not confined to the world of things and matters of making but includes the social domain, that is, the world of human action and interaction. It is here that a second art is called for: the art of *praxis*. The orientation here is towards the promotion of the human good, that is, of living life well (the Greek term is *eudamonia*). *Praxis* is 'about what sort of things conduce to the good life in general' (Aristotle 1980: 142). What we need to proceed here is not judgement about how to do things but rather judgement 'about what is to be done' (Aristotle 1980). Aristotle refers to this kind of judgement as *phronesis*, which is usually translated as practical wisdom.

Aristotle thus provides a powerful argument for the idea that teaching is an art and not a science and also provides us with precise definitions of 'art' and 'science'. The key insight here is that teaching takes place in the domain of the variable, that is, the domain of actions and possible consequences, and the reason for this, to put it bluntly, is that in teaching we work with 'living material', that is, with human beings who are capable of their own thought and action. What is also interesting about Aristotle's approach is the distinction he makes between two different arts: the art of making, for which we need *techne*, which is the practical knowledge and judgement about how to do things, and the art of doing, for which we need *phronesis*, the practical wisdom we need to judge what is to be done. In this regard we could say that teaching is a 'double art', which requires both educational craftsmanship – the *techne* of teaching – and educational wisdom.

The final point to make here is that the 'how' of teaching and the 'what for' of teaching should not be seen as disconnected from each other. It is not that in education we can first set the goals and then just find the most effective and efficient way of getting there. The reason for this lies in the simple fact that the ways in which we proceed in education, the ways we teach, the ways we engage with our students, the ways we focus their attention and the ways we encourage them to study are not just more or less effective interventions that happen behind the backs of our students (which is where the comparison between education and medicine already fails). On the contrary, our actions are in full view of our students. This means that in addition to judgements about the purposes of our teaching, judgements about the way we try to balance the different domains of purpose and judgements about possible trade-offs in achieving a balance, we also need to judge the ways in which we teach. And this judgement is not just technical – which is the question of effectiveness – and also not just moral – Are the ways in which we teach morally acceptable? – but also needs to be *educational*, that is, to be judged in terms of the ways in which they may or may not contribute to the overall ambitions we have with our teaching.

If teaching is an art and, more specifically a 'double art' of craft and wisdom, then it is important that teachers keep working on their own educational 'artistry' (Stenhouse 1988; Eisner 2002), that is, their ability to make situated judgements about educationally desirable ways of acting in the always new situations they encounter. It is here that the whole question of the ongoing improvement of education finds its 'home', because, to quote Lawrence Stenhouse (1988: 50), 'improving education is not about improving teaching as a delivery system [because] crucial is the desire of the artist to improve his or her art'. And once more I wish to emphasize that to think of teaching as an art in the nuanced way in which I have discussed it in this section provides a way to distinguish it from technicist accounts that seek to do away with the need for complex educational judgement and ongoing inventiveness in the educational situation.

9. Concluding Comments: Resisting Technicism, Reclaiming Artistry

I have suggested that in many contexts and settings a particular understanding of teachers and teaching has become near hegemonic. This is a technicist account of teaching which sees education as the mere production of 'learning outcomes' and sees the work of the teacher as that of implementing evidence-based interventions. While such a view of teachers and their teaching may sound attractive from a policy perspective that sees education as a matter of control, I have suggested that such a view has little to do with the reality of teaching. The problem we are facing, however, is that the 'global construction' of teaching is continuously being repeated at all kinds of levels and has begun to become a kind of 'common sense'.

While the construction of this common sense is not devoid of good intentions, it is nonetheless a problematic and misleading account of teaching, also because it demands from teachers to enact their teaching in ways that are sheer impossible to achieve – or are only possible if teachers themselves enact very strict forms of control over their students. The main intervention I have sought to make in this chapter is to present an alternative way to talk about teaching – one that highlights the fact that teaching is a purposeful activity and that there are a number of different domains of purpose that require attention in teaching and one that highlights that teaching takes place in the domain of the 'variable' and therefore never can be regulated by the kind of knowledge that actually doesn't take the particular nature of acting in this domain into account.

While language in itself may not have the power to interrupt technicist constructions of teaching, having alternative ways of talking 'in' and 'about' education is nonetheless an important resource for creating a critical distance from which judgement and action may become possible. In this regard having a different way to talk 'in' and 'about' education may be a crucial resource for teachers who are trying to navigate the real pressures that the technicist construction of teaching and teachers is exerting on them and that is continuing to influence the many local, regional and national educational structures and cultures that migrating teachers may find themselves in.

Note

1 Available online: https://ministers.dese.gov.au/tudge/initial-teacher-education-review-launched (accessed 17 April 2021).

References

Apple, M. (2000), 'Can Critical Pedagogies Interrupt Rightist Policies?', *Educational Theory*, 50 (2): 229–54.

Aristotle (1980), *The Nicomachean Ethics*, New York: Oxford University Press.

Benner, D. (2015), *Allgemeine Pädagogik. Eine systematisch-problemgeschichtliche Einführung in die Grundstruktur pädagogischen Denkens und Handelns*, 8, Auflage, Weinheim: Beltz and Juventa.

Biesta, G. (2009), 'Good Education in an Age of Measurement: On the Need to Reconnect with the Question of Purpose in Education', *Educational Assessment, Evaluation and Accountability*, 21 (1): 33–46.

Biesta, G. (2010), *Good Education in an Age of Measurement: Ethics, Politics, Democracy*, New York and London: Routledge.
Biesta, G. (2015), 'Resisting the Seduction of the Global Education Measurement Industry: Notes on the Social Psychology of PISA', *Ethics and Education*, 10 (3): 348–60.
Biesta, G. (2019), 'Reclaiming Teaching for Teacher Education: Towards a Spiral Curriculum', *Beijing International Review of Education*, 1 (2–3): 259–72.
Biesta, G. (2020), 'Risking Ourselves in Education: Qualification, Socialisation and Subjectification Revisited', *Educational Theory*, 70 (1): 89–104.
Biesta, G. and B. Stengel (2016), 'Thinking Philosophically about Teaching', in D. H. Gittomer and C. A. Bell (eds), *Handbook of Research on Teaching*, 5th edn, 7–68, Washington, DC: AERA.
Eisner, E. (2002), 'From Episteme to Phronesis to Artistry in the Study and Improvement of Teaching', *Teaching and Teacher Education*, 18 (4): 375–85.
Evers, J. and R. Kneyber, eds (2015), *Flip the System: Changing Education from the Ground Up*, London: Routledge.
Hopmann, S. T. (2008), 'No Child, No School, No State Left Behind: Schooling in the Age of Accountability', *Journal of Curriculum Studies*, 40 (4): 417–56.
Jansen, J. D. (1998), 'Curriculum Reform in South Africa: A Critical Analysis of Outcomes-Based Education', *Cambridge Journal of Education*, 28 (3): 321–31.
King-Rice, J. (2003), *Teacher Quality: Understanding the Effectiveness of Teacher Attributes*, Washington, DC: Economic Policy Institute.
Netolicky, D., J. Andrews and C. Paterson, eds (2018), *Flip the System Australia. What Matters in Education*, London and New York: Routledge.
Priestley, M., G. J. J. Biesta and S. Robinson (2015), *Teacher Agency: An Ecological Approach*, London: Bloomsbury Publishing.
Ravitch, D. (2011), *The Death and Life of the Great American School System: How Testing and Choice are Undermining Education*, New York: Basic Books.
Soskil, M. (2021), *Flip the System US: How Teachers Can Transform Education and Strengthen American Democracy*, 32–8, New York: Routledge.
Spady, W. G. (1994), *Outcome-Based Education: Critical Issues and Answers*. Arlington: American Association of School Administrators.
Stenhouse, L. (1988), 'Artistry and Teaching: The Teacher as a Focus of Research and Development', *Journal of Curriculum and Supervision*, 4 (1): 43–51.

2

Being Prepared for Diverse Classrooms
Boundaries of Professional Devices and the Dangers of Inclusive Teaching

Ayşe Yolcu

1. Introduction

The diversity in today's classrooms becomes more visible with the increase of migration all over the world. Students' immigration status in addition to other socio-demographic characteristics such as gender, socio-economic status, race and ethnicity are reported to explain the achievement gap in school subjects such as science or mathematics (Organization for Economic Co-operation and Development (OECD) 2013). In contemporary educational research, nevertheless, assuming a direct relationship between students' diverse background and their achievement in standardized tests has already proven to consolidate social and educational disadvantages (Gutiérrez 2008). Rather than reporting achievement gaps, teachers' work and teacher education are acknowledged as the key to ensuring equitable and socially just experiences for all in today's diverse classrooms (Darling-Hammond 2006; Villegas 2007). In particular, teachers are asked to handle different social and cultural backgrounds in effective ways where they need to understand the diverse backgrounds as an asset to build classroom pedagogies that are inclusive of 'culturally-other minority' or 'immigrant student' (Forghani-Arani, Cerna and Bannon 2019: 14).

In Turkey, educational policies indicate concerns with the increased diversity in classrooms, given that the country is one of the hosts of the world's largest refugee population. Particularly, they distress how those refugee children equitably progress their educational trajectory and how they are integrated into the current schooling system in Turkey. Despite educational and social inequalities are historical and systemic issues in Turkey (Ünal et al. 2010), diverse classrooms have been widely recognized and acknowledged following the migration of people over the last few decades. This visibility opens up a space for a discussion of diversity in multiple educational spheres and the need for teachers who can effectively address the issues of diversity in today's classrooms. Preparation of teachers with inclusive pedagogical skills and competencies becomes the key agenda in teacher education, especially when they have students with an immigrant background in their classrooms (Öztürk et al. 2017). Nevertheless, effective management of diversity is promoted as a way to maintain 'social cohesion' (Forghani-Arani, Cerna and Bannon 2019: 36) both in the classrooms and also in society, rather than teaching and learning the content. In a similar vein, the desire to maintain social cohesion is taken as an issue of safety in Turkish classrooms. That is, inclusive pedagogies are considered to support and initiate social interaction and harmony among students coming from diverse backgrounds to prevent conflict in both classrooms and society (Öztürk et al. 2017). Here, handling *diversity* governs the activity of teaching and makes kinds of teachers who administer the children in the schools (Popkewitz 1998). In these processes, teachers are recognized as responsible actors to contribute social progress and development by cultivating 'quality of individuals' (Directorate of Teacher Training and Development (DTTD) 2017b: 20) as they learn asset-based pedagogies where they draw upon children's lived experiences and interests. These pedagogies are considered inclusive since they aim at socially and culturally integrating diverse student populations with the current system of schooling. Configuring teachers as key actors in these acculturation processes with a concern for security, a governmental space is produced. Rather than taking for granted, this chapter critically examines the current teacher education discourses in Turkey, as making teachers particular kinds of people who are to be prepared for the organization of diverse classrooms.

In an era in which diversity has increasingly become visible in the classrooms, continual education of teachers has been one of the primary goals to include all students despite their differences (Darling-Hammond 2006). The professional development initiatives consider that education is a never-ending process and suggest the need for self-monitoring of teaching activities on a day-to-day basis. For example, teachers are instructed to be reflective about their teaching practices so that they could be adaptive to the new conditions such as the increased diversity in classrooms. However, reflective teachers are not born but made through a set of regulatory practices and meanings that are produced with temporal governing technologies (Fendler 2003). In similar ways, and as will be analysed in this chapter, contemporary professional development initiatives further contribute to the making of teachers of diverse classrooms with a set of regulations and control techniques to provide inclusive teaching for all.

As continual education of teachers becomes more and more common sense, the practices of administration of teachers are also changing. The governance practices in the teacher education field are understood as those mechanisms in societies of control (Deleuze 1992). These include faster and more frequent monitoring of teaching, accountability of teachers to multiple stakeholders and the impossibility of completion (Fendler 2008). For example, self-assessment tools and practices have been built into the continual education of teachers to promote teacher autonomy and position teachers as subjects of their teaching. These tools are considered to enable teachers to work on their preconceptions and biases regarding immigrant students (Öztürk et al. 2017). With the increasingly diversified classrooms, teachers are to be prepared to teach their content in equitable ways. Through fast and frequent self-evaluation, teachers continually monitor themselves so that they could commit themselves to see the positive traits of immigrant students and develop inclusive pedagogies. These pedagogies need to build on students' assets and capabilities rather than weaknesses that build on deficit orientations. Given that the context of classrooms cannot be known in advance, the ongoing teacher self-assessment does not only serve to develop inclusive pedagogies but also becomes a vehicle to control uncertain conditions through continual instructional adaptation. In these processes, teachers learn to see inequalities between students to reflect and modify their teaching approaches for diverse learners.

In this chapter, I aim to explore how practices and statements proposed to respond to classroom diversity function as control technologies of making the teacher and the regulation of inclusive teaching. Drawing on the works of Foucault (1991) on governmentality and Deleuze (1992) on societies of control, I examine how continual professional development and self-assessment tools function as regulatory practices to govern the teacher and culturally intelligible notions of teacher selves for today's diverse classrooms. Concerning Turkey, this chapter aims to explore how these tools and techniques construct a particular kind of teacher who is to be prepared to secure uncertain conditions as well as to maintain social cohesion. It makes visible the production of norms for 'inclusive' teachers of diverse classrooms through self-practised professional tools and how those norms are deeply connected with the values of self-monitoring and security in contemporary control societies.

I scrutinize how those formations of the teachers of diverse classrooms embody cultural rules of knowledge that generate distinctions and divisions between kinds of learners in the efforts to include all. Examining the constitution of teacher selves also enables an understanding of how particular kinds of students and their differences are made. That is, I analyse how teacher self and diverse classrooms are co-constituted within the network of inclusive pedagogies that simultaneously differentiate and divide children. Here, my point is to think about productive power, and how it operates in contemporary modern societies, which is different from domination or repression. Rather than the pressures experienced by teachers, this chapter tries to understand how teachers and students are generated as particular kinds of people (Hacking 2007). In doing so, this chapter explores the limits of contemporary education reforms and questions the theoretical moves built upon classroom diversity that simultaneously configures and governs the 'inclusive' teachers.

The chapter is organized as follows: I begin discussing how being prepared to teach in classrooms with diverse student population(s) exercises multiple governance and control modes for the teacher. Then, in the context of Turkey, I explore how governmental rationalities and technologies make 'inclusive' teachers of diverse classrooms. I specifically analyse the insistence of continual professional learning and self-assessment tools as professional devices of making and regulating the 'inclusive' teacher. Last, I examine the dangers of inclusive pedagogies as they divide and differentiate students in the effort to include. The analysis suggests that teachers are not the key actor of inclusive pedagogies. Rather, the emerging assemblage of 'inclusive' teachers with the aforementioned pedagogical devices configures and regulates the classroom differentiating discourses.

2. Being Prepared for Diverse Classrooms: Multiple Forms of Normalization and Control

Recent teacher education practices, international assessments of teachers and standards for teaching seek to prepare teachers for diverse classrooms (i.e. Forghani-Arani, Cerna and Bannon 2019). Nevertheless, the statements and practices to improve teaching quality do neither refer to an endpoint nor a single version of teaching that the teachers are prepared for. Rather, current discourses for teacher education concern teachers' continual professional development (Darling-Hammond 2006). While discourses focus on teacher autonomy and flexibility, teachers need to be prepared for diverse classrooms in which they can easily adapt their instruction to available circumstances.

Being prepared has an anticipatory mode of thinking to secure, control and normalize particular forms of actions and participation in contemporary societies (Anderson 2010). It provides a sort of uncertainty to the teacher education in relation to the ever-changing world and a new kind of teacher who is not fixed and stable but a dynamic individual having the potential to adapt their teaching in more situated and contextual forms (Heyck 2015). Since diverse classrooms cannot be known in advance, being prepared for diverse classrooms remains uncertain so that teachers are produced in flexible ways to adapt their instruction according to the context of their diverse classrooms.

Being prepared for diverse classrooms, nevertheless, operates as a discursive strategy of making teachers for inclusive teaching (e.g. Hacking 2007). Teachers are to be prepared to accommodate differences between students in diverse classrooms in which they learn to design their instruction based on students' assets (see Forghani-Arani, Cerna and Bannon 2019). Along with the emphasis on teacher autonomy and treating them as subjects of their instructional decisions, teaching practices include flexible, adaptive and ever-emerging ideas. For an 'inclusive' teacher, although an exhaustive list to do or a recipe of effective teaching procedures is not provided, teaching practices are regulated and controlled by the need for continual effort to improve those uncertain conditions. This represents the equitable teaching as a fluid, ever-changing and never-ending production process (Yolcu 2021) in which teachers are signified as adaptive, flexible and reflective to make inclusive and just decisions in diverse classrooms.

Contemporary educational practices do not suggest separating different students into different classrooms but insist on the heterogeneity of the student population in classrooms. Conventionally, schooling practices inequitably separate students into classrooms based on their abilities, needs, interests and social background (Oakes 2005), whereas today's educational vision supports diverse classrooms that include all students regardless of their abilities and social backgrounds. To achieve an inclusive vision for all students, new tools and technologies are invented. These tools, nevertheless, do not merely improve instruction but also make the teachers by working on their inner qualities in a way that they are to embody a particular set of actions (Popkewitz 1998). For example, the uncertain conditions of diverse classrooms are secured with pedagogical and professional tools in a way of cultivating the ability to live and learn together despite the differences. These shifting practices of schooling and processes of inclusive pedagogies do not simply assign new roles to teachers but actively configure teachers through internalizing particular subjectivities in the face of uncertain conditions of classrooms.

However, how to act and participate in the real world under uncertain conditions is not a new problem. Historically, for example, statistical technologies make the kinds of people and formulate what the normal is to control the population and state (Hacking 1990). The contemporary technologies of control are more related to the configuration of the spaces of security in which the issue becomes the administration of people in their own living time and spaces (Foucault 2007). These moving spaces are not enclosed in a disciplinary sense: People are not divided in advance. For instance, as immigrant students move into another country, they cannot be separated from the local population. Rather, these moving spaces are integrated with the local context. Moreover, these processes further produce multiple forms of heterogeneity in diverse classrooms, including immigrant background and other socio-demographic characteristics of the local population such as gender, socio-economic status, race and ethnicity. The diverse classrooms are usually taken as a security concern. So, control technologies across spaces and possibilities are installed, such as perpetual training, frequent and faster surveillance and self-assessment tools to maintain social order and cohesion in these heterogeneous and diverse spaces (Deleuze 1992).

In this configuration of governmental tools and techniques, multiple forms of power are operating in new domains. According to Foucault (2007), normalization is enacted in establishing interplay between the different distributions of normal without referencing oneself to the specific norm. It occurs through relying on 'material givens' in an environment, 'a matter of maximizing the positive elements, for which one provides the best possible circulation, and of minimizing what is risky and inconvenient' (Foucault 2007: 19). That is, making of 'inclusive' teacher, for example, is a matter of getting closer to the normal through the continuous control mechanisms but not necessarily requires conforming to the norms. Here, we have the positive regulatory function of uncertainty that takes and affirms the different qualities of children as a positive object of administration (i.e. looking for their assets to organize teaching) through continuous and scientific management of diversity.

Exploring power relations in the teacher education field requires a detailed examination of descriptions, techniques, methods and knowledge. The analysis of the complexity and uncertainty of diverse classrooms enables a detailed picture for the teachers who are to provide 'inclusive' learning opportunities for learners with diverse backgrounds. As argued in the following sections in the context of Turkey, making the teachers of diverse classrooms through a number of control techniques and rationalities does not strictly divide and differentiate teachers according to the normalized category but establishes several curves of normality that distinguish classrooms as secure or not. This analysis provides the examination of productive power in teacher education practices and highlights the limits of contemporary practices, aiming at the inclusion of all.

3. Cultivating the Sense of Responsibility for 'Inclusive' Teaching

With the changing demographic conditions of today's classrooms in Turkey, educational needs are reidentified, learning processes are repurposed and teaching competencies are modified to ensure inclusive experiences and success for all students regardless of their social and cultural background. The movement towards inclusive teaching is to generate an alternative space for all, in which teachers are considered as the key figures of safeguarding motivation, social integration and adjustment of foreign-born students in addition to promoting success and academic achievement of all (see Öztürk et al. 2017: 92). Being prepared for enacting these hopes, teachers are expected to gain a sense of responsibility for acquiring inclusive teaching competencies for diverse classrooms where they respect different habits of learning, get to know families and become aware of the cultural richness that foreign-born students bring to the classrooms.

Affirming cultural richness is not merely an improvement of teaching competencies in diverse classrooms. A humanitarian responsibility and moral anxiety are cultivated among teachers, since the immigrant students, particularly refugee students, are formulated as the victims of the global system. These reveal a concern of inclusion of those others into the current spaces of schooling through interaction and harmony along with the local population rather than conflict (Öztürk et al. 2017: 23–4). In parallel with the multicultural literature in Turkey that has been limited to develop tolerance and sensitivity towards cultural minorities (Özsoy and Bilgi 2016), the responsibilities of 'inclusive' teacher in diverse classrooms include a set of values such as 'respect and tolerance, generosity and hospitability' (Öztürk et al. 2017: 30–1) towards the victim other. More than creating a social cohesion in diverse classrooms, these discourses entail a hierarchy between the local students and culturally different, foreign-born or others (Özsoy and Bilgi 2016). That is, students are differentiated along a hierarchical continuum, from the citizens of Turkey and to the foreign-born and non-Turkish speakers. As teacher competencies for inclusive education are built on these assumptions, responding to the educational needs and interests of diverse students is built upon a set of values and morals that put the teacher in a position of a responsible saviour. Since those students located in the lower end are positioned as the victim other, the work of teaching is framed through a missionary lens (see e.g. Martin 2007), in which teachers are prepared to be the moral advocates of the migrant other in diverse classrooms. In addition to the hierarchical production of differences in the classrooms, this kind of 'inclusive' teacher is made based on particular notions of responsibility and morality. Here, diverse classrooms become normative in which the migrant others are positioned as in need of rescue from their own living and learning conditions without attending to their social and political contexts in their host countries.

The sense of responsibility towards migrant others usually takes the differences among students as an issue that needs to be resolved, albeit in positive ways, and characterizes the activity of teaching as management of diverse and heterogeneous classrooms. Nevertheless, that responsibility does not require teachers to dominate the students but to build a classroom culture where teachers are positioned with the students: 'Teachers position on the side of children, not as the other party in all evaluation processes. They also evaluate their own teaching skills, they are always open to learning, are enthusiastic and make people feel this' (Ministry of National Education (MNE) 2018: 21). These characteristics for the teachers indicate the management of the diverse classrooms is to configure a kind of teacher whose dispositions, sensitivities and responsibilities are transformed. That is, the responsibility of building an inclusive and equitable classroom culture configures the 'inclusive' teacher who needs to internalize particular characteristics such as being responsible and tolerant to differences or seeing the positive characteristics of diverse students. Nonetheless, cultivating the sense of responsibility for inclusive teaching is not a simple learning task. It does compromise a set of professional techniques and strategies to internalize those morals and values. As will be discussed through the professional devices of these formulation processes, teachers are asked to make their own teaching decisions, but the tools enable regulatory conditions to actualize those decisions.

4. Professional Devices of Making the 'Inclusive' Teacher

Continual professional development with necessary self-assessment procedures is configured as an important component of being prepared for inclusive teaching in diverse classrooms. As argued above, preparation for teaching in diverse classrooms cannot exactly be designed in advance and planned due to unforeseen circumstances. In this regard, continuous learning on a daily basis becomes one of the professional devices of making the 'inclusive' teacher. Those professional tools and techniques are considered as part of the intelligibility that makes the particular kinds of teachers as being prepared for diverse classrooms. In this regard, analysis of professional devices as material practices within the spaces of teaching and teacher education is a way to decentre the teachers and to analyse how 'inclusive' teachers are made in a field that relates knowledge and power (Popkewitz and Brennan 1997). Below, I examine two of these pedagogical devices, which are considered as useful tools to be prepared for organization and management of diverse classrooms. Despite the pragmatic nature of these strategies, my examination focuses on their boundaries and constitutive actions in the making of the teacher.

Continuous Professional Development

In the processes of learning inclusive teaching practices and so becoming an 'inclusive' teacher, the continual comparison is made with the traditional education where immigrant students fall in a 'disadvantageous position' (Öztürk et al. 2017: 39). To provide equitable and socially just experiences for all and to prevent adaptation difficulties, teachers need to learn to *differentiate* their available instructional practices with respect to diverse backgrounds. Here, the teacher is configured as a kind of person who is 'open to continuous development' (DTTD 2017a: 3) and 'adaptive to the emergent circumstances' (DTTD 2017b: 15) such as classroom diversity where they continually adjust and differentiate their instructional practices since their previous education and training is never seen enough to be the kind of teacher that is desired for inclusive teaching. Here, teachers are being positioned as always lack of knowledge and experiences. This generates a never-accomplished professional goal and a governmental space that limits the actions of teachers.

Continuous professional development can be an example of the contemporary mode of governance in teacher education. Far from the traditional models of domination and subordination, teachers are inculcated to be open for further training since the possibility of completion is foreclosed as in the control societies (Fendler 2008). Here, despite the continuous professional development is not obligatory for teachers, they are encouraged to take teacher seminars where they obtain skills and knowledge to handle effectively new classroom contexts such as diversity. Then, the education of teachers becomes a never-ending process and the completion would not be an option for a teacher. Although this can be a way to open up various possibilities for diverse classrooms, the need for lifelong learning more becomes a mode of conduct in the everyday life of teachers. This is particularly because that their conventional practices are seen as outdated or unsuitable for new and uncertain classroom conditions. For example, in the contemporary mathematics classrooms, teachers are expected to accommodate differences among students who come from diverse linguistic and cultural backgrounds, who have specific disabilities or who possess a special talent and interest in mathematics (National Council of Teachers of Mathematics (NCTM) 2014). Within the scope of these teacher education policies and related documents in Turkey, similarly, an inclusive teacher is configured as the one who is not insisting on those old-fashioned practices. Rather, the desired teacher is the one who continually adapts their teaching repertoire with innovative approaches to respond and manage the classroom diversity with the help of continual professional development.

Being open to continuous development, furthermore, reworks on teachers' characters and personal traits: 'The teacher should be willing, persistent, lively, energetic and creative, aware of the responsibility of self-development' (DTTD 2006: 17). The making of teachers in the migration context of Turkey incorporates both professional and personal dimensions of growth as lifelong learners (Popkewitz 2008). For example, teacher knowledge and skills are also expanded with values of respect and tolerance towards others. Addressing the issues of diversity in the classrooms is not merely a technical issue but contains a sense of responsibility of being a role model in their classrooms to constitute an equitable and inclusive society (Öztürk et al. 2017: 16). Hoping for social harmony and cohesion, teachers need to eliminate their fixed beliefs and attitudes towards students from diverse religious and ethnic backgrounds (Öztürk et al. 2017: 18–19). In this way, teachers begin to get to know students who are different from the local ones and teachers can start to accommodate their instructional practices with respect to diverse prior knowledge, interest, needs, learning styles and other characteristics of immigrant students. Nevertheless, the 'inclusive' teaching practices are not simply knowledge that teachers learn and implement in diverse classrooms. Rather, teachers are expected to internalize those practices, their rationalities and potential consequences. And, here, the formation of the teacher is not merely built on the teachers' action and participation as agents, but the material tools and techniques act in the configuration of the 'inclusive' teacher.

The Case of Self-Assessment Tools

As teachers are seen as the key players to transform education and to reduce educational inequalities, they are expected to 'take action knowingly and willingly' (Education Reform Initiative (ERI) 2019: 8). That is, teachers are seen as subjects of their teaching in which they should have the 'authority' over their practices. In this way, teachers are thought to have the capacity to transform education and become empowered to enact inclusive educational expectations (Education Reform Initiative (ERI) 2019: 10–16). Particularly, they 'should be able to develop critical thinking, problem solving, communication skills and aesthetic understanding and use them effectively' (DTTD 2006: 17). In parallel with their continuous learning and professional development, teachers are to monitor and evaluate themselves with respect to the national and international competencies for teaching such as the strong content knowledge, professional skills and the values of twenty-first-century world: 'It is very important for our teachers to identify their strengths and weaknesses in the light of national and international criteria by carefully examining competencies as well as their own individual and local needs' (DTTD 2017b: 16). Taking the teacher competencies as the criteria of evaluation, teachers are asked to assess their own teaching practices and continually evaluate themselves as competent or not.

Rather than an external control or coercion, the implementation of inclusive pedagogies depends on the teachers' own evaluation and assessment of their competencies through their use of self-assessment tools such as personalized maps, personal and professional plans and diaries. Self-assessment is considered as a professional responsibility and the use of these tools enables teachers to interrogate their competencies, identify their current situations and determine new professional goals and make plans to realize these goals (DTT 2017a: 10). For instance, teachers reflect on the teaching and learning processes in diverse classrooms through specifically 'keeping diaries' (Öztürk et al. 2017: 47). On a daily basis, they write and think about their own practices and experiences with foreign students. Keeping track of specific situations through crafting personal narratives in their own diaries, teachers are to self-validate the differences between students, and they 'knowingly and willingly' modify their instructional practices towards inclusive ends.

These tools and practices do not dictate a particular teaching self; nevertheless, they work on the inner qualities of teachers that normalize particular teaching actions or instructional moves that assume students' differences. As inclusive teaching suggests differentiating instruction based on the students' assets and capabilities, the self-assessment tools unpack teachers' own practices, develop skills of empathy and enable teachers to think from the 'eyes' (Öztürk et al. 2017: 47) of the learners. Although empathizing with foreign students is seen as a solution for the 'mismatch' between teachers and foreign students, documentation of feelings, reflections and thoughts judges teaching practices and gives value for them as 'inclusive' teachers.

5. 'Inclusive' Pedagogies as Making the Child and the Society

Making the inclusive teachers through the professional devices and enabling inclusive teaching with a sense of responsibility is enacted to secure the uncertain conditions of diverse classrooms. So far, I have discussed the ways in which the teachers are configured as particular kinds through considering professional tools and strategies that carry cultural and moral values in the field of teaching and teacher development. I have problematized the internalization of the need for continuous professional development and self-assessment as a mode of governance in the everyday life of teachers. Besides the administration of the teacher, securing diverse classrooms has been a way to make the children as a particular kind of person. The dangers become visible as the human kinds and their differences are produced in culturally intelligible ways despite the aims of including the migrant other.

In the context of inclusive education for diverse classrooms in Turkey, teachers are to provide differentiated learning environments, aiming at the cultivation of values and attitudes of democracy, respect and recognition of diverse cultures (Öztürk et al. 2017: 48). Building a classroom culture, based on harmony and cohesion, assumes that the conflicts in society are also prevented. Here, the aim is not merely teaching subject matter but teaching and learning processes include particular values that are compatible with the norms of local culture such as 'patriotism, honesty or environmental sensibility' (Öztürk et al. 2017: 46). The purposes of differentiated lessons are extended with 'socialization, communication, elimination of bias and prejudice, language acquisition and cultural integration and respect' (Öztürk et al. 2017: 47). These 'inclusive' teaching practices may seem like a pedagogical accommodation of differences of students with an immigration background but, in fact, incorporate an assimilation process based on cultural norms and values of the host countries.

In Turkey, teachers are considered as 'bridges' (DTTD 2017a: 1) between social values and next generations, and teaching in diverse classrooms is not merely consisting of teaching content and skills. Besides the accommodation of students' differences in affirmative ways, teachers' professional improvement and their work on their own biases and the development of tolerance towards others are not merely for improving the academic success of diverse learners. Rather, these personal characteristics become a role model for the immigrant students to safeguard conflicted situations both in the classroom and also in society.

Considering the teachers of diverse classrooms as a role model for all, particularly for the immigrant students, becomes a way to locate the children and their families as lacking of appropriate and acceptable role models. This reveals paradoxical situations where teachers are asked to implement asset-based pedagogies that value children's lived experiences and prior knowledge. Rather than recognition of differences in non-hierarchical ways, the cultivation of the particular norms of local culture through role models unveils the assimilative nature of these practices. As argued by Özsoy and Bilgi (2016), this is particularly due to the hegemonic position of the state that forces diverse students to assimilation by homogenizing them into the local culture and values.

Teachers are usually considered as a bridge between social and cultural values and the next generations. However, they are not directly transmitting those values to the students. Rather, the processes of teaching and learning make students as particular human kinds such as problem solvers, lifelong learners or able bodies through generating cultural thesis that governs their modes of conduct not only in the classrooms but also in daily life (Popkewitz 1998). That is, when inclusive pedagogies are exercised in diverse classrooms, the ability to live together and the values of social harmony are also cultivated so that children are made as particular human kinds who are able to maintain social cohesion despite the distinctions. The problem occurs when the differences are ranked on a hierarchy within the desire to build a society without social conflicts.

For example, teachers working in diverse classrooms are asked to develop a democratic attitude among students through cooperative learning environments in which students are to learn to work together, respect each other and communicate (Öztürk et al. 2017). Nevertheless, the learning products are differentiated based on student's prior knowledge and readiness. To illustrate, while the homework expectation is 'designing an encyclopaedia entry' (Öztürk et al. 2017: 54–5) for those students who have a robust prior knowledge, 'preparing a newspaper article' (Öztürk et al. 2017: 54–5) with a simple language is seen as enough for others. That is, despite diverse students learn together in a heterogeneous environment, the learning products are gradually differentiated.

By being prepared for such differentiation processes and taking the distinguished pedagogical measures, students are divided in the same classroom with respect to their prior knowledge, and the processes of teaching and learning work as technologies of governance. Despite the efforts to create an inclusive and equitable learning environment in diverse classrooms, differentiating the academic expectations while cultivating particular social and moral values further visualizes students' differences and makes them visible for pedagogical intervention. This way of pedagogical reasoning maintains the social hierarchies in diverse classrooms and generates an exclusive diverse society.

6. Final Remarks

In this chapter, I have examined the recent landscape of teacher education in Turkey that prepares teachers for diverse classrooms. The desire for continual development and the persistent use of self-assessment tools function as professional devices for making and regulating a particular kind of teacher who maintains social cohesion both in the classroom and society. These professional devices are not simple additions to the available teaching repertoire, but they actively participate in the formation of teachers of diverse classrooms. In addition to the configuration of 'inclusive' teacher as being prepared for uncertain classroom conditions such as diversity, enactment of 'inclusive' pedagogies simultaneously generates kinds of students and their distinctions. Here, diversity is seen and acted as a site to make the child who embodies particular knowledge and skills such as problem-solving, collaborative working or communication to maintain the social order in teaching and learning spaces.

Shifting the attention from the gaps in the achievement towards building inclusive classrooms is an important turning point for educational research and practice in the climates of migration all over the world. Nevertheless, as this chapter explores in Turkish educational contexts, responding to diversity with inclusive pedagogies is not far from limitations and dangers. Governing the activity of teaching in diverse classrooms with the use of self-monitoring techniques makes the teacher responsible towards the migrant other. Also, constructing inclusive teaching enables circulation of the cultural norms and values of the host country and differentiates the children as citizens versus foreign-born and non-Turkish speakers. These processes paradoxically recreate and maintain social hierarchies both in the classroom and in society despite the inclusive aims.

Rather than inculcating innovative teacher competencies to be prepared for the diverse populations and assimilative circulation of cultural norms and values, the emphasis needs to be built on the discourses and practices that govern the teacher and the work of teaching in diverse classrooms. This enables the problematization of how diversity becomes the object of teaching and learning. The particular attention to the governmental rationalities and tools unpacks the social and political contexts of migration instead of focusing on individual students.

References

Anderson, B. (2010), 'Preemption, Precaution, Preparedness: Anticipatory Action and Future Geographies', *Progress in Human Geography*, 34 (6): 777–98.

Darling-Hammond, L. (2006), 'Constructing 21st-Century Teacher Education', *Journal of Teacher Education*, 57 (3): 300–14.

Deleuze, G. (1992), 'Postscript on the Societies of Control', *The MIT Press*, October, 59: 3–7.

Directorate of Teacher Training and Development [DTTD] (2006), 'Öğretmenlik mesleği genel yeterlikleri' [General competencies for teaching profession], Ministry of National Education.

Directorate of Teacher Training and Development [DTTD] (2017a), 'Öğretmenlik mesleği genel yeterlikleri' [General competencies for teaching profession], Ministry of National Education.

Directorate of Teacher Training and Development [DTTD] (2017b), 'Öğretmen strateji belgesi' [Strategy document for teachers], Ministry of National Education.

Education Reform Initiative [ERI] (2019), 'Öğretmenler: Eğitim izleme raporu 2019' [Teachers: Education monitoring report], Eğitim Reformu Girişimi. Available online: https://www.egitimreformugirisimi.org/wp-content/uploads/2010/01/Egitim-%C4%B0zleme-Raporu-2019_Ogretmenler_.pdf (accessed 8 November 2021).

Fendler, L. (2003), 'Teacher Reflection in a Hall of Mirrors: Historical Influences and Political Reverberations', *Educational Researcher*, 32 (3): 16–25.

Fendler, L. (2008), 'Educationalising Trends in Societies of Control: Assessments, Problem-Based Learning and Empowerment', in P. Smeyers and M. Depaepe (eds), *Educational Research: The Educationalization of Social Problems*, 47–59, Singapore: Springer Science Business Media.

Forghani-Arani, N., L. Cerna and M. Bannon (2019), 'The Lives of Teachers in Diverse Classrooms', OECD Education Working Papers, No. 198, Paris: OECD Publishing.

Foucault, M. (1991), 'Governmentality', in G. Burchell, C. Gordon and P. Miller (eds), *The Foucault Effect: Studies in Governmentality*, 87–104, Chicago: University of Chicago Press.

Foucault, M. (2007), *Society Must be Defended: Lectures at the College de France, 1975–1976*, trans. D. Macey, New York: Picador.

Gutiérrez, R. (2008), 'A "Gap-Gazing" Fetish in Mathematics Education? Problematizing Research on the Achievement Gap', *Journal for Research in Mathematics Education*, 39 (4): 357–64.

Hacking, I. (1990), *Taming of Chance*, Cambridge: Cambridge University Press.

Hacking, I. (2007), 'Kinds of People: Moving Targets', *Proceedings of the British Academy*, 151: 285–318.

Heyck, H. (2015), *Age of System: Understanding the Development of Modern Social Science*, Baltimore: Johns Hopkins University Press.

Martin, D. B. (2007), 'Beyond Missionaries or Cannibals: Who Should Teach Mathematics to African American Children?', *The High School Journal*, 91 (1): 6–28.

Ministry of National Education (2018), *Güçlü yarınlar için 2023 eğitim vizyonu* [2023 education vision for strong futures]. Available online: http://2023vizyonu.meb.gov.tr/doc/2023_EGITIM_VIZYONU.pdf (accessed 8 November 2021).

National Council of Teachers of Mathematics (2014), 'Principles to Action: Ensuring Mathematical Success for All', NCTM National Council of Teachers of Mathematics. Available online: http://areaiihsmap.pbworks.com/w/file/fetch/109255672/Principles.To.Actions.ebook.pdf (accessed 8 November 2021).

Oakes, J. (2005), *Keeping Track: How Schools Structure Inequality*, 2nd edn, New Haven: Yale University Press.

Organization for Economic Co-operation and Development (2013), 'PISA 2012 Assessment and Analytical Framework: Mathematics, Reading, Science, Problem Solving and Financial Literacy', OECD Publishing, 11 February. doi:10.1787/9789264190511-en.

Özsoy, S. and S. Bilgi (2016), 'Multicultural Education Perspective in Turkey: Possibilities and Dilemmas', in J. Lo Bianco and A. Bal (eds), *Learning from Difference: Comparative Accounts of Multicultural Education*, 147–69, Basel: Springer International Publishing.

Öztürk, M., G. Ş. Tepetaş Cengiz, H. Köksal and S. Irez (2017), *Sınıfında yabancı uyruklu öğrenci bulunduran öğretmenler için el kitabı* [Handbook for teachers with foreign students in their classrooms], Ankara: MEB.

Popkewitz, T. S. (1998), *Struggling for the Soul: The Politics of Schooling and the Construction of the Teacher*, New York: Teachers College Press.

Popkewitz, T. S. (2008), *Cosmopolitanism and the Age of School Reform: Science, Education, and Making Society by Making the Child*, London and New York: Routledge.

Popkewitz, T. S. and M. Brennan (1997), 'Restructuring of Social and Political Theory in Education: Foucault and a Social Epistemology of School Practices', *Educational Theory*, 47 (3): 287–313.

Ünal, I., S. Özsoy, A. Yıldız, S. Güngör, E. Aylar and D. Çankaya (2010), *Eğitimde Toplumsal Ayrışma [Social Division in Education]*, Ankara: Ankara Üniversitesi Basımevi.

Villegas, A. M. (2007), 'Dispositions in Teacher Education: A Look at Social Justice', *Journal of Teacher Education*, 58 (5): 370–80.

Yolcu, A. (2021), 'Fluid Identities for Equitable Mathematics Teaching: Narrative Analysis of Prospective Teachers' Foregrounds', *Teachers and Teaching*, 27 (1–4): 82–94.

3

Mobility and Education

Susanne Ress

1. Introduction

The number of people on the move has been rising steadily over recent years (UNHCR 2020). Many of them are refugees, and many of them are teachers. One would think that today's hybridized and transnationalized world valorizes migrating teachers' experiences and knowledges for their internationality. Yet, by leaving and/or being forced out of their home countries in search for safety and opportunities, teachers' professional skills are not easily transferred, it seems. Teachers' beliefs, perceptions and practices become illusive objects of scrutiny. The very act of moving brings along judgement, valorization or devaluation of refugee teachers' repertoires. How can educational scholarship make sense of what happens to teachers whose movements do not succumb to the certainty of place?

Discourses of internationalization of education may serve to bind the seemingly disparate concerns for teacher shortages and simultaneous deference (or denial) of access to the European education labour market in ways that reaffirm divisions manifest in different notions of mobility. Who refugee teachers are and what they can do in the national education systems of their destination countries rests on divergent interpretations of different kinds of movements across spatial-temporal landscapes. Regardless of refugee teachers' actual experiences, these often-unspoken interpretations set them apart from their nationally trained colleagues in ways that risk reproducing colonial racializing differences that have long been unveiled by postcolonial and critical Black and ethnic scholarship (cf. Fanon 1967 [1952]; Said 1978; Ferguson 2006; Povinelli 2011; Weheliye 2014). Thinking about the making of teachers in the age of migration thus calls for sustained reflections on divergent and differently valued meanings associated with different forms of international movement.

This chapter offers some reflections on mobility as movement, meaning and practice in relation to education. It builds on previous research conducted to learn about African students' experiences in the context of Brazilian higher education (Ress 2019). It further makes use of a comparative perspective, which I have acquired over thirty years of working and living in the 'trenches of internationalization' (including Germany's Reunification in 1990). Propelled across time and space by life, work and research, each change from one geographical-ideational location to another required an act of translation to make my knowledges and experiences legible within the receiving contexts. Immersing myself into a new context often meant learning locally adapt understandings of difference.

Similarly, in her seminal TED Talk *The Danger of a Single Story* (2009), Chimamanda Adichie admits: '[B]efore I went to the U.S., I didn't consciously identify as African. But in the U.S., whenever Africa came up, people turned to me. Never mind that I knew nothing about places like Namibia. But I did come to embrace this new identity and in many ways I think of myself now as African.'

Adichie's recollection exemplifies the need to reframe one's identity as part of moving to a new place, which makes me wonder about the kinds of learning refugee teachers have to perform to be accepted by their destination countries' society. Alisha Heinemann (2017), for instance, building on ethnographic research and discourse analysis, provides a critical account of the cultural learning demanded of refugees upon their arrival in Germany and Austria. Both countries are nation states that consider themselves monolingual as if German was the only spoken language (despite widespread bi- and multilingualism). Consequently, newcomers must first learn to speak German before being granted access to the labour market and becoming German or Austrian citizens. To this end, they have to participate in language and culture learning courses to become acquainted with German and Austrian societies and value systems. These courses teach refugees about cultural expectations and norms and what constitutes a 'good' citizen, parent or labourer. According to Heinemann, course participants' responses to these courses are informed by their desire to be 'good' and 'not to make any mistakes', to avoid attention, both of which are deeply ingrained colonial logics that subdue people of colour to occidental/White/male-dominated discourses of self-worth (cf. Jugé and Perez 2006). Refugees 'adapt' to the cultural demands either readily, reluctantly or submissively (Heinemann 2017). They adjust their self-perception to mimic the destination country's/ culture's understanding of difference. Moving becomes an act of transforming oneself to mirror the expectations of those who inhabited the place one is moving to. Notions of mobility play into these expectations.

2. The Meaning of Mobility

Thinking about mobility in theoretical-philosophical terms is more than thinking about movement from one location to another. It is about figuring out the socio-historical, political, economic and cultural meanings of getting around between places. While locations and movements can be mapped onto cartographic representations of the earth's surface, there is more to it. Mobilities come with histories and rich senses of meaning. To better grasp mobility as something that is filled with meaning, it is useful to distinguish between the concepts of mobility and movement as well as place and location (Cresswell 2006). Movement and location are the brute facts. Locations are geographical points on a map whereas movement represents the line a subject/object forms when dislocating from point A to point B. Mobility and place are the dynamic equivalents of movement and location. They are socially constructed, filled with history, ideology and power. People give meaning to mobility and place through daily interactions and interpretations. Mobility, alongside place thus understood, is an embodied experience, which provides people with a frame of reference for making sense of life – a way of 'being in the world' (Cresswell 2006: 3). This conceptual perspective opens analytical space for recognizing mobility as fundamental aspect of human life from which rich narratives and indeed ideologies emerge.

The relationship between mobility and place can be constructed as either sedentarist or nomadic (Cresswell 2006). In a sedentarist understanding, the line between A and B is defined by the characteristics of the places that make up A and B. Refugee teachers' migration would be explained, for example, by war, lack of safety or socio-economic opportunities in their home countries whereas moving to European countries would promise the opposite. In this place-based understanding, mobility happens because places between which to move exist. Movement itself carries no distinctive meaning. Staying in (one's rightful) location comes to be seen as a form of preserving sociocultural formations or, in the case of refugee teachers, professional skills. A sedentarist understanding values place and rootedness over mobility. It is akin to governing notions of nationhood and citizenship that privilege people, who are bound to a place by blood and soil (or language). Membership to a collective in this instance comes to be understood in relation to or by belonging to a particular place.

In a nomadic understanding, mobility itself carries meaning. Mobility can be perceived as change in its positive or negative sense such as progress, freedom or learning. It is seen as a process of becoming and a way of (re)producing life. A nomadic understanding does not privilege location over movement. It rather values movement for its own distinctive sociocultural formations that produce meanings beyond simplified notions of departure and arrival. As such it enables a comparison between various mobilities rather than sole interpretations of movement in reference to place. The theoretical distinction between sedentarist and nomadic lenses should not imply that one holds value over the other, yet, a focus on mobility as the experience of movement rather than location creates space for stories that go beyond the socio-historical, political and cultural constellations that constitute place.

The distinction between sedentarist and nomadic conceptualizations of mobility is useful in another way. It affords a categorization for the frames of references employed in public and professional interpretations assigned to various forms of mobility. What kind of narratives are emphasized to explain movements such as refugee teachers' migration? Is mobility understood as tied to a place – sedentarist – or does it carry meaning in its own right – nomadic? European education discourses and policies are increasingly concerned with international student mobility and internationalization of teacher education. This particular internationality heralds a nomadic understanding in which mobility is valued as (intercultural, global) learning, self-realization, flexibility and tolerance or acquisition of competences relevant for labour markets (cf. Brodersen 2014; Falkenhagen, Grimm and Volkmann 2019). It sets itself apart from settledness (immobility) perceived as lack of individual thrive for learning and change. Educational policies that focus on internationality, transnationality and mobility mask forced migration caused by wars, crises and poverty and miss to address European and national policies that (often violently) prevent refugees' movement across borders or restrict their movement within receiving countries (Dubiski, Chehata and Thimmel 2016). Table 3.1 juxtaposes conceptualizations of mobility and immobility and their different connotations.

Dominant perceptions often associate refugee teachers' movements with negatively connoted understandings of mobility. Firstly, teachers' professional repertoires are primarily understood through place. Value is assigned based on the fact that these teachers have left the 'old' but not yet arrived at the 'new' place. If allowed access to the teaching profession, they first must undergo the kinds of

Table 3.1 Conceptualizations of Mobility and Immobility

	Mobility	Immobility
Sedentarist	Devaluing movement as destroyer of sociocultural formations and traditions *Negative connotation*	Valuing settledness as preserving sociocultural formations and traditions *Positive connotation*
Nomadic	Valuing movement as learning, change and (individual) freedom *Positive connotation*	Devaluing settledness as lack of flexibility or as dysfunctionality in relation to the mobility of human bodies *Negative connotation*

Source: Author's depiction.

retraining examined by Heinemann (2017). Despite refugee teachers' rich and diverse personal stories and identities, they are primarily imagined as holders of 'outdated' (out-of-place) knowledges and skills that (might) suit the place they have left but need adjustment to suit the 'better here'. Their journeys are rarely associated with learning in the way that internationalization of education discourses implies. Secondly, although refugee teachers are perceived as those being on the move, their everyday lives are far more often characterized by (involuntary) immobilities compared to the freedom of movement enjoyed by 'rightful' national citizens (Sarikakis 2012).

Applying a critical Black and ethnic/postcolonial lens unveils the racializing undertones of these perceptions. It shows the mutual constitution of mobility and race. Concentration camps and reservations established by European colonizers (Zimmerer 2008), missionary schools for Indigenous people (Derksen 2020), plantation economies fuelled by transatlantic slavery (Singleton 2001), forced settlements of nomadic people (Randall and Giuffrida 2006; Wilson 2014), the prison industrial complex (Sudbury 2017), border protection, visa and residency regulations (Stahmann 2012; Dempsey 2021), urban stop-and-frisk policies and racial profiling and practices of policing Black bodies on sports fields (Stuesse and Coleman 2014; Cresswell 2016) have created and recreated racializing power structures across time and space over and over again. Restricting and surveilling the movement of people perceived as culturally and racially 'other' has been leaving an excruciatingly violent mark on the global history of human mobility.

Marginalized people and subaltern groups have also entrusted movement and mobilities with positive expressions of self-affirmation, freedom, resistance and other forms of empowerment (Weheliye 2014; Masola 2018). Thinking about mobility and race simultaneously affords a perspective that shows how socio-historical constructions of race have relied on mobility (alongside and intersecting with language, religion, sexuality, employment and otherwise) and, at the same time, how race has been mapped onto mobilities rearticulating and reinscribing the colonial difference that is at the roots of global inequalities. Considering internationalization discourses and non-European teachers' migration as iterations of the same phenomenon, yet valued differentially, highlights the need for a much deeper understanding of what is at stakes in the making of teachers in the age of migration. Educational scholarship needs to develop sensibilities to detect the racializing work performed by notions of mobility while moving beyond simplified understandings of mobility through place or celebrations of internationalization. This requires holistic, socio-historically situated analyses of subject positions produced by intersecting discourses of internationalization, mobility and place. It further entails a closer and more critical look at the kinds of learning (hidden or otherwise) that asks of refugee teachers to (re)locate themselves in unfamiliar terrains of difference.

The subsequent sections draw on research conducted at the International University of International Integration of Afro-Brazilian Lusophony (*Universidade da Integração Internacional da Lusofonia Afro-Brasileira*, UNILAB) which was established by the Brazilian government under the presidency of Lula Inácio da Silva in 2011 to foster development cooperation with African countries through intercultural integration (Ress 2019).[1] It is used as a case study to exemplify how students from Guinea-Bissau, São Tome e Principe, Mozambique, Angola and Cape Verde had to relearn understandings of difference as they adapted to the Brazilian society. Though not necessarily wealthy, many had lived in the capital cities of their home countries and considered themselves urban middle class. They are part of transnational networks with family members living in Europe and North America, able to mobilize relationships and resources. Coming to Brazil confronted them with a complicated and ambiguous mixture of assigned identities as 'Black' and 'African'. A historicized conceptualization of internationalization of higher education paired with the Brazilian racializing gaze constructed the students as locked in place (and in the past) while their own aspirations engendered mobility with meaning. Both shaped students' everyday lives and their ability to traverse sociocultural boundaries in Brazilian society. It also subjected their movements in and outside of classrooms to intensive surveillance, especially in the early days of the university. Although, admittedly, Africa-Brazil relations constitute a different sociospatial context than Europe and most of the students did not become teachers, their experiences pose important questions about broader efforts to 'integrate' (or not) refugee teachers into European education systems.

3. Racializing Mobility

A short look into history first: At the turn of the twentieth century following the abolition of slavery, Brazilian scientists subscribed to the idea that Europeans are inherently superior to non-White people, proposing policies of whitening as a solution (Schwarcz 1999). Brazilian politicians and scientific and economic elites subsequently promoted European immigration to replace slave labour and heralded miscegenation to alter what they perceived as biological degeneracy in the Brazilian populace. The eugenic understanding of the mixing of races became a central feature of Brazilian national identity, from which the idea of racial democracy that dominated Brazilian thinking from the 1930s to the early 1990s developed. Racial democracy claimed that Brazilian society was unique for its smooth blending of European, Indian and African people and cultures and free of the anti-Black racism that affected the rest of the world, especially the United States and South Africa. Gilberto Freyre, a famous Brazilian sociologist, identified the extended patriarchic family of the plantations (*latifundios*) in the sixteenth and seventeenth centuries as a cauldron for interracial mixing that harmonized differences and diluted conflicts, thus enabling extraordinary assimilation, creating a new Brazilian people ([1933] 1986). Yet, this purportedly anti-racist vision of miscegenation was contingent upon the process of whitening. Freyre acknowledged that miscegenation could only occur because people believed in the supremacist ideology of whitening. According to this popular notion, many Black Brazilians believed their greatest chance for escaping poverty was to marry Whites and lighter-skinned 'mulattos' (Telles 2004).

In 2011, the Brazilian government placed UNILAB in Redenção, a small town in the rural interior of the state of Ceará in Northeast Brazil, because it was the first town to legally abolish slavery in 1883. It entrusted the university with the objectives to (1) develop public higher education in the previously underserved rural interior of the country, (2) redress racial inequalities in Brazilian society and (3) foster Africa-Brazil through intercultural integration.[2] To legitimize the triple mandate, the university founders relied on a narrative in which Brazil accrued a historical debt from transatlantic slavery, which it hoped to compensate at least symbolically through cooperation with African countries (Cesarino 2017).

This particular sedentarist narrative constituted 'Africa' as the place from which slaves originated (and from which they were extracted by colonial force) and 'Brazil' as the recipient and eventual abolisher of slavery. It afforded the founders with the possibility to imagine transatlantic slavery as a supposedly shared history. The university's founding narrative positions 'Brazil' as a postcolonial nation state that successfully fought against the cruelty of slavery and now celebrates the Africanness of its culture from a post-slavery stance. 'Africa' cannot join in this celebration since it cannot abolish the continent's role as the source of slaves. The experiences and relations of African states and people in the present are subsumed into an imagined relationship of Africans out of Africa in the past and not as the contemporary flows of people into Brazil for new experiences and opportunities. In this particular construction of history, Brazil sets itself apart in time and space and consequently reworks and reemploys the idea of the 'other' as 'other' in time and place.

Simultaneously, the presence of international Black students on campus (and in Brazil) was mobilized to represent Brazilian efforts of intercultural integration, for example, on the university website and in publications. From a Brazilian perspective, this produced a vision of internal development and increasing equity within the state, which was well aligned with then president Lula's general efforts to overcome racialized inequalities. It also expressed the desire for development as an attempt to overcome the wrongs of history, which further reconstructs 'Africa' as a place that is always already in the past and that has to be lifted out of this past through cooperation with the always already present Brazil and into a developed future. In the attempt to fabricate a founding narrative – that is, to rediscover the history of slavery and postulate it as the new foundation of Brazil as a nation – the university founders collapsed complex histories into a simplified and historicized image of Africa, which repeats the century-old colonial gesture of othering 'Africa' and 'Africans' in a new yet all too familiar way, in the name of development (Kothari 2006; Wilson 2012). In other words, upon arrival in Brazil, many of the international students were confronted with a racializing depreciation (and sometimes outright hostility) that stood in stark contrast to the sense they themselves assigned to their journeys.

4. Relearning Difference

In many African countries, young people came of age at times when national elites, multilateral organizations and First and Second World donor countries promised progress and development for everyone. In reality, young people often witnessed and survived political instability, proxy hot wars, internal armed conflicts and economic decline (Ferguson 2006). Many of them are aware of the contradictory conditions of their lives. They realize their marginality and limited ability to participate in global modernity (Bordonaro 2006; Dureau 2013). Still, they dream about better lives and actively engage in forging them (Vigh 2006). Like many youths around the world, young Africans turn to education for opportunities of social and geographical mobilities. Education provides a cultural repertoire that affords young people with symbols, perceptions and attitudes to make sense of the world and their lives within (Stambach and Hall 2016).

International student mobility, in many ways, entails the culmination of these dreams. It can offer students access to university education or better quality thereof (King and Raghuram 2013). They can acquire what they perceive to be valuable credentials (Beck 2008) and provide financial support to their families from afar (de Haas 2010). Apart from these material opportunities, the physical act of moving between places carries a symbolic meaning. International migration for educational purposes allows youth from African countries to imagine their escape from marginality.

Many international students at the university imagined their moving to Brazil as stories of global belonging and participation in modernity, a sentiment that they found frequently disappointed by the Brazil-centred approach to internationalization. The founders of the international university aspired to create an ambience characterized by mutual recognition, understanding and respect for cultural diversity. In line with the premise that cultural sharing leads to fuller integration the administration invested significant resources into cultural and athletic activities where Brazilian and non-Brazilian students could familiarize themselves with the habits and customs of students from other countries. Following such familiarization, deeper connections – including dating, regular socializing and intermingling in daily life – were expected to occur. In class, Brazilian and non-Brazilian students were also encouraged to reflect on their lives in the form of the so-called life project (*projecto da vida*) and to makes plans for their (professional) futures. The life projects encouraged students to perceive themselves as agents of the future. Asking students to scrutinize their ideas of the future through introspection displayed in the public space of the classroom constitutes an act of surveillance that could expose unduly misconceptions of value systems perceived as the norm (e.g. intercultural integration).

Locating development (economic, cultural and otherwise) in the life of the individual represents a mode through which to control the uncertainty and unpredictability of the future. The possibility of locating certainty within the individual as the locus of identity and therefore projectable future rests on the Enlightenment invention of the Self as a certain kind of norm – reason, calculability, objectivity and rationality. This norm, however, is only one side of the binary. The other side is the unreasonable person through which the reasonable person can be conceived (Popkewitz 1998). The idea that an otherwise uncertain, instable future can be pinned down (stabilized) within a projectable life project simultaneously resurrects the notion of a subject incapable of planning.

Moreover, professors often envisioned the future for Brazilian and non-Brazilian students differently by linking them, among other things, to divergent notions of mobility. For Brazilian students, professors emphasized that the university would open individual opportunities, for example, to study abroad. The same professors assumed that international students would return 'Africa' (as their 'rightful' place) to foster development.

International students' daily experiences at the university and in the community were characterized by high levels of segregation, economic hardship and anti-Black/anti-African sentiments. Unfamiliar forms of sociability expressed through subtle mechanisms such as laughter (Dahia 2008; DaMatta 2001; Martins 2008), perceptions about language (Castanheira, Street and Carvalho 2015; Lewis 2003), silence (Sheriff 2000) or Brazilian students' refusal to study or 'help out' (Abad-Merino et al. 2013) as well as lack of financial resources restricted their physical and social mobilities. For instance, Redenção is located roughly two hours by bus away from the Fortaleza (the state's capital, located near the coast). International students with limited resources could not easily travel this distance and had to rely on the small number of stores in town, in some of which they were treated as intruders.

Some of the international students were able to cross sociocultural boundaries – such as moving across the town's square undisturbed or joining student groups at a football match – more easily than others. These boundaries were strongest for students with darker skin and limited financial resources. In the Brazilian context, people's ability to move freely across socio-economic and ultimately racial boundaries is often associated with the funds that people have available, which is referred to as the 'whitening' capacity of resources (Schwartzman 2007). Mixed-race, international students recounted that they were able to pass as Brazilian as long as they did not speak, which would reveal their non-Brazilian accent. Resources (i.e. social, cultural, political and economic capital (Bartlett 2007)) and the perceived and/or assumed appearance of affluence all played a role in facilitating physical mobility in daily activities and more fluid social relationships for some of the international students.

Non-familiarity with Brazilian forms of sociability also shaped international students' physical movement in classrooms and across campus. While Brazilian students would frequently stand up during lessons to approach the professor's desk or interact with peer, international students were less inclined to being mobile in such an informal manner. They were less familiar with treading the boundaries between playing and teaching in this new environment, and they did not always feel confident about whether they knew the rules. Likewise, Brazilian professors were more at ease with debating Brazilian students (even calling them to order) than they seemed to be in interactions with international students. Sociability in the Brazilian contexts functions as an ordering principle, which holds racial distinctions (economically, politically, culturally and before the law) in place. Sociable acts such as 'hands on other's shoulders, the attribution of loving nicknames, the use diminutives, congratulations, flattery and other forms of enchanting interpersonal relations' (Agier 1995: 251) are expressions of fraternization, which serve to maintain distinctive (racial) groups in the social fabric of Brazil.

Being unable to adequately perform such gestures often immobilized international students in particular ways. The cafeteria was an important space where students' social relations and movements became subjected to surveillance. Professors, administrators and researchers frequently judged students' behaviour based on their conception of what constitutes successful integration – that is, the spatial mixing of bodies equipped with divergent physical features. It was generally assumed that Brazilian and non-Brazilian students could be easily distinguished by visual markers such as the colour of their skin or style of clothing and whether 'integration' was happening could be judged based on the 'appropriate' mixing among all students. Professors, administrators and researchers frequently screened the room to discern whether integration was indeed occurring. Since UNILAB was still small at the time of research (2011–15), professors knew many of the students individually. But beyond that they performed their surveillance by relying on their senses, which entrusted them – as they had themselves convinced – with the ability to register in the flicker of the moment the progression of integration. Needless to say, the purported ability to judge based on visual markers was an illusion which often failed the observer and led to a misjudgement of students' belonging, which again afforded some students with more liberty of movement than others.

International students, on the other hand, behaved in the cafeteria in ways that enabled them to create safe spaces where they could escape, temporarily and however imperfectly, the disciplining function of professors' surveillance. Sometimes students would sit together with their classmates, but usually they shared their meals with friends and peers from their respective countries. Meeting in the same place around the same time every day during the busy routines of the day gave international students a sense of comfort in an environment that constantly called on them to represent the vision of the university. Country-specific groups provided a source of familiarity in what was otherwise an unfamiliar environment. Students did not have to request membership to sit with their peers because they belonged. They also did not have to explain themselves, their doings and motivations or their accents. To put it differently, they could engage with others by drawing on a familiar set of norms and beliefs. These groups were not perfectly harmonious, to the contrary. Personal quarrels and fault lines of difference (e.g. gender, ethnicity, religion or language) caused tensions within national groups as much as they did across them. It meant, however, that students populated a space in which they could rely on what was culturally known without having to feel that they were violating implicit norms of sociability.

Students, who often felt marginalized by their Brazilian peers, described their tables as zones of comfort, a small oasis in which they could somewhat let down their guards. By joining these tables, students created spaces for themselves, where they could hide from the rhetorics of integration, which marked them as racialized 'other', for as long as it took to eat their meals. The groups that students had in mind when speaking of comfort and camaraderie were not forcefully mixed (as done by group work in classrooms in an effort to foster integration). Instead they emerged from a sense of familiarity. These groups were also social networks within which students exchanged resources and lent each other support navigating the exigencies of living and studying in Redenção. As such these groups functioned in parallel to Brazilian networks, which Brazilian students accessed by virtue of Brazilian forms of sociability.

International students came to Brazil for the purpose of higher education. They saw their own mobilities as 'door to the world' that would provide their families and themselves with opportunities. Not all of them remained certain in light of the difficulties they faced in terms of anti-Black/anti-African sentiments, the lack of resources and future perspectives they encounter in Redenção. In addition, administrators, professors, fellow students and researchers frequently called on them to represent integration. Especially in the beginning (2011–13) their every move in and outside of classrooms was monitored. Yet, they adapted to locally conceived notions of difference by seeking out (e.g. interactions with fellow non-Brazilian students) or avoiding (e.g. two female students did not cross the central town square, an otherwise very sociable space) particular spaces. Much like Chimamanda Adichie admitted in her talk, they learned to 'read' the presence of their bodies within the powerfully racializing structures of the classed hierarchies of Brazilian society.

5. Conclusion

Some might think it far-fetched to borrow from international students' experiences in Brazil to reframe refugee teachers' movements into Europe, risking to perpetuate racializing constructions of people from the Arabic-Islamic world. At the same time, it is important not to miss the metamorphotic abilities of race, the spectre that looms over seemingly more benign conceptualizations of difference, such as *culture, ethnicity, language* or *education* because '[t]o think about the danger of what is useful, is not to think that the dangerous thing doesn't exist' (Spivak 1993: 11). From the perspective of the Brazilian government under Lula and Afro-Brazilian activists, international students' moving into Brazilian higher education carried the symbolic meaning of racial justice, which in turn assigned students the racializing subject position of the form slave, which denied students their contemporary realities. Upon arrival in Brazil, students had to learn to navigate new norms and forms of sociabilities. Both – symbolic meaning and social hierarchies – carried deeply racializing meanings, which left international students with little room to manoeuvre. No matter their ideas of internationalization and integration, their thoughts and actions were always already interpreted within a racializing frame of difference.

In Europe, we also have particular narratives about the value and meaning of mobility that emerged from history. What are these narratives? We too valorize and instrumentalize mobility depending on motives, whether it represents the excitement of learning or regulating national borders. Movements, big and small, get monitored in cities, on trains and in classrooms; and our societies certainly seem convinced that migrating teachers need 'integration'. Asked provocatively, 'How else could "we" [white/European/settler/colonizer] allow natio-ethno-culturally diverse teachers to teach "our" children?' Such perspectives rest on a sedentarist notion of mobility, where movement is merely opposite to location. Location in turn represents the illusion of meaning fixed in place, be it a continent, country or body. Somehow it seems unimaginable – far too 'dangerous' for 'our' way of life – to envision 'being a teacher' as a transnational endeavour, one that is not permanently affixed to a specific place (or imagined nation state) but rather feeds of the fragility, uncertainty, vulnerability and illusiveness of the human condition on an earth that is on the move and where mobility is a 'geographical fact that lies at the centre of constellations of power, creation of identities and the microgeographies of everyday life' (Cresswell 2010: 551).

To keep moving – forward, backward, sideways, in circles or chaotic/totally unstructured – will increasingly depend on unbound, non-classificatory engagements with each other. Not a denial of differences or false neutrality but a way of finding connections between seemingly disparate experiences, to connect at a human level, not as parents, not as teachers, but as humans. 'Does knowledge have a geography? Does knowledge have a biography? The decolonial project is to disclose identity, ideologies, biographies etc. and not to hide the political project of education' (Ndlovu-Gatsheni 2021, personal conversation in the context of a scholar activist decoloniality group), which requires unlearning the foundations of education, re-evaluating common understandings such as, for example, teacher professionalism. Thinking of mobility and teachers' professional repertoires as relations that form networks rather than considering refugee teachers to be atomized, 'dis(miss)place-able' individuals could provide a starting point. Sharing all sorts of stories about movement across time and space, reading migration as aspiration rather than unfortunate event can encourage transnationally mobile ways of belonging and learning which are more akin to many people's realities in which 'moving' rather than 'staying' is the norm.

Notes

1 Research was conducted between 2011 and 2015 with a total of five months of ethnographic fieldwork. Fieldwork began when the first campus was inaugurated in Redenção in 2011. By the end of 2015, UNILAB had three campuses, two in Ceará and one in Bahia. It enrolled 2,666 undergraduate students (73 per cent Brazilian, 27 per cent non-Brazilian). The university employed 173 professors (87 per cent Brazilian, 13 per cent non-Brazilian). It offered seven undergraduate disciplines including agronomy, engineering of sustainable energies, public administration,

nursing, social sciences and humanities, teacher education in mathematics and science and pedagogy.
2 The political idea of Africa-Brazil relations under the Lula presidency was radically new in its decolonizing vision (Ress 2018). The claim of solidarity with African countries coincided with a remarkable shift in state discourses from 'racial democracy' to 'affirmative action' (Htun 2004). At the beginning of the 2000s, after decades of holding on to the false perception that socio-economic disparities were not also racial disparities, the Brazilian government introduced a number of affirmative action policies to democratize access to public employment and higher education (Paschel 2016). Reforms included a change to the national curriculum mandating the teaching of the history and culture of Africa and the Afro-Brazilian diaspora at all levels of education. The aim was to acknowledge the economic role of enslaved labour in the emergence of the Brazilian nation state and to value the African heritage in Brazilian culture.

References

Abad-Merino, S., A. K. Newheiser, J. Dovidio, C. Tabernero and I. Gonzáles (2013), 'The Dynamics of Intergroup Helping: The Case of Subtle Bias against Latinos', *Cultural Diversity & Ethnic Minority Psychology*, 19 (4): 445–52.

Adichie, C. (2009), 'The Danger of a Single Story' [Video file], 9 July. Available online: http://www.ted.com/talks/chimamanda_adichie_the_danger_of_a_single_story?language=de (accessed 28 February 2018).

Agier, M. (1995), 'Racism, Culture and Black Identity in Brazil', *Bulletin of Latin American Research*, 14 (3): 245–64.

Bartlett, L. (2007), 'Human Capital or Human Connections? The Cultural Meanings of Education in Brazil', *Teachers College Record*, 109 (7): 1613–36.

Beck, K. V. (2008), 'Being International: Learning in a Canadian University', PhD thesis, Faculty for Education, Simon Fraser University, Ottawa.

Bordonaro, L. (2006), *Living at the Margins. Youth and Modernity in the Bijagó Islands* (Guinea-Bissau), PhD thesis, ISCTE, Lisbon.

Brodersen, M. (2014), 'Mobility: Ideological Discourse and Individual Narratives', in J. Gerhards, S. Hans and S. Carlson (eds), *Globalisierung, Bildung und grenzüberschreitende Mobilität*, 93–108, Wiesbaden: Springer VS.

Castanheira, M. L., B. V. Street and G. T. Carvalho (2015), 'Navigating Across Academic Contexts: Campo and Angolan Students in a Brazilian University', *Pedagogies: An International Journal*, 10 (1): 70–85.

Cesarino, L. (2017), 'Anthropology and the South–South Encounter: On "Culture" in Brazil–Africa Relations', *American Anthropologist*, 119 (2): 333–41.

Cresswell, T. (2006), *On the Move: Mobility in the Modern Western World*, New York: Routledge.

Cresswell, T. (2010), 'Mobilities I: Catching up', *Progress in Human Geography*, 33 (4): 550–8.

Cresswell, T. (2016), 'Black Moves: Moments in the History of African-American Masculine Mobilities', *Transfers*, 6 (1): 12–25.

Dahia, S. (2008), 'A mediação do riso na expressão e consolidação do racismo no Brasil' [The Role of Smiling in the Expression and Consolidation of Racism in Brazil], *Sociedade e Estado Brasília*, 23 (3): 697–720.

DaMatta, R. (2001), *O que faz o Brasil, Brasil?* [What does Brazil, Brazil?]. Rio de Janeiro: Rocco.

deHaas, H. (2010), 'Migration and Development: A Theoretical Perspective', *International Migration Review*, 44 (1): 227–64.

Dempsey, K. E. (2021), 'Migrant Agency and Counter-Hegemonic Efforts among Asylum Seekers in the Netherlands in Response to Geopolitical Control and Exclusion', *Geopolitics*, 27 (2): 402–423.

Derksen, M. (2020), 'Educating Children, Civilizing Society: Missionary Schools and Non-European Teachers in South Dutch New Guinea, 1902–1942', *International Review of Social History*, 65 (1): 43–70.

Dubiski, J., Y. Chehata and A. Thimmel (2016), '"Youth on the Move"?! Mobilität und Learning Mobility', in U. Becker, H. Friedrichs, F. von Gross and S. Kaiser (eds), *Ent-Grenztes Heranwachsen*, 291–307, Wiesbaden: Springer VS.

Dureau, C. (2013), 'Visibly Black. Phenotype and Cosmopolitan Aspirations on Simbo, Western Solomon Islands', in S. Trnka, C. Dureau and J. Park (eds), *Senses and Citizenships: Embodying Political Life*, 33–54, New York: Routledge.

Falkenhagen, C., N. Grimm and L. Volkmann, eds (2019), 'Internationalisierung des Lehramtsstudiums: Modelle, Konzepte, Erfahrungen', in *Internationalisierung des Lehramtsstudiums*, 1–14, Paderborn: Ferdinand Schöningh.

Fanon, F. and C. L. Markmann ([1952] 1967), *Black Skin, White Masks*, New York: Grove Press.

Ferguson, J. (2006), *Global Shadows: Africa in the Neoliberal World Order*, Durham: Duke University Press.

Heinemann, A. M. B. (2017), 'The Making of "Good Citizens": German Courses for Migrants and Refugees', *Studies in the Education of Adults*, 49 (2): 177–95. doi:10.1080/02660830.2018.1453115.

Htun, M. (2004), 'From "racial democracy" to Affirmative Action: Changing State Policy on Race in Brazil', *Latin American Research Review*, 39 (1): 60–89.

Jugé, T. S. and M. P. Perez (2006), 'The Modern Colonial Politics of Citizenship and Whiteness in France', *Social Identities*, 12 (2): 187–212.

King, R. and P. Raghuram (2013), 'International Student Migration: Mapping the Field and New Research Agendas', *Population, Space and Place*, 19 (2): 127–37.

Kothari, U. (2006), 'An Agenda for Thinking About "race" in Development', *Progress in Development Studies*, 6 (1): 9–23.

Lewis, A. (2003), 'Everyday Race-Making. Navigating Racial Boundaries in Schools', *American Behavioral Scientist*, 47 (3): 283–305.

Martins, F. (2008), 'Racism in Brazilian Aquarelle - The Place of Denying', *International Journal of Migration, Health and Social Care*, 4 (2): 37–46.

Masola, A. (2018), '"Bantu Women on the Move": Black Women and the Politics of Mobility in The Bantu World', *Historia*, 63 (1): 93–111.

Paschel, T. (2016), *Becoming Black Political Subjects: Movements and Ethno-Racial Rights in Colombia and Brazil*, Princeton: Princeton University Press.

Popkewitz, Thomas S. (1998), *Struggling for the Soul: The Politics of Schooling and the Construction of the Teacher*, New York: Teachers College Press.

Povinelli, E. A. (2011), *Economies of Abandonment: Social Belonging and Endurance in Late Liberalism*, Durham and London: Duke University Press.

Randall, S. and A. Giuffrida (2006), 'Forced Migration, Sedentarization and Social Change: Malian Kel Tamasheq', in D. Chatty (ed.), *Nomadic Societies in the Middle East and North Africa*, 435–66, Leiden and Boston: Brill.

Ress, S. (2018), 'Race as a Political Issue in Brazilian South-South Cooperation in Higher Education', *Comparative Education Review*, 62 (3). doi:10.1086/698307.

Ress, S. (2019), *Internationalization of Higher Education for Development: Blackness and Postcolonial Solidarity in Africa-Brazil Relations*, London: Bloomsbury Publishing.

Said, E. W. (1978), *Orientalism*, New York: Pantheon Books.

Sarikakis, K. (2012), 'Access Denied: The Anatomy of Silence, Immobilization and the Gendered Migrant', *Ethnic and Racial Studies*, 35 (5): 800–16.

Schwarcz, L. M. (1999), *The Spectacle of the Races: Scientists, Institutions and the Race Question in Brazil, 1870-1930*, New York: Hill and Wang.

Schwartzman, L. F. (2007), 'Does Money Whiten? Intergenerational Changes in Racial Classification in Brazil', *American Sociological Review*, 72 (6): 940–63.

Sheriff, R. E. (2000), 'Exposing Silence as Cultural Censorship: A Brazilian Case', *American Anthropologist, New Series*, 102 (1): 114–32.

Singleton, T. A. (2001), 'Slavery and Spatial Dialectics on Cuban Coffee Plantations', *World Archaeology*, 33 (1): 98–114.

Spivak, G. C. (1993), *Outside in the Teaching Machine*, New York: Routledge.

Stahmann, R. (2012), '"Residenzpflicht" und räumliche Beschränkungen der Bewegungsfreiheit', in K. Barwig, S. Beichel-Benedetti and G. Brinkmann (eds), *Gleichheit*, 348–76, Baden-Baden: Nomos.

Stambach, A. and K. D. Hall, eds (2016), *Anthropological Perspectives on Student Futures: Youth and the Politics of Possibility*, London: Palgrave Macmillan.

Stuesse, A. and M. Coleman (2014), 'Automobility, Immobility, Altermobility: Surviving and Resisting the Intensification of Immigrant Policing', *City & Society*, 26 (1): 51–72.

Sudbury, J. (2017), 'Celling Black Bodies: Black Women in the Global Prison Industrial Complex', in M. Chesney-Lind and M. Morash (eds), *Feminist Theories of Crime*, 457–74, London: Routledge.

Telles, E. E. (2004), *Race in Another America: The Significance of Skin Color in Brazil*, Princeton: Princeton University Press.

UNHCR (2020), *Global 2020*. Available online: https://reporting.unhcr.org/sites/default/files/gr2020/pdf/GR2020_English_Full_lo,wres.pdf (accessed 16 July 2021).

Vigh, H. (2006), 'The Colour of Destruction. On Racialization, Geno-Globality and the Social Imaginary in Bissau', *Anthropological Theory*, 6 (4): 481–500.

Weheliye, A. G. (2014), *Habeas Viscus. Racializing Assemblages, Biopolitics and Black Feminist Theories of the Human*, Durham: Duke University Press.

Wilson, A. (2014), 'Ambiguities of Space and Control: When Refugee Camp and Nomadic Encampment Meet', *Nomadic Peoples*, 18 (1): 38–60.

Wilson, K. (2012), *Race, Racism and Development: Interrogating History, Discourse and Practice*, London: Zed Books.

Zimmerer, J. (2008), 'Colonial Genocide: The Herero and Nama War (1904–8) in German South West Africa and its Significance', in D. Stone (ed.), *The Historiography of Genocide*, 323–43, London: Palgrave Macmillan.

4

Shared (Hi)stories of (Invisible) Living in the In-Between?

Experiences of and Perspectives on Being, Becoming and Remaining a Teacher in Austria

Tina Obermayr and Marie-Claire Sowinetz

1. Introduction/Preliminary Remarks

'In the past, Austria has welcomed refugees and shown great solidarity during numerous wars and crises' (UNHCR 2018: 10; translated by authors).[1] In the 1950s, for example, 170,000 Hungarians came to the country; in the 1960s, 'after the [so-called] "Prager Frühling", Austria became a refuge for almost 200,000 people' (UNHCR 2018: 10; translated by authors), and also in the 1990s, 90,000 people fled to Austria due to the violent collapse of Yugoslavia (UNHCR 2018: 10). Flight movements can thus by no means be regarded as a sudden or new phenomenon in Austria (Kremsner, Proyer and Obermayr 2020: 17). Nevertheless, the year 2015 undoubted holds specific significance: 'Across Europe, the time between late summer and fall 2015 became rapidly known as the so-called "refugee crisis", exposing us to daily pictures of large numbers of forced migrants crossing the borders to the EU on foot or by train' (Kohlenberger and Buber-Ennser 2017: [1]). In 2015, more than one million refugees and migrants arrived in Europe, the majority made the journey across the Mediterranean Sea, risking their lives on unseaworthy boats, resulting in more than 3,700 people dead or missing (UNHCR 2019: 7). In Austria, a total of 89,098 people sought asylum in 2015 (Bundesministerium für Inneres/Ministry of the Interior 2016: 3). Between 2015 and 2020, the Ministry of Interior recorded 196,203 asylum applications. However, in total, 113,194 people have been granted asylum or subsidiary protection in Austria.[2] Among those who have arrived in the country – contrary to the publicly represented and constantly (re)produced assumptions – a large number are highly skilled and well educated (Buber-Ennser et al. 2016: 21), and many are academics (Kremsner, Proyer and Obermayr 2020: 19). Many of these persons were (and still are) unable to continue working in their original profession in Austria because – particularly – formal recognition processes make it almost impossible to do so (Kremsner, Proyer and Obermayr 2020: 19; see also Resch et al. 2019). This affects not only, but especially, teachers, as teacher training differs significantly between countries of origin and arrival (e.g. Resch et al. 2019: 256). As a well-known phenomenon or rather as a result (for all refugees who arrived over time), many of the teachers are forced to take jobs that do not match their qualifications (Kremsner, Proyer and Obermayr 2020: 19; exemplary see also Miller 2008); many reject professional aspirations, abandon their former (professional) identity and seek new paths, since the goal to (re-)enter their original profession in the country of arrival seems unattainable. Despite the barriers already mentioned, there are (still?) a lot of people who have not given up. For this study, we, the authors, have interviewed eight people with different (biographical) backgrounds and ideas about life to find out about their experiences of trying to gain a foothold as teachers on the Austrian labour market; what challenges they have faced (and still face), and how they contextualize their experiences. The interviewees cover a broad spectrum of experiences: some were prevented from entering teacher training, others had to (re)qualify by attending a time-consuming course tailored especially for displaced teachers as a first step before entering teacher training program; some entered the system without any major hindrance. The stories told by the interviewees provide not only insight into their individual lived realities but also give an idea of how refugees in general and displaced teachers in particular have to position themselves amid (individual) hope and despair, and (social) paradoxes of *belonging and non-belonging.*

2. Methodical Approach, Guiding (Research) Question and Data Basis

From a critical reflexive perspective, it seems necessary to mention the limitations of this 'mini-study' already at this early stage: due to the relatively small sample size, the results generated can certainly not be accepted as universally valid. Much more, and larger-scale, research is needed to generate further and more precise findings. Nevertheless, the study can provide profitable insights: it focuses on cases that pay attention to forms of governance, how refugees are affected and how their experiences are (not) considered/valued. We are aiming at pinpointing to effects of rules and legislation that are intended to help reintegrate in the labour market but, in turn, might create inequalities. In the light of this, we assume that single case studies can be used for researching effects on subjects that point to (hidden) structures and (im)possibilities of dealing with them. Similarly, the fact that only very few people could be reached – despite attempts to recruit interviewees from across the whole of Austria – is very meaningful. Concerning the interpretation of this fact, it is crucial to differentiate: on the one hand, it is possible that persons simply do not want to be found (and categorized). Being singled out as 'refugee teacher' can be perceived as positive and helpful. Still, at the same time, affected persons might not want to be labelled that way. They might understand it as an unwanted attribution from outside and therefore reject it. On the other hand, it can also be (cautiously) concluded that the focused group of people is still hardly visible in society, a specific speechlessness prevails and there are few possibilities and tools to break through this barrier. In this context, it should also be mentioned that the Viennese certificate course 'Educational Basics for Displaced Teachers'[3] – located at the Postgraduate Centre of the University of Vienna – was for a long time the only Austrian (re)qualification measure available for displaced teachers. The last cycle of certification of the certificate course was completed in summer 2020. Since September 2019, a similar program has also been available in Upper Austria[4] – in summary, the range and scope of possibilities for teacher (re)qualification for this demographic in Austria are scarce.

Sample

Based on previous research (e.g. Kremsner, Proyer and Schmölz et al. 2020) as well as personal experience, we already assumed[5] that despite interviewees being qualified teachers in their respective countries of origin, their refugee status in Austria influences their access to the labour market in a way that doesn't necessarily allow for an easy path into the teaching profession. Therefore, the search for possible participants was based on three different groupings:

1) displaced teachers that slipped into the system without major obstacles
2) displaced teachers that attended specific (re)qualification measures, such as the Viennese certificate course 'Educational Basics for Displaced Teachers'

3) displaced teachers that – so far – were not at all able to get into the teacher training system or work in their former profession.

The outreach began with a written invitation that was spread through different channels so as to reach people in different federal states. With the help of specific contact persons, the invitation reached previous alumni as well as current participants of the Viennese certificate course directly. Persons who easily slipped into the system could be identified with the help of local education authorities as well as personal contacts. While most replies to the invitation came from former teachers facing difficulties entering the school system in Austria, reaching displaced teachers who had easily found work in the education system was quite challenging. Possible explanations are the fact that many do not want to be singled out or have discarded the label 'refugee' for themselves. In addition, the study took place during the Covid-19 pandemic, that is, at a time when the teachers' time and personal resources were very limited.

Survey and Evaluation Method

In total, qualitative and semi-structured interviews were conducted in English and German[6] with eight people, five women and three men, between June and October 2020 (participants from Syria, from Iran and from Bosnia and Herzegovina). Due to the Covid-19 pandemic all interviews were conducted online, via tools such as Zoom. Apart from existing guidelines, particular care was taken when conducting the interviews to respond flexibly to the content provided. This seemed to be of particular importance for obtaining an authentic impression of their life experiences and realities. In addition, in order to capture the interview situation in its entirety, care was taken to ensure that both authors were always present: this procedure made it possible to capture not only what was being said but also as much as possible of valuable atmospheric aspects and to involve all impressions in the analysis. Finally, all interviews were anonymized, transcribed and analysed in accordance with Mayring's (1994) qualitative content analysis; the method of structuring content analysis was applied here in detail, by which 'a certain structure can be filtered out of the material' (1994: 169; translated by authors) with the help of a category system. The central point of the procedure was to find indications or – rather – answers to the research question: *what are the main experiences of displaced teachers on their way to (re-)enter the teaching profession in Austria and how are they contextualized in the (individual) narratives?*

3. Main Findings

Inductively formed key categories (presented below) were developed in the course of (repeated) reflexive examination of the data material. In order to systematically outline the results of the interviews as clearly as possible, it seemed sensible to follow a structure that would trace different stages on the way to (re-)entering the teaching profession in Austria. For this reason, the findings are subdivided into the main subareas: (1) *being*, (2) *becoming* and (3) *remaining a teacher* in Austria.

Being a Teacher

'Something like spring in your soul': Vocation and the prevented process of (professional) self-fulfilment

All interviewees who are constantly and patiently engaged in entering the school system and working as teachers in Austria agree that the teaching profession is not just a job but also a kind of vocation. Barring two, all interviewees reach far back when telling their biographies. It becomes clear that they have always felt close to the teaching profession. The interviewees state that they have pursued the teaching profession 'all along' and that being a teacher constitutes a self-evident, basic feeling. In addition, and through their statements, it also becomes visible that they all link being a teacher with an inner attitude and an extraordinarily deep identificatory attachment. This is particularly evident in the following interview excerpt: 'Ahm // being a teacher is not / I don´t think it´s a job or it´s a kind of work / it is kind of / it is a kind of religion, a kind of belonging' (interview 1, ll. 42-3). It is interesting to note that the interviewees seem to have a clear idea of what a teacher is and what constitutes a teacher as such: a teacher imparts knowledge without exception in a school context. According to the interviewees, teachers are characterized above all by the fact that they generally *want* to help. However, only those who *do* actually help are considered to be 'good' teachers, that is, their success is ultimately linked to the achievement of a goal that often remains unspecified (in the interviews, there is repeated talk of helping; however, it is not explained what is to be helped with in detail).

Due to the strong (emotional) attachment, which in the interviews is always underpinned by emotive expressions and terms (e.g. 'dream job' (interview 7, l. 6); 'I was so impassioned' (interview 1, ll. 24-5); 'the most important thing is the emotion' (interview 3, l. 12)) to the teaching profession as well as the (internalized) professional ethos,[7] many of the teachers (in varying degrees, but to a certain extent uniformly) feel that the situation in Austria has robbed them of a piece of their identity. Due to the lack of recognition of them as teachers, the perception of belonging – which can be taken from the passage just quoted – is, to a certain extent, shaken on several levels simultaneously, and a diffusion arises between self-image and the image of the other. The interviewees state that they are teachers out of deep conviction. For them, there is no doubt about being a teacher. Because they do not receive recognition as teachers from others, they feel radically misunderstood. Here, the subjective meaning of professional recognition becomes obvious. Professional self-actualization extends into and influences the private sphere. Based on this, it can be concluded that professional fulfilment and self-realization are mutually related and interact with each other. In addition, the external framework conditions complicate the process of self-realization, which is closely related to an internalized professional identity. Both aspects have – especially for those who remain without concrete contact persons or support networks and who do not gain access to (re)qualifying programs – far-reaching consequences: the severity of the barriers on the outside often shifts to the inside of the persons. One interviewee who is still trying to find a way to continue working as a teacher in Austria reports:

> I all the time try but / how can I say / it is kind like a battery, if you don't recharge, you lose your power, this is happening here [. . .] I like my profession [. . .] this is my / all my passion or something my life, my heart [. . .] I cannot explain / this [loving one's job] gives you / something like spring in your soul / but if you have winter / all the time winter, all the time winter and no one is calling, you have nothing. (Interview 4, ll. 248–66)

'My Experience Is Worth Nothing': Lack of Recognition and Starting Again from Point Zero

All interviewees pursued a professional career and led an independent life before they had to flee their respective countries. This changed dramatically with their arrival in Austria. While some were aware that they might not be able to easily continue to work in their former profession (e.g. 'Yes, I prepared myself internally to start from zero again' (interview 6, l. 177)), others were convinced that they could continue their careers as a teacher in Austria without any major difficulties: 'Because I am a [subject/language] teacher, I thought it would be easier because I don't have to learn a new language and I could teach [...] right away' (interview 3, ll. 31–4).

The university degrees that used to be so valuable in their countries of origin had no value in Austria. Hence, with their degrees not (entirely) recognized, it becomes impossible for them to work as teachers in the Austrian school system. However, it is not only the formal recognition that is denied; participants also expressed that their professional experience does not seem to be very highly valued either: 'Personally, I have twenty years of experience and I can't work as a regular teacher now, that's [sigh] okay [...] we can be assistants or work in after-school care or I don't know' (interview 5, ll. 156–8).

Almost all participants expressed that their professional experience(s) and skills are not considered enough or are not valued by school directors or their fellow colleagues:

'Some school directors don't value my experiences [...] because they think the school system in [country of origin] is not like in Austria. They believe Austria has the best school system; therefore, we only need the people who studied in Austria. That means my experience is not worth anything' (interview 3, ll. 139–41). If one compares the systems of teacher training in Austria and the countries of origin of the teachers, it becomes apparent that the degrees cannot be compared on a formal level (Kremsner, Proyer and Obermayr 2020: 32). Austrian teacher training consists of three central elements: subject one, subject two and Basics in Education Studies (Kremsner, Proyer and Obermayr 2020: 32, figure 2). In most other countries, teachers need to prove only one subject (Kremsner, Proyer and Obermayr 2020: 32). While teachers attribute more value to their experiences than to the aforementioned formal aspects surrounding teacher training, this seems to contradict the perspective of school directors or fellow colleagues. That experiences are 'not worth anything' thus suggests that they play a rather subordinate role in comparison. From a critical perspective, certainly both approaches seem to be reductionist; certainly, however, the second-mentioned perspective runs the risk of making teachers invisible as (professional) subjects who have both their own biographical experiences (as students) and teaching experiences in the professional context. It can be assumed that both forms of experience (pre)form and influence teachers' (pedagogical) thinking and acting – in the sense of a (pre-) understanding that affects individuals on an unconscious level (Meyer-Drawe 1984). The fact that little importance is attached to these experiences, in turn, seems surprising because experiences constitute the teacher to a certain extent. The more experience a teacher has, the more s/he is usually trusted to be able to respond adequately to the professional challenges in school.

When asked about her/his experience with colleagues in school, one participant who works as a teacher, said, 'They don't see me properly; they don't believe that I can do anything. Maybe because of my background, because I'm not born there, because I speak broken German, I don't know what it's about, although I can do much, and can do more than the same person' (interview 2, ll. 228–31).

Another participant who already works in the school system noted that even if you have a job as a teacher, you still often doubt yourself: 'When I write something down, I have to look over it more often and make sure I haven't made any embarrassing mistakes [. . .] you often have to write things down, it's good but it's constant tension, and that's why it's a bit more work every day than you would have in your home country' (interview 8, ll. 214–18).

Becoming a Teacher in Austria

'They Told Me It Was Going to Be Hard': Formal Administrative Recognition of Qualifications as the Central but Non-transparent Thematic Linchpin

Not all of the interviewees were aware, when seeking asylum in Austria, that there might be complications concerning recognition of the qualifications they had 'brought with them'. It must also be noted that in some cases there was little time to think about the professional future that awaited in the country of arrival since the focus was on reaching safety. Moreover, as interviews made increasingly evident, Austria was not a firmly planned destination. Sooner or later, however, it became clear to the individuals who had the desire to re-enter their profession that working as a teacher in Austrian schools would involve major hurdles, primarily due to the fact that their experience, qualifications and so on did not meet aforementioned (formal) Austrian standards. The analysis of the interview transcripts showed that this problem was not only communicated in 'neutral' terms by state authorities and/or specialist advisors – many interviewees stated that they were also partly advised to discard their wish, as there was little chance of it coming true anyway. 'It was like a shock. You come out of war, you're not in good shape – new country, new people, new language. Then you hear you can't work as a teacher, even though that's what you studied. I hear that to this day from my counsellor. They make us pessimistic' (interview 3, ll. 46–8).

The interviewee states that the confidence and hope conveyed from the outside is scant. Moreover, the phrasing 'they make us pessimistic' already points to a distinction between us/them and others, and that the person does not feel supported and recognized in her/his needs. This is again emphasized when the interviewee says: 'people who are responsible don't treat us well' (interview 3, l. 56). From the outside, it is suggested that there may be little point in holding on to the desire for this future, which is also latently underpinned by the fact that, oftentimes, no additional information all around the topic (re)qualification and professional (re-)entry in Austria was passed on. As one interviewee relates: 'I didn't know what the options were, no information on courses, or how to get into my job' (interview 5, ll. 78–9). It can be inferred from interviewees' accounts that they find the lack of self-efficacy particularly stressful – that they feel at its mercy. Despite the experienced lack of support from the employment service,[8] many of the individuals learned – often by chance – that (re)qualifying programs do exist to help them approach the goal of returning to their original profession. Interviewees who have been accepted into and completed such programs are ultimately annoyed to find that – despite their efforts – they experience little response from the authorities: 'When I had my certificate with me at the appointment with the employment service – I was very proud – I was offered a job: and it was as a dishwasher' (interview 3, ll. 103–4). Another person reports that s/he was offered a job as an office clerk (interview 7, l. 111). Thus, on the one hand, it seems constantly emphasized from the outside that what is lacking and must be rectified are the formal deficits, but that doing so will be difficult. On the other hand, as soon as a person takes on the task and completes the program, it is communicated that the extra effort was kind of worthless. One interviewee had this impression in the school where s/he did the internship required by the (re)qualification program: 'I believe that not all directors accept the certificate course. Not everyone knows what it is. They think it's just a course and maybe they think it's better if they take other teachers' (interview 3, ll. 135–7).

'Everything Is Just a Hope, You Know. We Should Wait and See': Dealing with Uncertain Future Perspectives

The complex issue of formal recognition or non-recognition is closely linked to the future prospects of the interviewed individuals. Interviews revealed that interviewees have been forced to come to terms with an uncertain and/or uncontrollable dimension of their future. The fact that returning to teaching is not obviously accessible or predictable was emphasized again and again. Thus, luck or coincidence is attributed a major role, both conceptually and in terms of content, which suggests that the interviewees feel at the mercy of a certain arbitrariness and powerlessness. Upon finally being able to join a (re)qualification program, one person states: 'I have been very lucky. Until now. I keep going and I believe in my luck' (interview 6, ll. 111–12). In regard to experiencing setbacks, another one says: 'I have a lot of new ideas, so I am hoping again' (interview 5, ll. 221–2). In general, the impression remains that the people interviewed show an extraordinary degree of resilience. Even though they keep coming back to how stressful and gruelling the situation is (especially for those who are forced to remain inactive), they hold on to their hope for a long time, despite feeling that more is expected of them – that they have to do more than so-called Austrian people: 'As refugees, we always have to prove that we are the good ones' (interview 2, ll. 273–3).

This quote makes clear in which context the respective people move – even if they are well aware of the injustice of the situation, they are in a sense forced to refer to it or to deal with it. The impression arises that these people have to continuously point out that they can do something profitable, which is also visible in the following quote: 'we can do a lot / and we are useful ... we can help' (interview 5, ll. 164–5). Elsewhere, references are made to the homogeneous composition of staff within Austrian schools ('unfortunately, almost all of the teachers are Austrians / we can be very helpful there, we can use our mother tongue' (interview 5, ll. 139–41)). At this point, it should be highlighted that even though Austria had to deal with refugees before, they have by no means entered all professions; academic professions in particular are lagging behind. In this respect, the teaching profession is a typical second-generation profession. With regard to the emphasis on mother tongue competencies, the question arises which expectations the teachers had in this context (especially with regard to the use of these competencies in the Austrian school context). Most interviewees state that they could help with translation problems at school (e.g. between parents and other teachers). It is questionable whether an exaggerated appreciation for language skills is desirable; this is because there is a certain danger that this easily could lead to a distortion of the understanding of the teaching profession (teacher vs. social/cultural translator). To achieve the goal of entering the teaching profession in Austria, the interviewed person is prepared to invest a lot of patience, valuable time and quality of life: 'For me, it is okay, even if it takes many years' (interview 5, l. 233). Ultimately, it is about giving everything possible: 'I am going to try hard' (interview 5, l. 213).

Remaining a Teacher in Austria

It was particularly challenging to find displaced teachers who easily transitioned into the Austrian school system. Possible explanations could be the limited number of people fitting this description – us not having found suitable channels to reach this particular group and/or (again) the limited amount of time available to teachers during the Covid-19 pandemic. Therefore, the category *remaining a teacher in Austria* contains statements by participants who managed to (re-)enter the school system, as well as statements that represent the efforts and struggle to try to continue working professionally as a teacher.

'I Have Rubber Tires, I Go Everywhere': Between Resignation, Resilience and the Pressure to Perform

Every interview provided proof of incredible resilience. While it is not the focus of this chapter to explore the struggle and trauma caused by a flight from conflict or war as well as by the asylum procedure and the ensuing integration process in Austria, this aspect should not be left unmentioned. In line with what many members of minority groups have consistently expressed, the participants of this study state feeling a pressure to perform better, work harder and prove themselves over and over again due to their 'refugee background'. Compared to other teachers, they face more scepticism from the outside; it seems like the pressure of having to prove their professional skills never really ends. One participant states:

> If you want to go even halfway towards school in Austria, you will have to work ten times as much. [. . .] You must prove yourself much more, be much more diligent and not think about whether it is fair, or you pity yourself. Life is just not a child's birthday party, I can't say that, because it's very exhausting. (Interview 8, ll. 202–6)

As described in the section '"They told me it was going to be hard": Formal administrative recognition of qualifications as the central but non-transparent thematic linchpin', all participants – including those who have completed (re) qualification programs – have experienced major setbacks. For some, remaining in the teaching profession appears to involve accepting certain jobs that fall well below their qualification level, before getting a regular contract as a teacher:

> Maybe I will try to apply for some other places in private schools but all in all I am hoping that *Bildungsdirektion* [Department of Education] says something / give us some positive news that we can work there / actually there is another organization [name of organization] / it provides afternoon support for primary school students and some of the people who did the course before, are working there, *Freizeitpädagogik* [leisure education]. (Interview 5, ll. 215–19)

All participants emphasized the aspect of vocation in relation to the teaching profession. However, the contrast between the struggle to (re-)enter the teaching profession and the statement from a participant who already works in the school system was striking. S/he stated that s/he is a trained teacher and worked as a trainer as well as an entrepreneur. Contrary to most other participants (and although leaving the school system for (professional) self-fulfilment can be interpreted as a contradiction), her/his explicit professional goal was not to return to work as a teacher in Austria but to be a contributing member of society and being seen as a person, not a number: 'I, with my hands I can do a lot, I can do almost everything . . . and is not so complicated for me that I integrate somewhere, they have only one goal that they work as a teacher, but for me, I never had many goals. My important goal / only one goal was, I should be there as a person, I am there. I am not a number' (interview 2, ll. 84–8).

'He Believed in Me . . .': Supporting Structures and Supportive Individuals

When asked what motivates and helps them to persevere despite the difficult situation and setbacks, all participants named individuals who have been particularly supportive. These people included family members, or people from the community, as well as people from the host society. Regarding those individuals who slipped into the system without major obstacles, it became evident that they named specific 'key persons' who significantly influenced their career path. The know-how and individual help of these persons enabled these displaced teachers to find a way into an Austrian school without detours. One interviewee describes how, 'He [the "key person"] is really my friend, he is like a mentor to me and he has always accompanied me' (interview 2, ll. 120–1).

What is striking is that not even these persons find secure, long-term employment (unless they sign up for further education measures). Also, for those displaced teachers who have been able to enter the Austrian school system, the topic of catching up with formal requirements plays or has played a decisive role. For example, one person is aware that changes in the status in the school system can occur at any time, summing it up as follows: 'my testimonies are recognized as testimonies, but they are not nostrified [recognition of academic certificates] [. . .] that has to happen. I have a limited future here as a teacher' (interview 2, ll. 256–8).

Another person explains that, at the beginning of his/her career in Austria, although s/he was able to enter the school system without any specific measures, s/he benefited from the insider knowledge of a person who was very sympathetic to her/him at the time and explained that s/he would have to take further steps in order to continue working for adequate pay:

> I had a special contract, always limited to a year. So, if they were satisfied, the contract was extended. My director said he was satisfied, but he said he knew my history and so on, if I make the decision to want to stay in school, then I have to make up for it [complete the Austrian qualifications], otherwise I am constantly poorly paid, and every time trembling: will [my contract] be extended or not? (Interview 9, ll. 170–4)

4. Conclusion

We named this chapter 'Shared (hi)stories of (invisible) living in the in-between'. Looking at the insights and results of the interviews conducted, it became apparent that the significance of the living in the in-between never completely fades away – and this relatively independently of which of the three interview groups the person is assigned to. In this context, one must look at what is being formulated in these interviews on an abstract level: while some of the persons try to find a place (in the Austrian school system) after graduating from a (re)qualification program and to convince responsible persons that they meet the demands made on them, others still struggle to find access to such programs and to become (professionally) visible as subjects at all. It seems that even those who have been able to enter the Austrian school system – more or less by coincidence and/or with the help of specific people – feel unable to settle into it (whether because of the ever-present need to catch up on pedagogical training or the feeling of constantly having to perform better and more than others). What remains is a latent floating feeling of not yet (?) having arrived – which is not specific to teachers per se but points to the pressure for having a profession and being a public person – based on the feeling of being valued and differentiated from other belonging. The question of the origin of these trends can be raised at this point. It can be assumed that one encounters powerful structures that are probably difficult to grasp because they are so deeply inscribed in society and the persons acting in it: it seems that the persons who have been at the centre of this contribution, but also their (professional) experiences and qualifications, are automatically associated with otherness and deficiency that needs to be compensated for. As the yardstick used for orientation here seems questionable, further reflection on the meaning of (hidden, but also obvious) Eurocentric structures and paternalism appears to be all the more important. This is especially because at this point it becomes evident how close the linkage between nation state and schooling is since social attitudes are mirrored in the school system. Thus, it is necessary to focus on the need for a fundamental change of paradigm not only within the educational system but also in society itself.

Notes

1. In the following article we use the terms 'refugee(s)' and 'displaced teacher(s)'. The term 'refugee' is used in its legal definition as it was first laid down in the 1951 Refugee Convention. The term 'displaced teacher' is *not* intended to *label* persons who used to work as teachers and had to flee their home country but to draw on the accomplishments and challenges that they had and have endured.
2. Own calculations based on asylum statistics from the Ministry of the Interior (details see: https://www.bmi.gv.at/301/Statistiken/start.aspx (accessed 19 October 2021).
3. Website Certificate Course (available in German only): https://www.postgraduatecenter.at/weiterbildungsprogramme/bildung-soziales/bildungswissenschaftliche-grundlagen-fuer-lehrkraefte-mit-fluchthintergrund/ (accessed 7 January 2021).
4. For further details, see: https://ph-ooe.at/lehrgang-anmeldung/lehrgaenge-201920/basiskurs-fachdidaktische-und-bildungs.html (accessed 12 November 2020).
5. Due to professional experience gained in the Public Information Department of UNHCR Austria and as a former research assistant in the Erasmus+ Project 'R/EQUAL – Requalification of (recently) immigrated and refugee teachers in Europe' (for further information see: https://blog.hf.uni-koeln.de/immigrated-and-refugee-teachers-requal/), specific expertise pre-structures and preforms our interpretive understandings. This shapes how we look at the research subject, the interpretation of the interviews, the questions we asked and, finally, links to our categories (see the following (sub)chapters). In short: we are not neutral observers, a fact we have also critically reflected on during the research process.
6. Since many people switched back and forth between German and English during the interview, we decided to uniformly translate all passages that were spoken in German into English.
7. According to Reichenbach (2018), the term *professional ethos* refers to the moral awareness and responsible attitude of a professional group with regard to the duties and standards to be observed in the exercise of the profession. Teachers are exposed to a variety of demands (ibid., 199), and high expectations are placed on them from different directions (parents, colleagues, society, etc.). In order to meet these

demands, not only professional competencies are required but also 'an inner attitude and situational wisdom' (ibid., 202; translated by authors).

8   During the asylum procedure, asylum seekers have minimal access to the labour market. They receive the so-called *Grundversorgung* (basic welfare), which ensures a modest livelihood but is significantly lower than Austrians' social benefits. As soon as they are recognized as refugees or receive subsidiary protection, they have unrestricted access to the labour market and are entitled to social benefits. Persons who receive this benefit and are fit for work must register with the Public Employment Service (AMS) where they receive support in finding a job (Auer et al. 2021: 1). To obtain more precise data on the integration of refugees in the labour market, the AMS monitors the employment situation of people who were granted asylum or subsidiary protection from 2015 onwards and subsequently registered with the AMS. Of control group 1 (protection granted in 2015 and registered with the AMS until mid-2016), 50 per cent have found a job as of June 2021. A crucial sector for refugees is catering, followed by temporary employment agencies, retail and construction (ibid.).

References

Auer, E., M. Gatterbauer, N. Grieger and I. Wach (2021), 'Daten und Fakten zur Arbeitsmarktsituation von Geflüchteten'. Available online: https://www.ams-forschungsnetzwerk.at/downloadpub/ams_spezialthema_07_2021.pdf (accessed 19 October 2021).

Buber-Ennser, I., J. Kohlenberger, B. Rengs, Z. Al Zalak, A. Goujon, E. Striessnig, M. Potancoková, R. Gisser, M. R. Testa and W. Lutz (2016), 'Human Capital, Values, and Attitudes of Persons Seeking Refuge in Austria in 2015', *PLoS ONE*, 11 (9): e0163481. doi:10.1371/journal.pone.0163481.

Bundesministerium für Inneres/Ministry of the Interior (2016), 'Asylstatistik 2015' [asylum statistic 2015]. Available online: https://bmi.gv.at/301/Statistiken/files/Jahresstatistiken/Asyl_Jahresstatistik_2015.pdf (accessed 3 January 2021).

Kohlenberger, J. and I. Buber-Ennser (2017), 'Who are the Refugees That Came to Austria in Fall 2015?', *ROR-n*, 1 October. Available online: http://www.ror-n.org/-blog/who-are-the-refugees-that-came-to-austria-in-fall-2015 (accessed 13 November 2020).

Kremsner, G., M. Proyer and T. Obermayr (2020), 'Die Ausgangslage und die Einrichtung des Zertifikatskurses "Bildungswissenschaftliche Grundlagen für Lehrkräfte mit Fluchthintergrund"', in G. Kremsner, M. Proyer and G. Biewer (eds), *Inklusion von Lehrkräften nach der Flucht*, 17–45, Bad Heilbrunn: Klinkhardt.

Kremsner, G., M. Proyer and A. Schmölz et al. (2020), 'Das Forschungsprojekt "Qualifizierung von Lehrkräften mit Fluchthintergrund"', in G. Kremsner, M.

Proyer and G. Biewer (eds), *Inklusion von Lehrkräften nach der Flucht*, 46–92, Bad Heilbrunn: Klinkhardt.

Mayring, P. (1994), 'Qualitative Inhaltsanalyse', in A. Boehm, A. Mengel and T. Muhr (eds), *Texte verstehen: Konzepte, Methoden, Werkzeuge*, 159–75, Konstanz: UVK Universitätsverlag Konstanz.

Meyer-Drawe, K. (1984), 'Grenzen pädagogischen Verstehens – Zur Unlösbarkeit des Theorie-Praxis-Problems in der Pädagogik', *Vierteljahrsschrift für wissenschaftliche Pädagogik*, 60 (3): 249–59.

Miller, P. W. (2008), 'Downgrading and Discounting the Qualifications of Migrant Professionals in England: The Case of Overseas Trained Teachers', *Education, Knowledge and Economy*, 2 (1): 15–25.

Reichenbach, R. (2018), *Ethik der Bildung und Erziehung*, Paderborn: Ferdinand Schöningh.

Resch, K., H. Terhart, G. Kremsner, C. Pellech and M. Proyer (2019), 'Ambivalenzen der Anerkennung beruflicher Qualifikationen von International ausgebildeten Lehrkräften mit Fluchterfahrung in Österreich unter Berücksichtigung europaweiter Entwicklungen', *Sozialwissenschaftliche Rundschau*, 59 (3): 255–74.

UNHCR (2018), 'Flucht und Asyl in Österreich: Die häufigsten Fragen und Antworten' [Flight and asylum in Austria: frequently asked questions and answers]. Available online: https://www.unhcr.org/dach/wp-content/uploads/sites/27/2018/01/AT_UNHCR_Fragen-und-Antworten_2017.pdf (accessed 17 November 2020).

UNHCR (2019), 'Desperate Journeys. Refugees and Migrants Arriving in Europe and at Europe's Borders. January–December 2018'. Available online: https://www.unhcr.org/desperatejourneys/ (accessed 5 January 2021).

Part II

International Perspectives on (Local) Politics of Education

Pedagogy and Research Cooperations in the Neoliberal Politics of Speed

Reflections for Critical Pedagogical Professionalization in Migration Societies

Nadja Thoma

1. Introduction

In recent years,[1] the Austrian migration regime, very similar to the German one, has institutionalized a number of models that foresee separate and temporary schooling of differently positioned groups of students in terms of their 'natio-ethno-cultural belonging' (Mecheril 2003).[2] Though often accompanied by a rhetoric of enabling language acquisition, participation and recognition, these measures of 'emergency education' (Proyer et al. 2021) have (re)produced students which are marked as 'migrants' or 'refugees' in deficit opposition to 'normal' youth. Scholars from relevant fields such as education and linguistics have repeatedly voiced their criticism of these measures: They state that deindividualizing ascriptions on social groups results in social, cultural and economic disadvantages (Karakayalı 2020). In addition, they have exposed some of the measures that operate under the label of 'inclusion' as 'exclusionary inclusion' (Alpagu et al. 2019b), attending to deficit-oriented perspectives towards the multilingualism of students rather than analysing inequality-promoting educational structures and their 'monolingual habitus' (Gogolin 1994) which have been discussed in the German-speaking academia for decades (e.g. Alpagu et al. 2019a; Dirim, Knappik, Thoma 2018; Plutzar 2010). Despite considerable criticism and protest from researchers and pedagogical professionals (e.g. see Flubacher 2021), the former Austrian chancellor, Sebastian Kurz, and former education minister, Heinz Faßmann, decided to maintain their agenda and thus contribute to a perpetuation of migration-related lines of differentiation and exclusion mechanisms.

Most recently, Flubacher pointed to the remarkable speed of such political developments in Austria. Taking what are known as 'German support classes' as a point of departure, she examined the role of speed within language integration policies and concluded that the Austrian case of politics of speed 'goes hand in hand with executive decreeing and a disregard of parliamentary democracy' and leads to an 'institutional lag and systemic confusion' (Flubacher 2021: 1). Such politics of speed are constitutive for neoliberal societies. However, they are even more significant when schooling for refugee students is provided in a provisional form, because temporary education measures are connected to belonging for a limited time (Dausien et al. 2020: 52–5), which poses special challenges both for the development of future perspectives for students and for pedagogical practice.

This chapter aims to advance scholarly understanding of the ways in which temporalities, more concretely, forms of acceleration, are relevant for pedagogical practice and reflection. Informed by critical theories from different fields of social science, and empirically based on interviews with pedagogical professionals, my analysis aims at revealing the coexistence of multiple temporalities in education and the challenges in making sense of and acting upon them. The chapter is divided into four parts. First, I introduce temporality as fundamental for understanding educational processes and practices. Second, I reflect on the relevance of time in relation to the methodological framework in research with refugee students conducted in Austria between 2017 and 2019. Third, I analyse interview data from teachers generated in this project. The concluding section addresses the consequences of acceleration in the implementation of segregated schooling in neoliberal migration societies, considers the roles of institutional temporalities and biographical time structures in educational settings and raises methodological questions about temporalities in research.

2. Temporality and Acceleration in Educational Theory

Despite the spatial turn in education (Gulson and Symes 2007; Manchester and Bragg 2013), there has been growing scholarly interest in time and temporality during the last decade,[3] which has become ever more relevant with the introduction of neoliberal educational policies. Recently, many scholars have criticized neoliberal rationalities which involve 'time compression' and require the delivery of learning 'content' in small chunks and quantifiable time units (Hartman and Darab 2012: 56) aimed at standardization and accountability (Chitpin and Portelli 2019). Neoliberal governmentality leads to the transformation of educational institutions along entrepreneurial logics (Brown 2003: 38) and goes hand in hand with a 'renaissance of contractualism' (Dzierzbicka 2006). Among more general critiques, scholars have argued that neoliberal education policies imply a marginalization of policies and practices which advocate social justice and equity (Grimaldi 2012), and that they appropriate the social justice discourse to motivate reforms (Bale 2019: 122). Most scholarly work on neoliberalism and education addresses notions of time in some way, often paying attention to acceleration processes.

Acceleration, however, is not a new phenomenon and has accompanied modern society since the middle of the eighteenth century, encompassing all areas of life (Rosa 2009). Rosa defines a society as an 'acceleration society', if 'technological acceleration and the growing scarcity of time . . . occur simultaneously, i.e., if growth rates outgrow acceleration rates' (Rosa 2009: 87). In addition, the introduction of new technologies 'almost inevitably brings about a whole range of changes in social practices, communication structures, and the corresponding forms of life' (Rosa 2009: 88). This results in a paradox which combines a general sense of 'speed-up' with the feeling of being 'time-poor'. Rosa's considerations can be applied particularly well to education and the challenges of the teaching profession. In addition to some studies that generally address teachers' stress and their strategies for dealing with time (Philipp and Kunter 2013; Richards 2012), Thompson and Cook described the phenomenon of 'curriculum pressure' as a 'tension between the perceived need to move through the curriculum (Thompson and Cook 2017: 32) and teachers' pedagogical desires in relation to students and content.

But how can learners and teachers cope with acceleration? While many researchers focus on slowness and/or 'laziness'[4] as a response (Hytten 2019: 150) to the logics of acceleration, as a form of resistance (Varkøy and Rinholm 2020) or as subversive, political act (Taylor 2019: 625), others conceptualize slowness as a prerequisite of *Bildung*. Dörpinghaus (2015), for instance, defines *Bildung* as a 'distance achievement of slowing down' (*Distanzleistung der Verzögerung*). More concretely, he conceives slowing down as a transition from usability to questions of meaning and sense. In contrast to behaviourist concepts of learning, he argues that slowing down allows learners not to respond immediately to a stimulus but to take time and thus create freedom (Dörpinghaus 2015: 476). He also argues that 'detours, errors, aberrations, pauses, and recursive temporal shapes' (Dörpinghaus 2015: 478)[5] prevent quick and naive solutions, enable people to distance themselves from the world and thereby learning to understand it.

However, Rosa emphasizes that deceleration is not a solution to the problems caused by acceleration (Rosa 2021: 13). Instead, he proposes the concept of resonance which he understands as a 'mode of relation' to the world which consists of different spheres and axes of resonance. He refers to school as one of the spaces in which axes of resonance are established. In order to create meaningful and dynamic relations between actors and their environment, their relationships need to be based on response, rather than echo, which is not possible if teaching focuses on right and wrong answers for the sake of efficiency and optimization (Rosa 2021: 416). Resonance is built on the experience of self-efficacy, which enables the individual to relate the self and the world in an appropriate way. The 'other' of resonance, in Rosa's view, is alienation, a mode of relation in which there is no responsivity and no inner connection (Rosa 2021: 418).

3. Methodological Reflections – Time and Interaction in Research Processes and Collaboration

The 'speedy pedagogy' criticized above is accompanied by 'speedy scholarship', characterized by 'the relentless pace of scholarship, teaching, and service' (Taylor 2019: 625) and the need to design and complete research projects quickly. In our research project 'Translating Wor(l)ds'[6] (*Zwischen Welten ÜberSetzen*), we put neoliberal requirements for publications and measurable output aside and focused on the students, their experiences, perspectives and needs. This approach required regular and time-intensive reflections both within the research team and with teachers and students. The actual living conditions of the students, however, often prevented them from taking time for the project and engaging in learning: Insecurity surrounding their asylum status was at the forefront, along with precarious housing and family situations, diverse care and interpreting responsibilities for family members (Thoma and Langer 2022; Thoma and Draxl, in print) and acquaintances. In addition, their (often unspoken) preoccupation with past experiences and with their social position and (educational) future in the Austrian migration society demanded attention and took up considerable time. They spent their time carrying out duties outside school and taking care of administrative matters for their families, which often resulted in their withdrawal from activities at school (for instance listening to music or sleeping during workshops), and they also devoted time to reflections and discussions, sometimes with the research team.

Methodologically, we combined two methods for which time, especially for interaction with research participants, is central, namely ethnography and biographical research. The ethnographic approach (Breidenstein et al. 2020; Jeffrey and Troman 2004) involved ongoing field visits over the course of a school year. On the one hand, the school as an institution with its tight organization and rigid time structures limited our open research stance, and in order to open up the institutional framework, it was necessary to build trust over a longer period of time through regular workshops and meetings outside of school. On the other hand, the school's framework and rules allowed us to be in regular contact with the students. In view of the institutional framework and the precarious living situation of the students, we did not conduct biographical interviews as part of the project but worked with a range of 'small stories' (cf. Georgakopoulou 2015) around the topics of school, arriving in Austria, languages and translation (Dausien and Thoma, in print). In addition, we were sensitized to listening to spontaneous biographical narratives beyond methodologically established narrative impulses and to giving them space (Völzke 2005: 13). We also tried to convey to the students that we were not interested in a time-efficient account of their educational or life situation (see Völzke 2005: 13), but that we were open to whatever they wanted to tell us and that they had time to do so.

Another aspect concerns the participatory approach of the project,[7] which was not limited to students and was aimed instead at examining cooperation with teachers. Two teachers were already involved in the conceptualization of the project during the application phase. During the field phase, we discussed excerpts from our field notes in research workshops together with the teachers and a school social worker. In doing so, we aimed to learn more about the professionals' perspectives while at the same time opening up possibilities for their participation in our academic work and for common knowledge production. Despite the overall interest of the teachers and very fruitful exchanges in these sessions, the teachers were occupied with completing various tasks at their school and with activities they were doing for the students on top of that. Therefore, regular workshops were not possible.

4. Dealing with the Logics of Acceleration – Teacher and School Social Worker Voices

In the following, I will analyse excerpts from five interviews with pedagogical professionals (four teachers and a social worker) with whom we collaborated within the research project. The interviews aimed at reflecting on the research cooperation and experiences with the class as well as the concept of the transition class in general. The interviews were conducted after the first year of the research project and had a length of between 50 and 140 minutes. Although not being asked specifically about time, the professionals focused on different aspects and facets of temporality, which will be discussed in what follows.

Academia Meets Pedagogical Practice – Struggling with Speed Expectations in the Research Cooperation

The following account is from a reflective conversation about the first project year with the teacher Marta Meier,[8] with whom we cooperated intensively. Here, she reflects on a workshop that took place during the first weeks of our cooperation and in which we presented biographical methods to the teachers.

> Ah I know that it took a very long time and that we didn't get as far as we wanted. And then I thought to myself, ah that will – so, time – having time. So, taking time and having time, that will become a topic in the project. (6) On the one hand, I liked it then, to really take time – on the other hand, I noticed that it doesn't quite satisfy me when things take so long and ahm – we sort of don't finish, yes. So that – it was like that, it's exactly the opposite of school, yes, it's just – hey, you have to get to the next point, it doesn't matter whether you've finished the section in between or not, let's go to stage two. Because – I don't know, you have to be there in September, or in June.[9]

Marta characterizes the workshop in terms of its duration and the joint activities which were not 'finalized'. She addresses her thoughts at that time, emphasizing that she thought that time relations would become an issue in the project. By switching twice between 'having time' and 'taking time', she constructs time once as a 'natural' datum and once as a resource that can or must be actively accessed and thus offers different interpretations of the professionals' scope for action. After a pause of six seconds, Marta addresses her ambivalent relationship to the topic, namely, on the one hand, a pleasure in taking time and, on the other hand, a lack of satisfaction with longer durations and activities that are not completed within a set period of time. She then contrasts temporality in the research project with that at school, presenting them as 'opposite'. Her characterization of time frames at school refers to an extensive 'curriculum pressure' (Thompson and Cook 2017: 32). Moreover, the generalizing 'you'[10] in the last lines characterizes the teacher as a lone struggler who is the only one responsible for working through content items on time. In Marta's problematization, the students with whom the contents are worked out are made invisible, hidden behind the time pace of teaching practice. Marta's professionally acquired *speeding through the school year*[11] also becomes relevant in the context of the research project, in a setting outside the school which was not directly connected to her pedagogical tasks or the curriculum content-wise. Marta addresses her lack of satisfaction, even though the research group had only made a very open 'plan' for the workshop and focused on the quality rather than the timely 'output' of the joint engagement.

What is not visible in this excerpt, yet was central in our ethnographic fieldnotes, was Marta's commitment beyond her teaching assignment, which she shared with another teacher: She was part of a drama group with students and in her free time helped students with housing and jobs and residency law. In many conversations with her, dismay about the legal status and social situation of the students and their families was a central theme. The fact that she was only paid for her time spent in the classroom, but felt responsible for the class far beyond that, led to a *speeding between class, social work and the research project*.

Speed and Underorganization in the Implementation of the 'Transition Classes'

A shared view in all interviews refers to the implementation of the transition classes and their duration being less than ideal. The school social worker Karina Kaiser says:

> They [transition classes, N.T.] only started on November 8 or so for whatever reason because everyone was already there beforehand – but even there you can the structural organization um exactly on the part of the school authorities – the

question would also be interesting to answer why you just let people kill time even longer yes and just deprive them of two months of entry.

Karina Kaiser complains that the school year, which in Austria usually starts in mid-September, did not start for the transition class until November, although the admission interviews had already taken place and the students were waiting to start school. Karina thus points to a mismatch of individual and institutional time. The phrase *even longer* refers to the time that Karina thinks students had already 'killed' while fleeing and living in refugee camps with little to no educational opportunities. She thus criticizes the institution for adding to the students' already 'lost' educational time.

Another aspect that was discussed in all interviews is the limited duration of the transition classes, namely one year. The teacher Tamara Teimel says:

> So I don't find the concept very well conceived, yes? To be honest, a bridge class like this is for ME somehow an emergency solution, if I may put it that way. I think – to be able to integrate the students really seriously, one year is too little. And I would organize it in a completely different way, yes? It is a wonderful idea – but this idea is not very successful – in my opinion – because it does not lead to anything – the students are still not inside the system [...] I think it needs a year in which they really arrive.

Tamara Teimel's wording refers not only to the speed in the implementation but also to the provisional nature of the entire measure, which does not create conditions for what Tamara sees as serious integration. She criticizes the concept with the argument that the students are not yet *in* the system and argues that they need a year to really arrive. This last remark points to the fact that, according to Tamara, the experience of flight does not end with arrival in the Austrian nation state but is a continuing process that should ideally be addressed pedagogically.

Karina and Tamara's conceptualizations of time reveal that they see it as organized along biographical logics in which past, present and future are linked, 'often across large intervals of time and areas of life that are institutionally separated' (Alheit and Dausien 2002: 14). Thus, their accounts situate the time in the transition class as a temporal phase which the students have to meaningfully connect into their lifetime and in which the resonance of past and present can be established, ideally with pedagogical support.

Speed and a lack of organization affected not only the class but also the teachers, more concretely the hiring arrangements: Barbara Bauer talks in detail about the difficulties she experienced with different contracts during her first years of service. Contracts of teachers in the transition class differed from 'normal' contracts and affected both the working conditions of individual teachers and the composition of the teaching team (see Dausien et al. 2020: 51). The demand for speed plays an important role in this context as well. Barbara tells how she was faced with a last-minute decision by the principal of her school. First, he explained to her that his efforts to give her a 'normal' contract had been unsuccessful and that she could only take on the transition class with a special contract, which was a significant downgrade.

> BB: And then he said - but now you have time to think about it until tomorrow. Then I said - well - is there an alternative? He said - no, but you can say you won't do it - then we'll have to leave the bridge class.
>
> Int: Aha - great. ((laughs))
>
> BB: Then I said, well, then there's really no alternative - and he said - yes - and then - yes, he knows it's stupid and - then he said anyway, well, the only thing he can tell me is that if I want to stay somewhere for a weekend longer - then I can stay one day - I don't have to come. That's the only thing we can offer - but he knows it's stupid.

With the argument 'but now you have time', the school principal normalizes the extremely short period of time within which Barbara must decide on an important employment issue. Her question about an alternative reveals that a rejection of the contract would mean the end of the transition class at the school. Here, the decision about an educational measure at the school is not made at the ministerial or the school district level but is placed in the hands of an individual teacher. Her knowledge that only the acceptance of poor contract conditions could make the continuation of the transition class possible adds to the time pressure. The direction that the conversation ultimately takes shows that the principal was aware of the negative conditions. His offer that Barbara be given a day off after a vacation weekend as compensation for the bad contract reveals how the lack of organization of the transition classes left schools alone to find acceptable solutions for their teachers.

Institutional Time Regimes versus Biographical Time - Dealing with Pedagogical Dilemmata

In describing how a student was expelled from school a few weeks after the start of the school year, Karina Kaiser argues:

> [If] you are constantly kicked in the ass, metaphorically speaking, um, you can't get involved in school - yes - and then of course everything else is subordinate to the basic need for security - the very existence - yes that - is not possible -

with everything that has been experienced still in the back of your mind um – yeah what can't be processed at all, so even if you were to give people a therapist at their side for twenty-four hours – it simply doesn't change what they have experienced and that it takes time to re-orientate themselves in a completely foreign country without a family, and so on and so forth – these are all massive wounds.

Karina focuses on the lack of asylum-related security, which does not allow students to fully engage with school and learning. She argues that the time needed to come to terms with past experiences and to orientate oneself in the new environment cannot be 'compressed' and that uncertainty about one's own existence certainly does not help to increase school engagement. Karina's reflections on the students' time commitment to the school reveal her awareness of the friction between the time regime of the institutions on the one hand and the biographical logics and time structures of her students on the other. The task of dealing with these two logics presents a pedagogical dilemma (Helsper 2010) for which there is no simple or institutionally established solution. Similar considerations also concern cooperation in the research project, as the following observation on time constraints shows.

In her reflection on her experiences in the project Marta also addresses what she thinks the students' perspectives were:

Yes, exactly. I just think that when you have really big problems, you find – academic questions probably disturbing – I don't, but I'm just making assumptions about how they experience it, yes? So they have often – ahm – when we said, So, there is now another meeting – What for? What for, what for? I have English, I have German, I have that. I don't know where my cousin lives, I don't know w-what do I know. Why do I have to go back to the media room now? Yeah, I don't think I can pass the exam. Why do I have to go to the media room? I want to copy out the homework, yeah, or something. Can you explain math to me? [. . .] But I think that's a normal stress reaction. It's not just them, it's all the other students.

In this account, academia, or more specifically, the participatory research project, is portrayed, to some extent, as a somewhat luxury activity that bypasses the basic needs of the students and is therefore not suited to opening up meaningful axes of resonance. The teacher addresses 'very big problems' of the young people, against the background of academic questions which might be 'disturbing'. She then refers to questions that students asked in light of upcoming project meetings in the media room of the school and their explanations for why participation in the project was not considered meaningful. At the centre of the questions is the threefold 'what for', which refers to the overarching goal of the joint project work. In reported speech, the teacher cites the commitments of students, which competed with the academic project, namely school subjects (English, German), fears related to upcoming exams, struggling with homework and specific school subjects, and private challenges, such as worries about relatives.

The teacher's reflections point to a multitude of requirements that refugee students have to meet simultaneously in order to be successful in their new educational system. Her quick enumeration of the many tasks and concerns vividly paints a picture of young people struggling with the 'politics of speed' (Flubacher 2021): The multiple private difficulties and challenges, which are only indicated here with the concern about the cousin's whereabouts, compete with the educational expectations and time limits that students want and/or have to meet and for which the migration regime provides insufficient preparation. The teacher's account evidences that she is well aware of the competing activities, which, from the students' view, must be done at the same time. This hinders the formation of forms of resonance which are associated with experiences of self-efficacy (Rosa 2021: 418) and makes it more challenging to create biographical continuity.

5. Conclusion

In this chapter, I have analysed how pedagogical professionals in neoliberal migration societies make sense of temporality. In closing, I would like to summarize the research findings and point to current challenges in teacher education. The speed in the implementation of transition classes and other separating schooling measures for refugee students are part of what Rosa terms 'situationalist' politics (Rosa 2009). These politics are characterized by the 'primacy of the short-term' (Luhmann, as cited in Rosa 2009: 106) and by a 'muddling through' (Rosa 2021: 106) that leads to temporary 'solutions' and to a shift of decision-making processes to others, in this case, to school leaders who ultimately pass on decisions to individual teachers. This results in 'difficulties of synchronization' (Rosa and Scheuerman 2009: 13) and thus to 'institutional lag' and 'systemic confusion' (Flubacher 2021) which must be dealt with by professionals. The provisional structure of the transition classes is evident on several levels, such as their late start in the school year, the short duration of the programme and the non-standard work contracts for teachers.[12]

In sum, acceleration in educational policies contributes to the perpetuation of already-existing power relations and inequalities among students. This has the effect of institutionalizing new inequalities among teachers and preventing the generation of resonance and biographical continuity, which are essential in educational settings.

In addition, my findings are consistent with other scholarly work focusing on time and curriculum pressure (e.g. Thompson and Cook 2017). Much more importantly, they reveal that professionals are not only concerned with their own time: Rather, they are aware of the conflicts between the temporal logics of the institution and the biographical organization of time in which students reflexively connect their (educational) experiences at school to past experiences and the future (see, e.g. Alheit and Dausien 2002). This process is complicated and possibly hindered by the 'temporal regime' (Del Percio 2021: 4) of the nation state that determines their right to asylum and affects further (educational) opportunities. Thus, teachers need to make sense of and act upon the temporality of hastily introduced and short-lived educational measures and their coexistence with students' experiences which require resonant educational contexts (see Rosa 2021). These findings imply that training courses on 'time management' or 'work-life balance', which ultimately follow neoliberal (time) logics, are not sufficient in preparing teachers for the complex logics of temporality in educational institutions. Rather, schools in neoliberal migration societies need professionalization strategies that sensitize teachers to the biographical temporal logics of students and how to address and meaningfully link them to the temporal logics of the institution.

Moreover, the findings raise methodological questions and challenges. The analysis has revealed that the institutional logics of temporality in schools also affect research collaborations. Aside from their duties at school, students deal with manifold responsibilities like language brokering, administrative jobs and care activities for their family members, and teachers support students well beyond the assignments of their profession. Under these conditions, research collaborations, especially those with participatory approaches, represent an additional time commitment on the part of teachers who are already overwhelmed with other tasks. Thus, beyond the many aspects of the involvement of educational professionals and researchers in research topics (e.g. Czejkowska 2011; Messerschmidt 2016), research collaborations with students and pedagogical professionals require an additional and continuous reflection on the multiple temporal logics that are relevant in research projects. Common ways of exploring and negotiating temporalities are necessary in building meaningful relationships and spaces of resonance between research participants and in contributing to a more comprehensive theoretical understanding of time in education.

Notes

1 I would like to thank the editors of this book as well as Amer Alkojjeh and Michael Connors Jackman for their helpful comments to an earlier version of the chapter.
2 In German, these groups are often referred to as 'with (or without) migration background'. For the historical development of this category see Stošić (2017).
3 Obviously, researchers who draw attention to the importance of time do not see space and time as independent but as interwoven categories: see, e.g. Lingard and Thompson (2017), *The concept of 'timespace'* or the manifold references to what Harvey (1989) terms *Time–space compression*.
Time and temporality have been considered from very different perspectives in educational philosophy and theory which I cannot discuss here. See, e.g. Decuypere and Vanden Broeck (2020); Fischer (2018); Nieke, Masschelein, Ruhloff (2001); Schmidt-Lauff (2012); Tesar (2016).
4 Employing a coloniality perspective, Shahjahan advocates for 'being lazy' as a 'transformational heuristic device' (2015: 489). With his intentionally provocative formulation, he draws attention to colonial logics of categorizing individuals according to opposing categories and portraying 'others' as having 'deficit models' of time (2015: 490).
5 This quote was translated by the author. Dörpinghaus' conceptualization is consistent with Masschelein and Simons's perspective on school: Drawing on the ancient Greek meaning of σχολή (scholè), they define school as a place of 'the spatialisation and materialisation of "free time"' (Masschelein and Simons 2015: 86).
6 The project *ZwischenWeltenÜberSetzen* (2017–19) was funded by the Austrian ministry of Science and Education in the funding scheme Sparkling Science (SPA06-229). Project site: https://zwischenweltenuebersetzen.univie.ac.at.
7 The funding scheme required participatory approaches; on the difficulties of implementing such approaches in social science studies, especially when it comes to the biographies of the research subjects (cf. Dausien et al. 2020).
8 All names have been pseudonymized.
9 The original transcripts were translated by the author.
10 The German 'du' is the singular form of 'you'.
11 I am referring to Furman's phrase 'speeding through the school day' (Furman 2018: 433).
12 In addition, there were no nationally defined admission requirements, no curriculum and, most important for the students, the certificate they obtained

with the successful completion of the transition class did not include a formal entitlement to a further educational measure which, among other reasons, resulted in the students' feeling that they had 'lost time' (cf. Alpagu et al. 2019a: 218; Dausien et al. 2020: 35).

References

Alheit, P. and B. Dausien (2002), 'The "Double Face" of Lifelong Learning: Two Analytical Perspectives on a "Silent Revolution"', *Studies in the Education of Adults*, 34 (1): 3–22.

Alpagu, F., B. Dausien, A.-K. Draxl and N. Thoma (2019a), 'Die Bedeutung von Deutsch und Mehrsprachigkeit im schulischen Kontext. Erfahrungen aus einem Projekt mit einer "Übergangsklasse" für geflüchtete Jugendliche', *ÖDaF-Mitteilungen*, 35 (1+2): 207–23.

Alpagu, F., B. Dausien, A.-K. Draxl and N. Thoma (2019b), 'Exkludierende Inklusion - eine kritische Reflexion zur Bildungspraxis im Umgang mit geflüchteten Jugendlichen einer Übergangsstufe', *Schulheft*, 176: 51–63.

Bale, J. (2019), 'Neoliberal Education Policy and the Regulation of Racial And Linguistic Difference in Ontario Schools', in S. Chitpin and J. P. Portelli (eds), *Confronting Educational Policy in Neoliberal Times*: 117–31, New York: Routledge.

Breidenstein, G., S. Hirschauer, H. Kalthoff and B. Nieswand (2020), *Ethnografie: Die Praxis der Feldforschung*, 3rd edn, München: UVK-Verlag.

Brown, W. (2003), 'Neo-Liberalism and the End of Liberal Democracy', *Theory & Event*, 7 (1). Available online: https://muse-jhu-edu.uaccess.univie.ac.at/article/48659.

Chitpin, S. and J. P. Portelli (2019), 'Introduction', in S. Chitpin and J. P. Portelli (eds), *Confronting Educational Policy in Neoliberal Times*, 1–7, New York: Routledge.

Czejkowska, A. (2011), 'Hang in there! Normalisierende Interventionen und mögliche Spielräume', *Vierteljahrsschrift für wissenschaftliche Pädagogik*, 87 (4): 618–31.

Dausien, B., N. Thoma, F. Alpagu and A.-K. Draxl (2020), 'ZwischenWeltenÜberSetzen: Zur Rekonstruktion biographischer Erfahrungen und Kompetenzen geflüchteter Jugendlicher im Zugehörigkeitsraum Schule'. Available online: https://phaidra.univie.ac.at/o:1115870.

Dausien, B. and N. Thoma (in print), 'Small Stories' as Methodological Approach. *Reflections on Biographical Narratives Based on an Ethnographic Research Project With Refugee Students*, Forum: Qualitative Social Research.

Decuypere, M. and P. Vanden Broeck (2020), 'Time and Educational (re-)forms—Inquiring the Temporal Dimension of Education', *Educational Philosophy and Theory*, 52 (6): 602–12.

Del Percio, A. (2021), 'Speeding up, Slowing Down. Language, Temporality and the Constitution of Migrant Workers as Labour Force', *International Journal of Bilingual Education and Bilingualism*, 1–13. doi:10.1080/13670050.2021.1954386.

Dirim, İ., M. Knappik and N. Thoma (2018), 'Sprache als Mittel der Reproduktion von Differenzordnungen', in İ. Dirim and P. Mecheril (eds), *Heterogenität, Sprache(n), Bildung: Eine differenz- und diskriminierungstheoretische Einführung*, 51–62, Bad Heilbrunn: Klinkhardt.

Dörpinghaus, A. (2015), 'Theorie der Bildung. Versuch einer "unzureichenden" Grundlegung', *Zeitschrift für Pädagogik*, 61 (4): 464–80.

Dzierzbicka, A. (2006), *Vereinbaren Statt Anordnen. Neoliberale Gouvernmentalität macht Schule*, Wien: Löcker.

Fischer, W. (2018), 'Zeit und Biographie', in H. Lutz, M. Schiebel and E. Tuider (eds), *Handbuch Biographieforschung*, 461–72, 2nd edn, Wiesbaden: Springer.

Flubacher, M.-C. (2021), 'The "Politics of Speed" and Language Integration Policies: On Recent Developments in Austria', *International Journal of Bilingual Education and Bilingualism*, 1–11. doi:10.1080/13670050.2021.1954387.

Furman, C. (2018), '*Stopping Time* to Attend as a Care of the Teaching Self', *Philosophy of Education*, 1: 429–41.

Georgakopoulou, A. (2015), 'Small Stories Research: Methods - Analysis - Outreach', in A. de Fina and A. Georgakopoulou (eds), *The Handbook of Narrative Analysis*, 255–71, Chichester: Wiley Blackwell.

Gogolin, I. (1994), *Der monolinguale Habitus der multilingualen Schule*, Münster, New York, München and Berlin: Waxmann.

Grimaldi, E. (2012), 'Neoliberalism and the Marginalisation of Social Justice: The Making of an Education Policy to Combat Social Exclusion', *International Journal of Inclusive Education*, 16 (11): 1131–54.

Gulson, K. N. and C. Symes, eds (2007), *Spatial Theories of Education. Policy and Geography Matters*, London and New York: Routledge.

Hartman, Y. and S. Darab (2012), 'A Call for Slow Scholarship: A Case Study on the Intensification of Academic Life and its Implications for Pedagogy', *Review of Education, Pedagogy, and Cultural Studies*, 34 (1–2): 49–60.

Harvey, D. (1989), *The Condition of Modernity*, Oxford: Blackwell.

Helsper, W. (2010), 'Pädagogisches Handeln in den Antinomien der Moderne', in H.-H. Krüger and W. Helsper (eds), *Einführung in Grundbegriffe und Grundfragen der Erziehungswissenschaft*, 15–34, 9th edn, Opladen: Budrich.

Hytten, K. (2019), 'Ethical Scholarship and Information Overload: On the Virtue of Slowing Down', in A. Chinnery (ed.), *Philosophy of Education 2017*, 149–61, Urbana: Philosophy of Education Society.

Jeffrey, B. and G. Troman (2004), 'Time for Ethnography', *British Educational Research Journal*, 30 (4): 535–48.

Karakayalı, J. (2020), 'Rassismuskritische Perspektiven auf Segregation in der Schule – zur Einleitung', in J. Karakayalı (ed.), *Unterscheiden und Trennen. Die Herstellung von natio-ethno-kultureller Differenz und Segregation in der Schule*, 7–22, Weinheim and Basel: Beltz Juventa.

Lingard, B. and G. Thompson (2017), 'Doing Time in the Sociology of Education', *British Journal of Sociology of Education*, 38 (1): 1–12.

Manchester, H. and S. Bragg (2013), 'School Ethos and the Spatial Turn', *Qualitative Inquiry*, 19 (10): 818–27.

Masschelein, J. and M. Simons (2015), 'Education in Times of Fast Learning: The Future of the School', *Ethics and Education*, 10 (1): 84–95.

Mecheril, P. (2003), *Prekäre Verhältnisse: Über natio-ethno-kulturelle (Mehrfach-) Zugehörigkeit*, Münster, New York, München and Berlin: Waxmann.

Messerschmidt, A. (2016), 'Involviert in Machtverhältnisse', in A. Doğmuş, Y. Karakaşoğlu and P. Mecheril (eds), *Pädagogisches Können in der Migrationsgesellschaft*, 59–70, Wiesbaden: Springer.

Nieke, W. and T. Gatzemann (2001), *Bildung in der Zeit. Zeitlichkeit und Zukunft – pädagogisch kontrovers*, Weinheim and Basel: Beltz.

Philipp, A. and M. Kunter (2013), 'How Do Teachers Spend Their Time? A Study on Teachers' Strategies of Selection, Optimisation, and Compensation over Their Career Cycle', *Teaching and Teacher Education*, 35: 1–12.

Plutzar, V. (2010), 'Sprache als "Schlüssel" zur Integration? Eine kritische Annäherung an die österreichische Sprachenpolitik im Kontext von Migration', in H. Langthaler (ed.), *Integration in Österreich. Sozialwissenschaftliche Befunde*, 123–42, Wien and Bozen: Studien Verlag.

Proyer, M., G. Biewer, L. Kreuter and J. Weiß (2021), 'Instating Settings of Emergency Education in Vienna: Temporary Schooling of Pupils with Forced Migration Backgrounds', *International Journal of Inclusive Education*, 25 (2): 131–46.

Richards, J. (2012), 'Teacher Stress and Coping Strategies: A National Snapshot', *The Educational Forum*, 76 (3): 299–316.

Rosa, H. (2009), 'Social Acceleration: Ethical and Political Consequences of a Desynchronised High-Speed Society', in H. Rosa and W. E. Scheuerman (eds), *High-Speed Society. Social Acceleration, Power, and Modernity*, 77–111, Pennsylvania: Pennsylvania State University Press.

Rosa, H. (2021), *Resonanz. Eine Soziologie der Weltbeziehung*, 5th edn, Berlin: Suhrkamp.

Rosa, H. and W. E. Scheuermann, eds (2009), *High-Speed Society. Social Acceleration, Power, and Modernity*, Pennsylvania: Pennsylvania State University Press.

Schmidt-Lauff, S. (2012), *Zeit und Bildung. Annäherungen an eine zeittheoretische Grundlegung*, Münster, New York, München and Berlin: Waxmann.

Shahjahan, R. A. (2015), 'Being "Lazy" and Slowing Down: Toward Decolonizing Time, Our Body, and Pedagogy', *Educational Philosophy and Theory*, 47 (5): 488–501.

Stošić, P. (2017), 'Kinder mit "Migrationshintergrund". Reflexionen einer (erziehungs-) wissenschaftlichen Differenzkategorie', in I. Diehm, M. Kuhn and C. Machold (eds), *Differenz - Ungleichheit - Erziehungswissenschaft*, 81–99, Wiesbaden: Springer Fachmedien Wiesbaden.

Taylor, A. (2019), 'Slow(ed): Lessons on Slowness Within Projects of Inclusivity', *Philosophy of Education Archive*, 625–38. Available online: https://educationjournal.web.illinois.edu/ojs/index.php/pes/article/view/364/250.

Tesar, M. (2016), 'Timing Childhoods: An Alternative Reading of Children's Development Through Philosophy of Time, Temporality, Place and Space', *Contemporary Issues in Early Childhood*, 17 (4): 399–408.

Thoma, Nadja and P. C. Langer (2022), 'Educational Transitions in War and Refugee Contexts: Youth Biographies in Afghanistan and Austria', *Social Inclusion*, 10 (2): 302–12.

Thoma, N. and A.-K. Draxl (in print), *Transforming Language Brokering Policies at School: Learning from Students with Transnational Biographies'*, European Educational Research Journal..

Thompson, G. and I. Cook (2017), 'The Politics of Teaching Time in Disciplinary and Control Societies', *British Journal of Sociology of Education*, 38 (1): 26–37.

Varkøy and Rinholm (2020), 'Focusing on Slowness and Resistance: A Contribution to Sustainable Development in Music Education', *Philosophy of Music Education Review*, 28 (2): 168–85.

Völzke, R. (2005), 'Erzählen - Brückenschlag zwischen Leben und Lernen', *Sozial Extra*, 29 (11): 12–15.

6

Unravelling the Nuanced Experiences of Multilingual Internationally Educated Teachers in Bridging Programmes

A Focus on Language

Clea Schmidt, Henrike Terhart, Rory Mc Daid and Michelle Proyer

1. Introduction

Teaching is an increasingly mobile profession (Cho 2010; European Union n.d.). A review of the international literature and cross-disciplinary empirical work on international teacher mobility and migration undertaken by Bense (2016) provides a comprehensive outline of global patterns. This study identified key challenges for internationally educated teachers (IETs) including barriers to recertification, significant unpaid and volunteer work in schools in the hope of securing a teaching position, adjustment to the new curriculum, classroom management, language barriers and differences in approaches to teaching and learning. Bridging programmes address some of the most prominent challenges, though they often focus on the development of individual IETs' skills, knowledges and competencies when systemic barriers, not individual limitations, remain the most salient obstacles to diversifying the teaching force transnationally (see Schmidt and Schneider 2016).

The term 'bridging programme' is used for services that support people in the transition from one, usually professional, situation to another. Using the metaphor of a bridge, as a construction that connects a path interrupted by water or by a chasm, bridging programmes support people in the transition from one activity to another (study to work) or in re-entering the activity in another place. In this chapter, we use the term for programmes that support IETs re-entering the teaching profession in another country (for a discussion of terminology related to IETs, see Schmidt and Schneider 2016). Bridging programmes for IETs are provided in different countries of the Global North. They differ in terms of duration, structure and objectives.

The four programmes featured in the current research have (or had) a duration of eight to twelve months of full-time or part-time study. They usually have prerequisites in terms of prior university (teacher) preparation and consist of pedagogical and didactic content, language courses in the language(s) of the teaching jurisdiction, (supervised) school practicum or school experience and counselling of programme participants. The focus of the current chapter stems from our extensive experience administering and researching IET bridging programmes and a recognition that language issues are under-represented in both curriculum and scholarship around barriers (Schmidt and McDaid 2015). Our overarching question is: *What tensions arise from the hegemonic negotiation of the meaning of language(s)* and *what expectations of their linguistic abilities are IETs confronted with?*

We begin by delineating our theoretical framework of *translingual activism* (Pennycook 2006, 2010, 2015, 2019) and follow with an overview of our studies' four bridging programme contexts: Austria, Canada, Germany and Ireland. We then describe the methodologies used in each study and the amplified analysis (Heaton 2004) undertaken to collaboratively analyse our respective findings and identify common themes. Subsequent sections include findings, analysis, recommendations and conclusions for IET programmes and related actors. The chapter is based on reviews of relevant literature carried out in previous work by the authors (e.g. Schmidt 2010; Schmidt and Schneider 2016 Schmidt and Mc Daid 2015; Resch et al. 2019; Kremsner, Proyer and Biewer 2020; Proyer et al. 2022; Terhart 2022a+b).

2. Theoretical Framework

The theoretical lens of *translingual activism* (Pennycook 2006) informs both our argument about the need to explicitly attend to issues of translingualism and linguicism in IET bridging programmes and our analysis of comparative findings drawn from the four research sites. A translingual perspective is inclusive and refers to 'the deployment of a speaker's full linguistic repertoire without regard for watchful adherence to the socially and politically defined boundaries of named (and usually national and state) languages' (Otheguy, García and Reid 2015: 283). Linguicism in contrast describes discriminatory stances where specific languages or language varieties (in our case those of the host countries) are valued over others (Skuttnab-Kangas and Phillipson 1995). Alistair Pennycook (2006) introduced the term 'translingual activism' to respond to the problematic ways that multilingualism tends to be benignly and unproblematically viewed in terms of a 'more is better' mentality in many linguistically diverse societies. Multilingualism as a concept also tends to ignore the nuanced language proficiency that can involve not only more than one language but also more than one variety. Pennycook's (2006) critique underscores that simply framing heritage languages and additional language learning as positive does not in and of itself facilitate understanding of the complex dynamics informing language use in highly charged contexts of politicized transnationalism, nor does it counter linguicism. As he elaborates:

> we need to ask what meanings are being borne by languages, what cultural politics underlie the learning and use of different languages. It is not enough to assume that more is better – multilingualism, multilingual language policies, more foreign language education – in simple numerical terms. (Pennycook 2006: 111, drawing on Pennycook and Makoni 2005)

In addressing this central question of the cultural politics which underlies the learning and use of different languages, translingual activism challenges

> normative assumptions that define languages along statist and institutional lines and connects this translingual focus to an activist pedagogy that does not seek to bring students into conformity with central norms. (Pennycock 2019: 180)

This concern resonates with the four of us as IET programme developers and researchers who have grappled with the place of language and challenging linguistic discrimination in the bridging programme curriculum, in the field placement settings and in the academic and professional relationships IETs have with mentors, students and families and prospective employers. Across all of these situations, our participants may engage in language practices (Pennycock 2010) which are used by interlocutors to delegitimize their translingual competencies. Language practices can include conflating accent with intelligibility. As one previously documented example regarding the hegemonic discourse on language and accent, Schmidt (2010) previously documented an example of a multilingual IET who was placed for practicum in a bilingual school to teach in one of her heritage languages, Ukrainian. Though the school endorsed a philosophy promoting the positive nature of heritage language learning and the school principal was of the same multilingual and immigrant background as the IET, the IET faced harsh and undue criticism from the principal when she mispronounced a word in English. In this instance, the context of positive multilingualism was trumped by an intolerance of error in the dominant language of the wider society, necessitating a more nuanced consideration of how various languages matter differently in a range of settings and how advocacy manifests (or not) and by whom.

The above incident and other language experiences documented in the current analysis support what Pennycook (2015) offers as a solution to benign yet uncritical views of multilingualism in the form of translingual activism. Though he frames this concept in terms of English and English language teaching, we argue that it has relevance in other contexts where multilingual IETs are frequently disadvantaged when faced with local language standards and dominant language ideologies. In these settings, three elements identified by Pennycook (2015) are salient:

1) decolonizing and provincializing the dominant local language (especially English)
2) expanding notions of resourcefulness and resourceful speakers, and
3) engaging critically and politically with language pedagogy and ideology.

All three of these have a particular relevance for all or some of the projects analysed in this chapter. According to Pennycook, an activist pedagogy of (English) Language Teaching demands awareness of the 'collusionary, delusionary, and exclusionary effects of English' (Pennycock 2019: 180). He explains that English 'colludes with many of the pernicious processes of globalization' (Pennycock 2019: 180) and excludes many through the operation of a segregational class dialect. Of particular relevance for our work is the argument that English (in Canada and Ireland) as well as German and German dialects (in Austria and Germany) also mislead many learners of the language through the 'false promises it holds out for social and material gain' (Pennycock 2019: 180). The transformative potential of English has been well established in the literature with, for example, Rory Mc Daid (2011) analysing that the minority language learners in his study viewed English language learning as an elixir for all that negatively affected their migrant status in their primary schools.

3. Overview of Bridging Programme Contexts

Bridging programmes at universities and teacher colleges for IETs have been provided in different countries of the Global North. They vary in terms of duration, structure and objectives and target both pre- and in-service IETs. The four programmes we refer to in this chapter had a duration of two to three semesters (sometimes more in the case of Canada), offered full-time or part-time studies and had graduated up to four cohorts at the time of the research. Credit hours given for the programmes ranged between twenty-four (German programme), to forty (Austrian programme), to sixty and above (Canadian programme). The Irish programme is a non-credit professional development programme. Content included pedagogical and didactic topics as well as language courses (mostly non-credit) in the languages of the programme (German or English). Graduating from the Viennese programme offered direct entry to the regular teacher education programme to complete a second necessary school subject qualification in Austria or teaching on a limited-term basis or other kinds of pedagogical work. In the Cologne programme, there is the possibility to apply for a temporary position as a teacher with accompanying further training through the regional district government of the federal state of North Rhine-Westphalia. The IETs taking part in this programme *ILF – Promoting International Teachers* then act as mentors for the new participants in the bridging programme. Manitoba offered, in addition to the academic and professional bridging programme, a mentorship initiative for employed teachers (both this and the bridging programme were discontinued due to lack of funding). The Migrant Teacher Project (Ireland) works as a labour activation project, which aims to further enhance qualified teachers' professional development and opportunities for securing employment.

Entry requirements of the bridging programmes consisted of language requirements (at level of B2 for the European programmes) and a teaching certificate (most at the undergraduate level). Language-related issues were integral parts of the programmes where participants were sensitized to country- or region-specific language contexts and teaching concepts.

The bridging programmes supported the professional re-entry of IETs; however, they typically did not lead to a degree equivalent to a local teaching qualification. Even in contexts where teaching certification was obtained, there was no guarantee of entry into the profession. The programmes were financed either by public funds and/or donations and were supported by the universities as projects of a university in social responsibility.

4. Empirical Synopsis of Research in Four Countries of the Global North

Methodological Overview

Four independently conducted research studies were carried out in Austria, Canada, Germany and Ireland (see Table 6.1). For purposes of this chapter,

Table 6.1 Overview Methodology of the Primary Research Studies as a Basis for the Transnational Secondary Study

	Methodology	Sources	No Participants	Language of Study	Research Question/Focus
AT	Grounded theory and situational analysis (Clarke 2005)	Semi-structured focus group discussions	Five focus group discussions with three to five participants (twenty in total)	German and English	Evaluation of the course at different stages of the programme and with different cycles (Kremsner, Proyer and Biewer 2020).
CA	Critical ethnography (Quantz 1992)	Semi-structured interviews, focus group discussions with programme graduates	Twenty	English	What insights do bridging programme participants have about the programme since graduating (Schmidt 2010)?
DE	Grounded theory (Glaser and Strauss 1967; Strauss and Corbin 1994)	Semi-structured interviews	Twenty (before and after the bridging programme)	German and English	How is the process of trying to re-enter the teaching profession as an internationally educated teacher interlinked with professional biographical development tasks (Terhart 2021)?
IE	Critical phenomenology (Weiss, Salamon and Murphy 2019)	Semi-structured interviews Student reflective writings	Ten Seventy-four	English	What are the experiences of a variety of migrant teachers as they look to re-enter the profession in Ireland (Mc Daid and Nowlan 2022)?

common issues and themes were discussed collaboratively and analysed using a secondary qualitative analysis (Medjedović and Witzel 2010). The studies were based on reflective writings, semi-structured interviews and focus groups held with IETs as well as teaching staff and school administrators and were carried out in the years 2018–19 (Germany) 2010–18 (Canada), 2017–20 (Austria) and 2018–21 (Ireland).

Janet Heaton (2004: 38), who has developed five types of secondary analysis, refers to the reuse of data by combining two or more primary studies to compare them or to obtain a larger sample as amplified analysis. In this case the four primary studies were collectively considered to illuminate tensions of hegemonic structures on language(s) issues facing IETs seeking to resume their careers in the Global North. By combining research linked to different bridging programmes in different national contexts, the range of experiences of IETs is further amplified. The different national contexts in which the data were collected and are referred to by the IETs as well as other actors serve to prevent 'methodological nationalism' (Wimmer and Glick Schiller 2003), which usually leads to the unquestioning selection of a nation state as the frame of reference by ignoring processes of de-territorialization and deconstruction of the spatial conditions of the social.

In contrast to a national framing, the secondary analysis shows that there are underlying topics that run through the data collected in the four countries. The result is a transnational research perspective that takes into account transnational processes and practices by considering global power relations. We consider, what tensions arise from the hegemonic *negotiation of the meaning of language(s)* and *what expectations of their linguistic abilities are IETs confronted with?*

Empirical Synopsis

The following analysis draws on the four independent primary research studies from the four countries and identifies key areas of tension regarding the role of language(s) for IETs.

a. Internalizing Expectations from the School Community of Speaking a Further Language 'Perfectly' in the Hope That This Will Enable to Re-enter School as a Labour Market

As part of a bridging programme offering support for teachers from abroad, the teachers taking part in the Cologne programme emphasized their knowledge, experiences and professional qualifications in interviews held before and after participation (Terhart 2022a). Their strategies to highlight arguments for re-entry can be seen as counter-narrative to formal de-professionalization they experience as teachers (see also Cho 2010). In comparison, the IETs mainly identify the level of their language skills in German as an additional language as a key problem for working as a teacher in another school system again. In Germany as well as Austria, language proficiency in German at the level of C1 up to C2 of the European reference scheme is mandatory to enter the teaching profession. This level is close to native language command. Especially, in the interviews prior to participating in the Cologne programme, language was perceived as the central barrier IETs had to overcome to re-enter their former profession: one teacher describes that 'Language is important. Must be developed. (–) Yes, then everything comes' (G_2018_2). A Math teacher who had already made several attempts to work in the educational sector in Germany and worked in educational services before he attended the bridging programme notes:

> I was a teacher and I like my job and I have tried to work as a teacher here. You have to be a realist. I have language problems. Otherwise (–) I have without language/ I could control the class here and if I can speak well, surely I can teach here too. (G_2018_3)

Participants in the Irish study identified very similar issues, with one teacher estimating their language proficiency as not good enough: 'I have an accent so is this an issue to understanding and communicating well' (I_2018_15). Furthermore, in the Viennese study the handling of specific dialects spoken across Austria and even within Vienna was discussed by participants of the Austrian programme. Fear around speaking accented language as a marker of difference was generated directly by and internalized because of school systems whose actors value dominant varieties and are sceptical if not outright hostile towards educators without these varieties (Schmidt 2010).

It can be argued that in the Cologne research the strong focus of IETs on linguistic abilities in the dominant school language(s) as the primary barrier to re-enter the profession tended to strengthen the self-positioning as a well-qualified teacher with broad pedagogical experiences, especially if the language barriers before and after participation in the programme were perceived as manageable, as one teacher states: 'The obstacle between (–) me and my profession is the [German] language' (G_2018_12). Compared to the topic of language proficiency in German, further barriers such as the non-existent formal equivalence of foreign qualifications, or insecurities regarding a new school system, and/or being labelled as a migrant/refugee teacher were mentioned comparatively rarely in the interviews with IETs at the start of the Cologne bridging programme. Despite difficult circumstances, participants were convinced that they could work as teachers in Germany successfully if they improved their language proficiency in German during the programme. However, the responses after participation in the bridging programme were complemented by their professional experiences in terms of formal differences, the experiences of not being recognized as a professional teacher and specific expectations regarding teacher qualifications, for example, lesson planning and design in Germany. The above-mentioned phenomenon held true for many of the participants in the Austrian programme as well. High command of German was perceived as a threshold and preoccupied many of the activities. While striving to acquire a very high level of language competence in German as participants internalized the need to do so, personal efforts were made to study subject-specific terms. These were not covered in the foundational German course in Vienna which was criticized by participants.

This strong focus on the language proficiency of the IETs in the respective dominant language is not surprising, since this expectation is present for recently immigrated people in all four countries in general. The emphasis on acquisition of the official language in a school system in which IETs wish to work, including the often simultaneous devaluation of other linguistic skills or accents, is also evident in international research on IETs (for critical discourse on language proficiency of teachers trained abroad see Abramova 2013; Myles, Cheng and Wang 2006; Amin 2000; for discrimination because of accent see Lippi-Green 1997). The findings in the four bridging programmes can be framed by drawing on Pennycook's (2019) analysis regarding English that the promise and expectations associated with acquiring the dominant language are often not fulfilled. By focusing on language acquisition, unequal assessment at other levels (e.g. formal recognition of qualifications, more difficult access for female teachers wearing a hijab) is downplayed yet exacerbates unequal treatment for teachers. The 'false promises' (Pennycook 2019: 180) associated with the acquisition of the dominant language, in our perspective at least, is understood as 'fragile promises'.

b. Using the Language Proficiency and Knowledge Arising from the Migration Situation for Career Opportunities versus Criticism of a Narrow Focus on the Role of Being an Othered Teacher

In our studies, the complex role of teachers' multilingual proficiency became apparent. In the Cologne interview study the IETs referred to their language proficiencies and knowledge arising from their migration situations and experiences of being refugees in Germany. The focus here was on matching their own language skills with the languages of many (newly arrived) students to serve as a linguistic liaison. Some teachers explicitly emphasized their multilingual skills at school, for example, when the English teacher Mr Massoum reported that he promoted himself as a multilingual professional to the colleagues at school at the beginning of his first internship: 'When I did my internship in [city name], I introduced myself and then I said I speak four languages if anyone needs' (G_2019_3). Before the first internship, another English teacher also noted the ability to contact those parents who did not speak the German language:

> Perhaps also contact with the parents, because I have heard that some Turkish parents do not have (–) contact with the school so often because they cannot speak German. So, this could also be helpful for the rest of the teachers. I could be a kind of translator. (G_2018_4)

This theme of IETs using multilingualism to their advantage in obtaining employment and then continuing to draw on their multilingual capabilities to better serve their school communities is a complex one involving aspects of pragmatism, a strong linguistic identity that is affirmed by the school and advocacy. Some of the teachers saw significant value in this, with one participant from the Irish study claiming, 'For me, it is brilliant to see the eyes shine of students when I talk to them in Polish' (I_2019_7). We are mindful of Santoro's (2007) research documenting the exploitation of many culturally and linguistically diverse educators who are called upon too often to serve in extraordinary capacities as 'diverse others' without awareness or acknowledgement that such demands are essentializing, may be burdensome or that the responsibility for addressing the needs of diverse families rests with the entire school community and not only teachers from the same minoritized backgrounds.

However, as our findings demonstrate, multilingualism and when and how it is employed, and by and for whom, is anything but straightforward. Some IETs who participated in our respective studies experienced how proficiency in different languages reflected in the school communities could be advantageous in initially securing a teaching position, provided hiring personnel recognized the need for multilingual attributes among staff. Yet the extent to which IETs chose to continue to serve as linguistic liaisons once they were employed varied and depended on whether IETs felt like they were contributing meaningfully to the needs of linguistically and culturally diverse families, the extent to which their multilingual expertise was appropriately acknowledged by school leadership and the need to balance their various commitments. In the Manitoba context, one IET shared in the context of a post-bridging programme focus group:

> My journey started with [my practicum] school. The job just came from nowhere; I didn't apply for that job. The principal was looking for someone in that school so she just called me and I gave an interview. They were impressed because I offered additional things I can bring to the school other than teaching, which was culture, cultural dances, languages, and I think that was the strong point. Being on term I then got permanency. Until now they have just called me, 'Mrs. C. can you come to the office, there is someone who needs translation'. I am more than happy to go and help. And we also often translate the website in Punjabi, so I am the one who always does that. So having other languages helped me to fit in that school system. (C_2018_1)

This positive view of sharing multilingual attributes and serving as a translator when called upon was tempered somewhat by another IET who at the time of data collection had been working for several years in a large, linguistically diverse urban secondary school in Canada catering to many immigrant students. Despite the diverse demographics of the student population, the teaching staff in this school was overwhelmingly White, Manitoba-born and monolingual English-speaking. This IET, while willing to serve as a linguistic liaison and translate on occasion, was wary of some of his colleagues' efforts to volunteer him for such roles and was not prepared to offer his services on demand in what could easily become an onerous task. As he explained:

> I just want to add, as I mentioned I work in a school with more than sixteen hundred students, and I do make the phone calls in Punjabi, but my admin is aware, they are not going to ask me, 'OK, Mr. S., you have to make twenty phone calls.' There was a comment in our staff meeting when they said, 'Oh, Mr. S. can do this'. And I said, 'you know, I am willing to do a few phone calls, and maybe one letter a month. I'm not ready to make twenty phone calls from 3:30 to 5:30 after school because I do have other things to do.' (C_2018_2)

In the research in the four different national contexts, it becomes clear that the IETs frequently support students and families who speak the dominant language as an additional language during their practical experiences in schools based on their proficiency in other languages and their knowledge of multilingual didactics gained in some programmes. It is a challenge to recognize the skills that exist through migration and at the same time not attribute them to any particular person in an essentializing way. To mitigate the problems and to enact the activist stance advocated by Pennycook, it would be advisable for *othering* processes (fundamentally elaborated by Spivak 1985) to be recognized and reflected upon by all participants as far as possible and to ensure that IETs have agency in determining the various additional tasks they take on to support the wider school community. This way IETs can be part of school communities being acknowledged as resourceful speakers in multilingual societies.

c. *The Need for Linguistic Advocacy among Powerbrokers within the Wider Education Systems*

Regardless of whether IETs are willing to serve as linguistic liaisons and under what circumstances, the advocacy Pennycook prioritizes must be assumed by more than the IETs themselves. As one school superintendent in Manitoba noted in Schmidt's (2010) early ethnographic work:

> One aspect we're missing and [we're] silent on is some of our prejudices, and we have prejudice around accents. And superintendents need to be brought on board why this is an important issue, you know because it reflects the diversity in our communities and so on, but they also have to be armed with knowledge about how they share that with the community more broadly. (C_2010_6)

A school principal in the Irish study identified the very particular issue relating to proficiency in both Irish and English which is necessary for employment in Irish primary schools:

> When it comes to questions for example to do with Irish we would expect the teacher to have a high standard of Irish. So when we interview teachers at the moment and say you have got three of four teachers of the same level and we start the conversation in Irish and if the person can't speak Irish they are gone. I can't see that changing in our school because we are going to use people in the classroom and unless somebody has a standard that they are able to teach and they have to be fluent to teach Irish. (I_2018_23)

These quotations draw attention to a bias that should be critically addressed with Pennycook's translingual activism (2006). By pointing out a too narrow and prejudiced understanding of language the school superintendent refers to the need to address the notions of resourcefulness and resourceful speakers and suggests engaging critically and politically with language pedagogy and ideology (see the theoretical framework of this chapter) at the level of the administrative structure of the school system. While the Irish principal is being very honest in outlining what happens in their school, there is no sense in which the linguistic resources of those attending for interview are adequately valued.

By addressing the importance of the school system and its capacity for including IETs, a problematic effect of bridging programmes is addressed at the same time: Offers for IETs focus on providing highly skilled immigrants with information and further qualification to gain a foothold in the yet unknown school system as a labour market. An important component of this is the support of the required linguistic skills, which relate to one language (German in Austria and Germany) or to two languages (English and Irish in Ireland and English and French in some parts in Canada). Without denying the importance of support for re-entering another school system, the strong focus on IETs introduces a bias into the discussion. This is because the impression is created that if these teachers only try hard enough and make up for their 'deficits', they can be successful in the respective school system. In this way, ignored is the fact that the respective school system also must fulfil some prerequisites in order to enable corresponding opportunities for IETs. This refers, on the one hand, to the formal requirements that are set by educational authorities and which, due to their complexity, make access very difficult without a great deal of individual support. Therefore, the development of structures that enable access in the presence of defined prerequisites is necessary. On the other hand, school actors and overarching organizations must be prepared to accept new colleagues and recognize their qualifications. Some schools are highly qualified in acknowledging IETs in a resourceful way and addressing them as resourceful speakers; other schools have greater difficulties in overcoming a deficit-oriented perspective and in seeing the strengths of the IETs and at the same time offering the support that may still be needed.

5. Conclusion and Recommendations

Based on Pennycook's concept of translingual activism, the chapter brought together selected findings of four studies from Austria, Canada, Germany and Ireland in a secondary analysis to conduct an amplified analysis. The joint work on the material was initiated by the authors as we discussed the bridging programmes for IETs in the four national contexts, which revealed some commonalities. These relate not only to the elements of the bridging programmes offered but also to IETs' experiences with barriers regarding language(s) to re-entry into their profession. It became apparent that the strong focus on the dominant languages English and respective German in the context of international teacher mobility was evident along the empirical material on different dimensions. By choosing the concept of translingual activism as a theoretical heuristic, the focus was placed on the complexity of multilingualism and school on three dimensions:

First, IETs internalized expectations from the school communities that they speak the official school language 'perfectly' in the hope that this would facilitate re-entering teaching as a labour market. This created pressure (from the teachers themselves) that language skills in the dominant language needed to be developed in ideally a very short time. The hopes associated with the acquisition of a further language partly outweighed the additional formal and informal burdens of being recognized as a professional teacher in Austria, Canada, Germany and Ireland. Notwithstanding this, some teachers showed – secondly – an attention to their various linguistic skills, which they wished to use beneficially in their work as teachers. Language proficiency and knowledge arising from the migration situation were seen as a career opportunity by some. However, the emphasis on the language skills and knowledge related to migration could also limit the teacher profile and narrow the focus on the role of being an *othered* teacher (Santoro 2007). In this case, a support system for linguistic advocacy among powerbrokers within the wider education systems is needed and can be carried out by bridging programmes as a third dimension. However, bridging programmes themselves need to reflect on their own involvement in the system of linguistic dominance and submission. Bridging programmes can play a role in questioning language hierarchies and ideas and ideologies of norm(ality) regarding teachers and the representation of social reality in the school systems. For example, bridging programme staff should have linguistic expertise to avoid misjudging IETs or reifying linguistic stereotypes. This way, opportunities to decolonize language hierarchies arise.

The concept of translingual activism strengthens the demand to question the respective discourse on dominant local language(s) by expanding notions of resourcefulness and resourceful speakers to engage critically and politically with language pedagogy and ideology. Taking into account Pennycook's critique on the delusion of the transformative potential of learning the dominant language(s), it becomes apparent that 'false promises' (Pennycook 2019: 180) are part of the strong focus on language acquisition, even though the support of learning the official school language is of great importance. This way bridging programmes for IETs can support a deeper understanding against superficial understandings of celebrating diversity without reacting on deeply embedded forms of privilege and discrimination that may occur as linguicism.

We would therefore like to recommend that any attempts to support IETs in re-entering their profession should always take the multilingual setting as well as the language ideologies regarding migration into account. Linguistic supports should be accompanied by explicit attention to issues of linguicism IETs are likely to encounter. Bridging programmes can take the role of linguistic allies giving support not only to the framework of existing formal national structures but also point out the hidden agendas regarding the use of language(s) within a singular school as well as in the respective national or regional school system, including the requirements for access to the teaching profession. Bridging programme leaders can also serve as important liaisons between IETs and the school contexts they are preparing to enter, to help uncover unreasonable expectations and biases before these are imposed on and internalized by IETs. In addition to the teachers' obligation participating in such programmes, it must also be considered the development stakeholders from education policy and administration, teacher training institutions as well as school management and colleges.

References

Abramova, I. (2013), 'Grappling with Language Barrier: Implications for Professional Development of Immigrant Teachers', *Multicultural Perspectives*, 15 (3): 152–7.

Amin, N. (2000), *Negotiating Nativism: Minority Immigrant Women ESL Teachers and the Native Speaker Construct*, PhD Thesis, University of Toronto, Canada.

Bense, K. (2016), 'International Teacher Mobility and Migration: A Review and Synthesis of the Current Empirical Research and Literature', *Educational Research Review*, 17: 37–49.

Cho, C. L. (2010), '"Qualifying" as a Teacher: Immigrant Teacher Candidates' Counter Stories', *Canadian Journal of Educational Administration and Policy*, 100: 1–31.

Clarke, A. E. (2005), *Situational Analysis: Grounded Theory after the Postmodern Turn*, Thousand Oaks: Sage Publications.

European Commission (n.d.), *The EU Single Market. Regulated Professions Database*. Available online: https://ec.europa.eu/growth/tools-databases/regprof/index.cfm (accessed 13 July 2021).

Glaser, B. G. and A. L. Strauss (1967), *The Discovery of Grounded Theory: Strategies for Qualitative Research*, Hawthorne and New York: Aldine de Gruyter.

Heaton, J. (2004), *Reworking Qualitative Data*, London: Sage Publications.

Kremsner, G., M. Proyer and G. Biewer (2020), *Inklusion von Lehrkräften nach der Flucht: Über universitäre Ausbildung zum beruflichen Widereinstieg* [Inclusion of teachers after forced migration. Via university training to professional re-entry], Bad Heilbrunn: Verlag Julius Klinkhardt.

Lippi-Green, R. (1997), *English with an Accent: Language, Ideology, and Discrimination, in the United States*, New York: Routledge.

Medjedović, I. and A. Witzel (2010), *Wiederverwendung qualitativer Daten. Archivierung und Sekundärnutzung qualitativer Interviewtranskripte* [Reuse of qualitative data. Archiving and secondary use of qualitative interview transcripts], Wiesbaden: VS Verlag für Sozialwissenschaften.

Mc Daid, R. (2011), 'GŁOS, VOCE, VOICE: Minority Language Children Reflect on the Recognition of Their First Languages in Irish Primary Schools', in M. Darmody, N. Tyrrell and S. Song (eds), *The Changing Faces of Ireland: Exploring Immigrant and Ethnic Minority Children's Experiences*, 17–33, Rotterdam: Sense Publishers.

Mc Daid, R. and E. Nowlan (2022), 'Barriers to Recognition for Migrant Teachers in Ireland', *European Educational Research Journal*, 21 (2): 247–64

Myles, J., L. Cheng and H. Wang (2006), 'Teaching in Elementary School: Perceptions of Foreign-Trained Teacher Candidates on Their Teaching Practicum', *Teaching and Teacher Education*, 22 (2): 233–45.

Otheguy, R., O. García and W. Reid (2015), 'Clarifying Translanguaging and Deconstructing Named Languages. A Perspective from Linguistics', *Applied Linguistics Review*, 6 (3): 281–307.

Pennycook, A. (2006), 'Postmodernism in Language Policy', in T. Ricento (ed.), *An Introduction to Language Policy: Theory and Method*, 60–76, Oxford: Blackwell.

Pennycook, A. (2010), *Language as a Local Practice*, London: Routledge.

Pennycook, A. (2015), 'Language Education as Translingual Activism', *Asia Pacific Journal of Education*, 26 (1): 111–14.

Pennycook, A. (2019), 'From Translanguaging to Translingual Activism', in D. Macedo (ed.), *Decolonizing Foreign Language Education: The Misteaching of English and Other Colonial Languages*, 169–85, New York: Routledge.

Pennycook, A. and S. Makoni (2005), 'The Modern Mission: The Language Effects of Christianity', *Journal of Language, Identity, and Education*, 4 (2): 137–55.

Proyer, M., C. Pellech, T. Obermayr, G. Kremsner and A. Schmölz (2022), '"First and Foremost, We Are Teachers, Not Refugees": Requalification Measures for Internationally Trained Teachers Affected by Forced Migration', *European Educational Research Journal*, (21)2: 278–292.

Quantz, R. A. (1992), 'On Critical Ethnography (With Some Postmodern Considerations)', in M. Le Compte, W. L. Millroy and J. Preissle (eds), *The Handbook of Qualitative Research in Education*, 447–506, San Diego: Academic Press.

Resch, K., H. Terhart, G. Kremsner, C. Pellech and M. Proyer (2019), 'Ambivalenzen der Anerkennung beruflicher Qualifikationen von international ausgebildeten Lehrkräften mit Fluchterfahrung in Österreich unter Berücksichtigung europaweiter Entwicklungen' [Ambivalences of the recognition of professional qualifications of internationally trained teachers with flight experience in Austria, taking into account Europe-wide developments], *SWS-Rundschau*, 3: 255–74.

Santoro, N. (2007), '"Outsiders" and "others": "Different" Teachers Teaching in Culturally Diverse Classrooms', *Teachers and Teaching*, 13 (1): 81–97.

Schmidt, C. (2010), 'Systemic Discrimination as a Barrier for Immigrant Teachers', *Diaspora, Indigenous, and Minority Education*, 4 (4): 235–52.

Schmidt, C. and R. McDaid (2015), 'Linguistic Barriers Among Internationally Educated Teachers in Ireland and Canada: A Critical Comparative Analysis', *Australian Review of Applied Linguistics*, 38 (3): 172–83.

Schmidt, C. and J. Schneider (eds). (2016), *Diversifying the Teaching Force in Transnational Contexts: Critical Perspectives*, Rotterdam, NL: Sense Publishers.

Skuttnabb-Kangas, T. and R. Phillipson, eds (1995), *Linguistic Human Rights. Overcoming Linguistic Discrimination*, Berlin and New York: Mouton de Gruyter.

Spivak, G. C. (1985), 'The Rani of Sirmur: An Essay in Reading the Archives', *History and Theory*, 24 (3): 247–72.

Strauss, A. L. and J. Corbin (1994), 'Grounded Theory Methodology: An Overview', in N. K. Denzin and Y. S. Lincoln (eds), *Handbook of Qualitative Research*, 273–85, Thousand Oaks: Sage Publications.

Terhart, H. (2022a), 'Teachers in Transition. A Biographical Perspective on Transnational Professionalisation of Internationally Educated Teachers in Germany', *European Educational Research Journal*, 21(2): 293–311.

Terhart, H. (2022b), 'Lehrerinnen mit Fluchterfahrungen: Frauen als Teilnehmende in Weiterqualifizierungsprogrammen für geflüchtete Lehrkräfte' [Female refugee teachers. Women as participants of bridging programmes for refugee teachers], in S. Farrokhzad, K, Scherschel and M. Schmitt (eds), *Geflüchtete Frauen. Analysen, Lebenssituationen und Angebotsstrukturen*, [Refugee women. Analyses, living situations and service structures], 143–163, Wiesbaden: Springer VS.

Weiss, G., G. Salamon and A. V. Murphy (2019), *50 Concepts for a Critical Phenomenology*, Evanston: Northwestern University Press.

Wimmer, A. and N. Glick Schiller (2003), 'Methodological Nationalism, the Social Sciences and the Study of Migration: An Essay in Historical Epistemology', *The International Migration Review*, 37 (3): 576–610.

Career Jumpers on Their Way to Teacher Professionalism – Challenges and Opportunities Based on Different Working Backgrounds

Miriam Voigt and Inka Engel

1. Career Jumpers and Lateral Entry Teachers in Germany

The terminology of career jumpers (*QuereinsteigerInnen*) and lateral entry teachers (*SeiteneinsteigerInnen*) must first be considered. The terms are usually differentiated, and only in rare cases are they used synonymously. Career jumpers are defined as persons who, usually, enter the preparatory service without previous teacher training (Bertelsmann Stiftung et al. 2018: 8). In contrast, lateral entry teachers go directly into the teaching profession without previous teacher training and without preparatory service (Bertelsmann Stiftung et al. 2018: 8). They usually complete appropriate introductory and further training courses in parallel, primarily in the pedagogical sector, but also in the subject-specific sector, in order to obtain the qualification for a second teaching subject (Autorengruppe Bildungsberichterstattung 2020).

A study published in 2017 by the Bertelsmann Stiftung predicts an enormous shortage of teachers in 2030, with demographic developments leading to a requirement for 28,100 additional classes and thus around 42,800 additional full-time teachers in 2030. The predicted shortage of teachers is already leading to increased competition between schools for well-trained teachers (Klemm and Zorn 2017: 8). As a result, more and more schools hire career jumpers and lateral entry teachers (Böhmann 2011). This development is hardly surprising since the demand for and supply of teachers has always fluctuated. The demand and supply of teachers is also not balanced in the school year 2019/20. Historically, the oversupply and shortage of teachers alternate, resulting in old ways of balancing the situation. As a result, teachers who complete their training faster or are differently trained – the so-called career jumpers or lateral entry teachers – have always been hired in times of teacher shortages (Reintjes et al. 2020).

In addition to a growing number of pupils due to the influx of refugees, reasons for the present shortage of teachers include a current wave of retirements, the partial reduction of one year of schooling in some federal states in Germany and the acute Covid-19 pandemic. Thousands of teachers are not able to provide face-to-face instruction due to pre-existing illnesses as part of the at-risk group, meaning that the current shortage of available teachers is worsening. Approximately thirty-six thousand new teaching positions must be filled by the 2020/21 school year. Berlin, for example, has 2,547 full-time positions advertised for the current school year, which is the same number as previously advertised over thirty years ago. To ensure that no lessons are cancelled, the schools rely on non-specialist teachers, lateral entry teachers and career jumpers (Andres and Kuhn 2020).

The school system in Germany is characterized by federalism and is developed under the supervision of the state (Grundgesetz 2017). The KMK (*Kultusministerkonferenz*/Standing Conference of the Ministers of Education and Cultural Affairs of the Federal States in Germany) coordinates the cultural and educational policies of the German federal states within the federal system. As a supra-regional but not overarching instrument of mutual coordination, it is of supra-regional importance in matters of cultural policy, with the aim to form a common will and represent common concerns (Rürup 2007: 161). Voting often involves consensual decision-making, which is voluntary in its implementation (Cortina et al. 2005: 155–8). Even though a partly uniform strategic orientation is specified, it is implemented differently to a very different extent in the individual states. Recently, on 5 December 2013, the resolution *Gestaltung von Sondermaßnahmen zur Gewinnung von Lehrkräften zur Unterrichtsversorgung* (Special Programme for Recruiting Teachers to Provide Teaching) of the KMK officially addressed the issue of dealing with the identified and expected shortage of teachers. The resolution explains that, in principle, the traditional way of recruiting teachers is through graduates with a master's degree in education and subsequent preparatory service, ending with a state examination. Only if the needs of specific school forms and subjects cannot be complied with using these traditionally trained teachers, can the German federal states turn to career jumper or lateral entry teachers for their education programme. This programme is based on the standards of the KMK and on a common agreement between the German federal states. Two different special measures are described as minimum requirements. In the first special measure, there is an option that graduates with a master's or equivalent university degree that refers to at least two subjects related to the teaching profession can be directly integrated into the preparatory service where basic educational science competence is taught. Future teachers recruited through this special measure who complete their training with the (second) state examination or a comparable state-certified qualification in the respective federal state are to be given preference over teachers recruited through the second special measure. Those recruited under the second special measure include graduates with a master's or equivalent university degree that covers only one subject related to teaching. It is recommended that these recruits qualify for a second teacher training-related subject by means of in-service studies in order to complete their state examination with an in-service training period. The German states are also free to implement additional special measures specific to their own federal state (KMK 2013). The KMK usually refers to both new and alternatively recruited groups of teachers as lateral entry teachers. Nationwide, however, there are both career jumpers and lateral entry teachers, whose distinction can be seen as complementary to the two special measures of the KMK resolution. However, these terms are not consistently used or defined. Some federal states do not differentiate between career jumpers and lateral entry teachers and use the terms synonymously, while others differentiate the concepts more specifically and have a clearer understanding of both terms in order to distinguish them from each other. The most common, and therefore that which is used here, is the difference in completing their preparatory service, also known as the clerkship, between these two alternative entry methods to the teaching profession. After their master's degree, which is completed in subjects relevant to the teaching profession, career jumpers complete a preparatory service together with traditionally trained teacher trainees. This training path is similar to the first and preferred special measure described by the KMK. Lateral entry teachers, on the other hand, start their teaching career directly without any preparatory service. Although they have usually studied a relevant subject, they often attend introductory and continuing education courses that accompany the teaching profession, thus attaining a pedagogical prerequisite virtually parallel to the profession and often leading to qualification in a second subject related to the teaching profession (Autorengruppe Bildungsberichterstattung 2020). This alternative entry into the teaching profession corresponds to the second special measure described by the KMK. It is difficult to differentiate between career jumpers and lateral entry teachers, and probably because of this there are hardly any statistics that distinguish between the two. It is nevertheless possible to identify general demand and how it is covered. These so-called demand coverage gaps explain the shortage or surplus of teachers differentiated according to school type and take into account forecasted demand as well as coverage in the form of expected available traditionally trained teachers.

As early as 2017/18, it was predicted that, for the school year 2020/21, there would be a shortage of 2,150 teachers at the primary level, 900 at the primary/secondary level one, 2,320 at the secondary level one, 370 at the secondary level two (vocational schools) and 940 in the special school sector. Even if this hardly seems to have any influence on the total number of teachers in Germany, these figures show a teacher shortage that poses major challenges for schools. Only the upper secondary level had a projected surplus of 3,250 jobs. Here, it is usually only in specific subjects, currently mainly in the field of natural sciences, that have an additional need for teachers. These figures do not take into account the already-existing shortage of teachers in certain types of schools, which would lead to far more serious balance sheet figures. Considering the unfilled vacancies in 2018 and 2019, and the needs of 2020, this, for example, would result in a cumulative deficit of 2,750 teachers at vocational schools. These shortfalls, as well as the proportion of career jumpers and lateral entry teachers – which was 12.5 per cent in total in the 2017/18 school year – are by no means evenly distributed between the federal states. There are considerable differences between needs, and thus also the number of career jumpers and lateral entry teachers, in the school system.

The proportion of career jumpers and lateral entry teachers in the public school system in the 2017/18 school year was 46.6 per cent in Saxony, around 41.5 per cent in Berlin, over 25 per cent in Brandenburg and just under 21 per cent in Bremen. In Lower Saxony, around 17 per cent were career jumpers and lateral entry teachers, Saxony-Anhalt recorded 12.7 per cent, Thuringia 11.4 per cent, North Rhine-Westphalia 10.3 per cent, Mecklenburg-Western Pomerania 7.7 per cent, Schleswig-Holstein 2.8 per cent, Hamburg 2.9 per cent and Baden-Württemberg 2.2 per cent. In Rhineland-Palatinate, the proportion of career jumpers and lateral entry teachers hired in the 2017/18 school year was only 0.7 per cent, with none at all in Bavaria, Hesse and Saarland (Klemm 2019). There is a strong east-west divide in the area of teacher shortages and the associated recourse to career jumpers and lateral entry teachers. Although the proportion of career jumpers and lateral entry teachers has already quadrupled since 2012, the figures for the 2020/21 school year show a similar picture. This indicates that the proportion of career jumpers and lateral entry teachers into the public school system is increasing, a trend that has been reinforced by the acute Covid-19 pandemic.

Currently 40 per cent of new hires in Berlin are career jumpers and lateral entry teachers, while in Brandenburg, for example, 34 per cent do not have a full teaching qualification. In the western German states, it is specific subjects, for example, the natural sciences, and certain types of schools that need to be filled with career jumpers and lateral entry teachers due to the applicant situation (Andres and Kuhn 2020). According to the different teacher needs, there is still a generally evident east-west as well as north-south divide in the distribution of the recruitment of career jumpers and lateral entry teachers in Germany. In addition to the different school types and subjects, an extension to the last concession made by the KMK resolution where states can take further specific special measures to recruit non-traditionally trained teachers is also being implemented to varying degrees in the federal states. Accordingly, the recruitment processes vary from an eighteen-month preparatory service in Berlin parallel to seventeen hours of independent teaching, to a one-year basic pedagogical in-service qualification in Mecklenburg-Western Pomerania, to the possibility of career jumpers and lateral entry teachers being included in the teaching profession in Saarland where this is not currently an option (*Ministerium für Bildung und Kultur*/Ministry of Education and Culture 2019).

2. EPIK – a Model of Teacher Professionalism

With the increasing employment of career jumpers and lateral entry teachers in the public school system, the discussion about their existing or absent competences or strengths, as well as any limitations as they relate to traditionally trained teachers, is also intensifying. General competency models for teacher professionalism are used to explain which competencies career jumpers and lateral entry teachers should bring with them. The underlying competencies of teacher professionalism are illustrated, for example, in the EPIK model – a working group on the development of professionalism in an international context. This model was chosen here because it is particularly open to non-didactic and pedagogical skills. It enables a variety of development perspectives that can be applied to school development, teacher training and continuing education and pedagogical concepts. The model is based on five domains of professionalism for teachers, which are presented as individual pieces of a puzzle, providing an overall picture of the competencies relating to the teacher's personality and the school environment. In the so-called EPIK model these competencies include the ability to reflect and discourse, professional awareness, personal mastery, the ability to differentiate and collegiality (Herzog-Punzenberger 2012). All these areas are explained from the perspective of the subject and the structure. On the one hand this means individual competence, which is explained in this context so that the focus is on the teacher, while on the other hand it also includes the structural conditions that often form the basis for the (further) development of the necessary competences of teacher professionalism.

The capacity for reflection and discourse focuses on the sharing of skills and knowledge. Self-observation, enabled by social competence and distance from one's own teaching, as well as reflection and communication skills in conversation with school and out-of-school actors are included in this area. Professional awareness refers to the teachers' perceptions of themselves as experts. A self-confident but also self-critical representation of the teachers' professionalism to the outside world and their perception of their own creative area and scope are issues relating to the subject. In terms of structure, the focus is on the organization promoting professional awareness, opportunities for further qualification as well as open career paths. Personal mastery, or individual ability, aims at a situation-appropriate and effective use of the skills and knowledge of the teacher. Appropriate structures enable the teacher to find their own way, to promote an open culture of error and to facilitate learning. The ability to differentiate, for example, in methods and tasks, ideally to an individual approach to the different abilities and personalities guides the student. On the one hand, this includes knowledge about the different learning types, integration and communication skills of the pupil body, while on the other hand, it includes a corresponding competence in observation and empathy. Accordingly, diversity must be recognized as a resource and heterogeneity must be promoted and recognized from a structural perspective. The area of collegiality includes successful cooperation and the formation of a professional community both in schools and with extracurricular partners. In terms of the subject, this requires a corresponding openness and social competence and a provision of the prerequisites for productive cooperation through an appropriate space, time and continuity (Schratz et al. 2011; Schrittesser 2013). Teacher professionalism and the necessary competencies are accordingly characterized by scientific knowledge, practical experience and the routine habituation of the corresponding activities in everyday professional life. The need for dual professionalism, which includes a scientific-reflective and a pedagogical-practical habitus (Helsper 2001), illustrates possible limitations that lateral entry teachers or career jumpers might have. Although they often have a subject-specific background, and thus a scientific-reflective habitus, they usually do not have any pedagogical training and, if they have not undergone regular formal training, are often inadequately prepared for the teaching profession in a fast-track process (Schmoll 2018; Engel and Voigt 2019: 51–2).

3. 'New' Competences of Career Jumpers and Lateral Entry Teachers

As the numbers of career jumpers increases in Germany, the discussion in the media about their lack of educational competences is also gaining presence. The most popular statement is from the German president of the teachers' association Heinz-Peter Meidinger, who, in 2019, said that career jumpers were pedagogical laymen working in primary schools without any sufficient preparation or quality guidelines. Meidinger describes the situation as a 'crime against children' (Vitzthum 2019). He points out that career jumpers teach children with the knowledge of a two-week crash course in education and didactics. This shows that politicians in Germany do not give recognition to teachers' professionalism (Vitzthum 2019). This often-quoted interview based on a discussion about career jumpers was started between the experts. The Education and Science Union in the state of Hesse emphasized that 'Nobody would let a nurse operate on their open heart', says GEW deputy chairman Tony Schwarz. 'Career changers would be used to make the teaching figures look good, while the quality is declining' (Kölner Stadtanzeiger 2020). In addition to these critics, it is true that career jumpers or lateral entry teachers often work with children from underprivileged social environments, for example, in primary schools in Berlin (Richter et al. 2018).

But let us take a different look at this discussion. A well-known educational researcher in Germany, Professor Klaus Klemm, refers to a study conducted by the Institute for Quality Development in Education. This study shows that for German and English lessons in the ninth grade, pupils taught by career jumpers who have studied the relevant subjects achieve approximately the same performance as those taught by teachers with basic training in the subject. On the other hand, if teachers teach other subjects, this leads to a weaker performance (Irle 2019). Klemm points out that in this case professional competence is more important than didactic competence. 'It would therefore be more appropriate to let the career changer with a degree in English teach English than the classically trained teacher without a specialized degree. It is certainly different in elementary school, where didactic and pedagogical competence plays a much greater role' (Irle 2019). The study of Lucksnat et al. found similar results. They analysed career jumpers and traditionally educated teachers in the subject of mathematics in the 'Sekundarstufe I' (Lucksnat et al. 2020), which is equivalent to the second level of the International Standard Classification of Education. Since professional competence was viewed as being equal in both groups, the difference was observed in the psychological-pedagogical and didactic skills. Lucksnat reveals that this knowledge, for example, structuring lessons or organizing both the class and the learning process, is inferior in the group of career jumpers (Lucksnat et al. 2020). One should note that this study was published in 2020 from data collected in 2009 and only refers to the subject of mathematics. This lack of studies applies to German research as a whole. Either the studies are not up to date, they analyse regional areas of career jumpers, for example, in a single federal state, or they analyse only one subject in a special school. There is an absence of holistic studies relating to the issue, so the discussion about competences from career jumpers remains on the surface.

As described above, education policymakers and researchers highlight a lack of competence for career jumpers. But the question of what added value career jumpers could bring to the school can also be asked. This question can be discussed on two levels since career jumpers can have competences which are relevant to the level of teaching as well as to the level of school development. In terms of the level of teaching, one characteristic of career jumpers is their former working background, for example, in the field of economics. In this field, the competences of entrepreneurship or intrapreneurship gain weight in the discussion on future skills (Kichherr et al. 2018: 3). Besides technology and digital competences or skills, both classical skills, such as 'adaptability, creativity, and perseverance' (Kichherr et al. 2018: 6), and entrepreneurial thinking are important in working life. 'Those who possess these classic skills will find new situations easier to handle and be able to analyse and solve problems in an increasingly volatile and complex working world' (Kichherr et al. 2018: 6). In this context, entrepreneurs and intrapreneurs are defined as follows: every successful, self-employed entrepreneur should have entrepreneurial skills, while every employee in the company should be an intrapreneur, a so-called co-entrepreneur, if possible, who successfully helps shape their company and contributes and implements new creative ideas. Intrapreneurs think profitably, initiate new processes, motivate their colleagues, are able to network and are risk averse. They aim to position the company successfully in the market and to use their ideas profitably (Schönebeck 2010: 11–14). The results of the ASCOT initiative show how important intrapreneurship skills have become in everyday working life. ASCOT is a programme funded by the BMBF (the German Federal Ministry of Education and Research) to conduct competence measurements in various professional fields between 2011 and 2015 to assess the performance level of young people. On the basis of the results, the researchers demanded, among other things, that 'for the promotion of a creative, innovative entrepreneurial thinking and acting . . . both in the operational and at school training practice increased learning opportunities for the perception of business opportunities and for the generation of new ideas are to be created' (Bundesministerium für Bildung und Forschung/Ministry for Education and Research 2015: 10). It can therefore be concluded that the teachers themselves must have intrapreneurial or entrepreneurial competences in order to be able to convey these in their teaching (here, especially in economics) through complex teaching-learning arrangements (Aff and Geissler 2014: 31). It can also be assumed that teachers who have already gained working experience in the business world have intrapreneurial competences and can thus pass these on to their pupils. This unquestionably represents added value and something positive in competence transfer at the teaching level.

These intrapreneurial competences of career jumpers or lateral entry teachers can also have a positive impact on the level of school development as the roles and tasks of school management and teachers undergo profound changes due to the development of increasing school autonomy in Germany. At the beginning of the twenty-first century, following the first publications of the PISA results, a paradigm shift in education policy took place in Germany. This is visible, above all, in external evaluations, competence standards and comparative work in schools (Raidt 2010: 11). In addition, changes in school practice determine the current picture of the economy and autonomy of the school. Schools have been assigned autonomous tasks with the aim of giving school actors more freedom in the pedagogical, organizational and financial areas (Munin 2001: 15). This does not mean complete responsibility for individual schools but rather the option to make independent decisions within a framework given by the state. These effects, in turn, are controlled by the state, for example, through standardized tests (Steiner-Khamsi 2002: 133). Accordingly, concepts such as partial autonomy and school autonomy or personal responsibility aptly illustrate the implementation (Sparka 2007: 4). Here, economy means efficiency, competition and marketing and is consistent with the characteristics of extended self-administration and school autonomy. Both processes of change in the school system complement and enrich each other and have an impact on its structures, processes and ultimately on the actors (Krautz 2007: 81–9; Lohmann 2002: 92–4). The associated mission statement moves away from purely administrative processes towards a school as a learning organization and accordingly includes the learning ability of the individual school and an emphasis on 'entrepreneurial-managerial virtues of organisational action' (Höhne 2015: 29). The deregulation of the school system thus not only enables the transfer of economic models of thinking, it also increasingly confronts the individual schools with new or changed requirements with the aim of increasing effectiveness and efficiency (Höhne 2015: 29). For this reason, and also through the initiation and implementation of school economic development processes, the actors are now forced to consider economic principles such as increasing competition in the school market or output orientation in a field that was previously purely pedagogical (Steiner-Khamsi 2002: 133–42; Höhne 2015: 7–9). Therefore, also at the level of school development, career jumpers or lateral entry teachers with a business-related background can add value and contribute their skills in this context. As traditionally trained teachers often have no further business background, unless they can receive further training in this area, for example with an additional degree in school management or quality development, lateral entry teachers and career jumpers can be at an advantage.

4. Conclusion and Outlook

One must differentiate between the competences of career jumpers or lateral entry teachers. One the one hand, it is apparent that this group of teachers has a less pedagogical-practical habitus; their professionalism comes from a working background and related experiences. In terms of the EPIK model, they might possess these competences in general without these referring to the school system or the teacher's role. On the other hand, career jumpers and lateral entry teachers do bring other relevant competences which provide added value for the pupils and the school's development.

Nevertheless, as the numbers of career jumpers and lateral entry teachers increases, and will continue to increase in the near future, one must think of new professional concepts in teacher training. In terms of the EPIK model as a basis for these professional concepts, one could extend the model by including the competences of intrapreneurship or digital skills, which are also becoming increasingly important due to the Covid-19 pandemic and digitization of the whole education system.

Besides a theoretical new orientation, system changes and recommendations for action can also be defined. A distribution mechanism should be established so that career jumpers or lateral entry teachers not only work with pupils from underprivileged social environments. This group of teachers must be equally distributed among schools so that no *two-tier system* and no social inequality is created. Furthermore, a mentoring system in individual schools could be recommended. Career jumpers or lateral entry teachers and traditional teachers work in tandem and help each other based on their respective strengths and competences. Traditionally trained teachers pass on their competences in the pedagogical field to career jumpers or lateral entry teachers, who in turn, for example, could share their entrepreneurial competences and experiences. This exchange should be organized and guided by the school management. It is essential that the two groups of people respect and accept each other and their different training paths as equal. It is the task of the school management to establish this culture and to avoid a two-class society being established among the teaching staff. However, there should be more compulsory further training for teachers so that they can better take on new challenges, such as the digitization of the education system. University curricula concerning the scientific and practical competences of trainee teachers should also be aligned.

All in all, it can be concluded that there is a vast desiderata in the research concerning the competences of career jumpers and lateral entry teachers. Recent empirical studies on this group of teachers are rare. Both nationwide and cross-school-type quantitative surveys and qualitative methods should be used to obtain new, meaningful results.

The EPIK model provides a very good basis for considering the competencies of teachers. A general expansion of this and other competence models to include less traditional competencies, which also specifically relate to a professional background acquired prior to teaching, would have to be questioned. The further development of models is ultimately to be seen in a constant development of societal requirements and school challenges and should never be viewed as complete. If the current focus is on digital and intercultural skills in the German education system, in future there must also be a focus on entrepreneurial skills in the sense of developing self-reliance in schools. Teacher training in Germany still offers many starting points for an individualized education, which, with different focuses and additional certificates, offers at least the possibility of a colourful expansion of competencies.

References

Aff, J. and G. Geissler (2014), 'Entrepreneurship Erziehung in der Berufsbildung', *Berufsbildung*, 68 (147): 29–31.

Andres, F. and A. Kuhn (2020), 'Länderüberblick zum Schulstart. Wo die meisten Lehrkräfte fehlen', *Das Deutsche Schulportal*, 24 August. Available online: https://deutsches-schulportal.de/bildungswesen/ueberblick-der-bundeslaender-neues-schuljahr-wo-die-meisten-lehrkraefte-fehlen/ (accessed 2 November 2020).

Autorengruppe Bildungsberichterstattung (2020), 'Bildung in Deutschland 2020. Ein indikatorengestützter Bericht mit einer Analyse zu Bildung in einer digitalisierten Welt'. Available online: https://www.bildungsbericht.de/static_pdfs/bildungsbericht-2020.pdf (accessed 10 November 2020).

Bertelsmann Stiftung, CHE Centrum für Hochschulentwicklung GmbH, Deutsche Telekom Stiftung und Stifterverband für die Deutsche Wissenschaft (2018), Monitor LehrerInnenbildung (2018), 'Lehramtsstudium in der digitalen Welt'. Available online: https://www.monitor-lehrerbildung.de/web/publikationen/digitalisierung (accessed 28 February 2021).

Böhmann, M. (2011), *Das Quereinsteiger-Buch. So gelingt der Start in den Lehrerberuf*, Weinheim: Beltz.

Bundesministerium für Bildung und Forschung (2015), *Technologiebasierte Kompetenzmessung in der beruflichen Bildung (ASCOT)*. Available online: https://www.bmbf.de/pub/ASCOT.pdf (accessed 10 July 2018).

Cortina, K., J. Baumert, A. Leschinsky and K. Mayer (2005), *Das Bildungswesen in der Bundesrepublik Deutschland. Strukturen und Entwicklungen im Überblick*, Reinbeck: Rowohlt Taschenbuch Verlag.

Engel, I. and M. Voigt (2019), 'Rekrutierung von QuereinsteigerInnen', *Journal für LehrerInnenbildung*, 19 (2): 50–7.

Grundgesetz der Bundesrepublik Deutschland. Edition 2017.

Helsper, W. (2001), 'Praxis und Reflexion. Die Notwendigkeit einer "doppelten Professionalisierung" des Lehrers', *Journal für Lehrerinnen und Lehrerbildung*, 1: 7–15.

Herzog-Punzenberger, B. (2012), *Nationaler Bildungsbericht Österreich Band 2: Fokussierte Analysen bildungspolitischer Schwerpunktthemen*, Graz: Leykam.

Höhne, T. (2015), *Ökonomisierung und Bildung: Zu den Formen ökonomischer Rationalisierung im Feld der Bildung*, Wiesbaden: Springer.

Irle, K. (2019), 'Lehrkräftemangel "Fachkompetenz schlägt didaktische Kompetenz"', *Gewerkschaft Erziehung und Wissenschaft GEW*, 10 July. Available online: https://www.gew.de/aktuelles/detailseite/neuigkeiten/fachkompetenz-schlaegt-didaktische-kompetenz/ (accessed 07 October 2020).

Kichherr, J., J. Klier, C. Lehmann-Brauns and M. Winde (2018), 'Future Skills: Which Skills are Lacking in Germany?', *Stifterverband*. Available online: https://www.future-skills.net/which-skills-are-lacking-in-germany (accessed 13 October 2020).

Klemm, K. (2019), *Seiten- und Quereinsteiger_innen an Schulen in den 16 Bundesländern. Versuch einer Übersicht*, Friedrich-Ebert-Stiftung: Netzwerk Bildung, March. Available online: http://library.fes.de/pdf-files/studienfoerderung/15305.pdf (accessed 3 November 2020).

Klemm, K. and D. Zorn (2017), *Demographische Rendite adé*, Bertelsmann Stiftung. Available online: https://www.bertelsmann-stiftung.de/de/publikationen/publikation/did/demographische-rendite-ade/ (accessed 13 January 2021).

KMK Sekretariat der ständigen Konferenz der Kultusminister der Länder in der Bundesrepublik Deutschland (2013), 'Gestaltung von Sondermaßnahmen zur Gewinnung von Lehrkräften zur Unterrichtsversorgung, Beschluss der Kultusministerkonferenz von 05.12.2013'. Available online: https://www.kmk.org/fileadmin/Dateien/veroeffentlichungen_beschluesse/2013/2013_12_05-Gestaltung-von-Sondermassnahmen-Lehrkraefte.pdf (accessed 4 November 2020).

Kölner, Stadtanzeiger (2020), 'Schulen auf Quereinsteiger angewiesen: Kritik von GEW', *Kölner Stadtanzeiger*, 13 January. Available online: https://www.ksta.de/schulen-auf-quereinsteiger-angewiesen-kritik-von-gew-33730628 (accessed 7 October2020).

Krautz, J. (2007), 'Pädagogik unter dem Druck der Ökonomisierung. Zum Hintergrund von Standards, Kompetenzen und Modulen', *Pädagogische Rundschau*, 67 (1): 81–93. Available online: http://schimmelbildung.blogsport.de/images/krautz__paedagogik_unter_dem_druck_der_oekonomisierung_paedagogische_rundschau.pdf (accessed 12 August 2018).

Lohmann, I. (2002), 'After Neoliberalism – Können nationale Bildungssysteme den "freien Markt" überleben?', in I. Lohmann and R. Rilling (eds), *Die verkaufte Bildung: Kritik und Kontroversen zur Kommerzialisierung von Schule, Weiterbildung, Erziehung und Wissenschaft*, 89–209, Opladen: Budrich.

Lucksnat, C., E. Richter, U. Klusmann, M. Kunter and D. Richter (2020), 'Unterschiedliche Wege ins Lehramt – unterschiedliche Kompetenzen?: Ein Vergleich von Quereinsteigern und traditionell ausgebildeten Lehramtsanwärtern im Vorbereitungsdienst', *Zeitschrift für Pädagogische Psychologie*, 1–16. doi:10.1024/1010-0652/a000280.

Ministerium für Bildung und Kultur (2019), *Stellen an allgemeinbildenden Schulen*, Saarland: Ministerium für Bildung und Kultur, 5 December. Available online: https://www.saarland.de/mbk/DE/portale/bildungsserver/lehrkraefte/stellenausschreibungen/stellenallgemeinbildendeschulen/stellenallgemeinbildendeschulen.html (accessed 3 November 2020).

Munin, H. (2001), *Schulautonomie*, Weinheim: Beltz Springer.

Raidt, T. (2010), 'Bildungsreformen nach PISA: Paradigmenwechsel und Wertewandel', MA diss., Heinrich-Heine Universität Düsseldorf, Düsseldorf.

Reintjes, C., G. Bellenberg, C. Kiso and J. Korte (2020), 'Ausbildungskonzepte für Seiteneinsteiger*innen: Notlösungen als Dauerzustand', *Pädagogik*, 20: 7–8.

Richter, D., A. Marx and D. Zorn (2018), *Lehrkräfte im Quereinstieg: sozial ungleich verteilt? Eine Analyse zum Lehrermangel an Berliner Grundschulen*, Gütersloh: Bertelsmann Stiftung.

Rürup, M. (2007), *Innovationswege im deutschen Bildungssystem. Die Verbreitung der Idee 'Schulautonomie' im Ländervergleich*, Wiesbaden: VS Verlag für Sozialwissenschaften.

Schmoll, H. (2018), 'In sieben Tagen zum Lehrer', *Frankfurter Allgemeine*, 17 August. Available online: https://www.faz.net/aktuell/politik/inland/bildung-in-berlin-in-sieben-tagen-zum-lehrer-15743043.html (accessed 3 November 2020).

Schönebeck, G. (2010), 'Intrapreneurship – Eine empirische Analyse der Barrieren und Widerstände im Unternehmen', PhD thesis, Fakultät VII - Wirtschaft und Management, Technische Universität, Berlin. doi:10.14279/depositonce-2536.

Schratz, M., A. Paseka and I. Schrittesser (2011), *Pädagogische Professionalität: quer denken – umdenken – neu denken: Impulse für next practice im Lehrerberuf*, Wien: facultas.

Schrittesser, I. (2013), 'Organisation der Lehrerbildung in Österreich: Modelle und Empfehlungen', in I. Schrittesser (ed.), *Lehren Lernen – die Zukunft der Lehrerbildung*, Tagungsband des Österreichischen Wissenschaftsrats 2012, 115–30.

Sparka, A. (2007), 'Schulautonomie in der Bewährung. Ein Vergleich: Das Bundesland Nord-Rhein- Westfahlen und die Niederlande', MA diss., Universität Dortmund, Dortmund.

Steiner-Khamsi, G. (2002), 'Die verkaufte Bildung', in I. Lohmann and R. Rilling (eds), *School Choice — wer profitiert, wer verliert?*, 133–55, Opladen: Budrich.

Vitzthum, T. (2019), 'Das ist ein Verbrechen an den Kindern', *Die Welt*, 30 December. Available online: https://www.welt.de/politik/deutschland/plus204584106/Lehrerverbandschef-Das-ist-ein-Verbrechen-an-den-Kindern.html (accessed 7 October 2020).

8

The Colleague-Outsider Conundrum
The Case of Zimbabwean Migrant Teachers in South African Classrooms

Kudzayi Savious Tarisayi

1. Introduction

The past two decades in South Africa have been characterized by the recurrence of violent outbreaks targeting foreigners. The recurring attacks on foreigners have been regarded as unabating (Tarisayi and Manik 2020). There is burgeoning literature that examines and explains the causes of violence on foreigners in South Africa (Bond, Amisi, Cele and Ngwane 2011; Hickel 2014). However, there is a dearth in literature focusing on the relationship between Zimbabwean migrant teachers and their South African counterparts in school spaces. Premised on the phenomenon of violence against teachers from outside South Africa, this chapter strives to analyse this relationship between Zimbabwean migrant teachers and their South African counterparts drawing from a qualitative multisite case study conducted in two selected provinces. The chapter begins with an introduction that provides a background to the study. The background also provides a literature review on the concepts of Afrophobia (xenophobia) in South Africa, integration of immigrants as well as unpacking of the concepts of belonging. The scapegoating theoretical framework guiding this chapter is explained as well as the research methodology. Lastly, the researcher presents the findings and their discussion.

Earlier scholarship conceptualized the violence on foreigners in South Africa as xenophobia; however, recent outbreaks suggest a more complex and nuanced phenomenon. The recent outbreaks in violence targeting foreigners in South Africa exhibit a new peculiarity of xenophobia. There is an apparent deviation from the norm, usually revealed in xenophobia and xenophobic attacks in other parts of the world. Essentially by definition, xenophobia usually targets foreigners in general. Conversely, South Africa's violence offers a variant of xenophobia which entails the targeted attacks on Black foreigners from other African countries. Thus, due to this deviation from what was previously reported and conceptualized as xenophobia this chapter leans towards the contemporary view that South Africa's violence is Afrophobia. Afrophobia which entails 'Africans targeting other Africans' (Tarisayi and Manik 2019: 7) in South Africa. South Africa is a multiracial society and in the words of Archbishop Desmond Tutu it is a 'Rainbow Nation' composed of 'rainbow people'. Tutu cited in Buqa (2015: 1) explained: 'They tried to make us one colour: purple. We say we are the rainbow people! We are the new people of the new South Africa!' However, the increase in migration after the country's transition to democracy in 1994 can be construed as adding other shades of colour to the rainbow nation. South Africa is receiving migrants from several countries, including Zimbabwe, Lesotho, Swaziland, Malawi, Mozambique, Nigeria, Ethiopia, Pakistan, China and European countries. Essentially, there is an apparent representation of almost all races in the migrants received by South Africa. However, recent violent attacks (September 2019) have only targeted Black foreigners from other African countries. Thus, giving justification to the view that the violent attacks are essentially Afrophobic and not entirely xenophobic. A study carried out by the South African Migration Project (SAMP) showed that South Africans are 'particularly intolerant of non-nationals, and especially African non-nationals' (Black et al. 2006: 105). Hence, general intolerance of non-nationals is understood in this chapter as xenophobia while intolerance of Black foreigners from other African countries is viewed as Afrophobia.

Furthermore, there is a plethora of literature from the Global North on the integration of migrants in the host countries. However, there is seldom interest in the integration of migrants in the Global South. Krumm and Plutzar (2008: 2) state that 'integration aims at giving the immigrants an opportunity to take part in the political, social, economic and cultural life of their new country'. Additionally, in the Global North, there are concerted efforts to facilitate immigrants' integration as exemplified by the development of the migration management strategy in Europe (Krumm and Plutzar 2008; Nieuwboer and Rood 2016). However, these scientifically based claims often remain unsatisfied by the rather discriminatory and at times racist practices in many parts of the Global North as well. Despite the elaborate body of literature and research efforts, more often than not suggestions remain unrealized. Krumm and Plutzar (2008: 2) state that the Council of Europe promotes the cooperation 'between the countries of origin and the receiving countries and the establishment of a climate favouring the integration of migrants into the host society'. Thus, there is an effort by an international body in Europe to promote the management of migration and integration of migrants. Resolution 1437 (2005), I.4 of the Parliamentary Assembly of the Council of Europe states:

> The concept of integration aims at ensuring social cohesion through accommodation of diversity understood as a two-way process. Immigrants have to accept the laws and basic values of European societies. On the other hand, host societies have to respect immigrants' dignity and distinct identity and take them into account when elaborating domestic policies.

Additionally, the European Commission published the *Handbook on Integration* that articulates that 'it is necessary to change and adapt all kinds of public services, housing, admission to the labour market and education programmes to the needs of immigrants' (Krumm and Plutzar 2008: 2). More recently, the Parliamentary Assembly of the Council of Europe (PACE) in 2019 adopted a resolution and publication of a report in support of refugees. The report highlights the urgent need, in the face of Covid-19, for parliaments to actively promote solidarity towards refugees and migrants at home and abroad (United Nations High Commissioner for Refugees 2021). Essentially, contemporary literature reveals that in Europe there is cooperation and political will to facilitate the integration of migrants. However, this chapter draws from a study carried out in a country located in a continent yet to embrace the importance of cooperation between the countries of origin and the receiving countries in facilitating the integration of immigrants. Okunade (2021) states that the African Union decided to move towards a 'borderless' Africa. Most notable was the adoption of the African Union Protocol on the Free Movement of Persons in Africa at the AU Assembly in Addis Ababa in 2018. Hirsch (2021: n.p.) argues that 'the rationale for the protocol is that African development will be enhanced by the freer movement of people across national borders within the continent'. Thus, while efforts at continental level have been seized with promoting the free movement of people on the continent, not much has been done on the integration of immigrants within countries on the continent.

A number of factors can be identified in migration literature that are pertinent in promoting integration of immigrants in general and teacher migrants in particular. Belonging plays an integral role in the integration of immigrants in host countries. Hagerty et al. (1992) (cited in Salami et al. 2019: 29) views belonging as 'the experience of personal involvement in a system or environment so that persons feel themselves to be an integral part of the system or environment'. Key features of an immigrant's 'sense of belonging include the experience of being valued, needed, and accepted as well as a person's perception that his or her characteristics articulate with, fit with, or complement the system or environment' (Salami et al. 2019: 29). Additionally, language plays an instrumental role in the integration of immigrants; Nieuwboer and Rood (2016) noted the centrality of language skills in the integration of immigrants in Europe. The Parliamentary Assembly of the European Council (2014) cited in Nieuwboer and Rood (2016: 30) declared that 'socially relevant functional language skills, which encourage communication and integration are more important'. Hence, it can be argued that acquisition of language skills is essential in the integration of immigrants in the host countries. Additionally, scholarship on monolingual habitus and linguicism locates language at the epicentre of integration of immigrants (Rem and Gasper 2018; Ruhlmann and McMonagle 2019). Ruhlmann and McMonagle (2019) highlight issues of othering and linguicism in the exclusion of immigrants in Germany. Other studies in South Africa have established that language skills were an essential survival strategy for immigrants (Sinyolo 2012; Tarisayi and Manik 2019). In this chapter the concepts of belonging and language were pertinent in unpacking the relationship between Zimbabwean migrant teachers and their South African counterparts.

2. Theoretical Framework

Several theories have been proffered to unpack the experiences of migrants in general and migrant teachers in particular. These theories include the isolation hypothesis, scapegoating hypothesis, biocultural hypothesis, power theory and power-conflict theory. In this chapter the researcher drew from the scapegoating theoretical lens to analyse the relationship between Zimbabwean migrant teachers and South African teachers in school spaces. The scapegoating theory of xenophobia argues 'prejudice and discrimination as a means by which people express hostility arising from frustration' (Odiaka 2017: 6). Harris (2002: 172) explains, 'The scapegoating hypothesis of xenophobia states that the foreigner is used as a scapegoat, someone to blame for social ills and personal frustrations. In this way, the foreigner becomes a target for hostility and violence.' Social ills within South Africa are blamed on the foreigners according to the scapegoating theory. Perennial problems related to limited resources such as housing, education, health care and employment are linked to the influx of migrants

(Tshitereke 1999; Harris 2002). Black et al. (2006) argue that many migrants find shelter in informal urban settlements which are sites of high poverty, unemployment, and housing shortages. This essentially puts pressure on the already limited resources. In contemporary times, social ills such as crime and drugs are blamed on the migrants according to the scapegoating theoretical lens. For Tshitereke (1999) the phenomenon of xenophobia entails frustrated people venting their anger on the 'frustration-scape goat'. Essentially, migrants become the frustration scapegoats according to the scapegoating theoretical lens. In this chapter, the way South African teachers relate to their Zimbabwean migrant counterparts resonates with the shared frustration that is captured by the scapegoating hypothesis. Odiaka (2017) terms the shared frustration among perpetrators of xenophobia 'commonness of experience'. Claassen (2017: 4) states that the scapegoating theory 'holds that poverty produces frustration, and consequently aggression, with aggression then displaced onto some innocent but weak third party'. Drawing from the scapegoating theory, this chapter argues that teachers from outside South Africa are targeted despite being innocent because they are considered a weak third party. Widespread poverty in South Africa feeds into the growing frustration with the government of South Africa and resultantly aggression against immigrants. The migrant teachers are targeted within South Africa's school spaces because there are construed as weak third parties. The next section presents the research methodology.

3. Research Methodology

The study on the relationship between the Zimbabwean migrant teachers and their South African counterparts in school spaces was within the interpretivist paradigm and it was qualitative. Creswell and Poth (2018: 45) state that qualitative research provides 'a complex, detailed understanding of the issue'. This study provides a detailed understanding of the relationship between migrant teachers and native teachers working in a country that has experienced recurring outbreaks of violence against foreigners. A multisite case study was carried out in two selected provinces in South Africa. Cohen, Manion and Morrison (2018: 376) explain case studies proffer 'a unique example of real people in real situations, enabling readers to understand ideas more clearly than simply by presenting them with abstract theories or principles'. The researcher purposively sampled eighteen Zimbabwean migrant teachers in two provinces in South Africa. Data was generated using two focus group discussions (one focus group per province) and twelve semi-structured interviews. Focus group discussions and semi-structured interviews were used to triangulate and probe themes emerging from either of the two data generation methods. Lambert and Loiselle (2008) aver that combining individual interviews and focus groups enhances qualitative research data. The researcher utilized thematic analysis (Braun and Clarke 2006).

4. Findings

This section presents and discusses the findings from this study. The chapter noted that the colleague-outsider conundrum was exhibited in teacher collegiality in school spaces. The sense of belonging of teachers from outside South Africa was affected by othering associated with the colleague-outsider conundrum. Additionally, there was weaponization of Indigenous languages to perpetuate the colleague-outsider conundrum. Lastly, the conundrum between teachers from outside South Africa and local South African teachers was revealed by the non-recognition of foreign-earned teaching experience. These findings are explained in detail in this section under the themes: teacher collegiality, sense of belonging, Indigenous languages and the colleague-outsider conundrum and non-recognition foreign-earned teaching experience.

Teacher Collegiality

The study revealed that being a migrant teacher in South African classrooms affected interactions with other local South African teachers, learners and parents. One critical relationship that was affected according to the participants in the study was teacher collegiality. Tarisayi, Munyaradzi and Chidarikire (2020: 92) view teacher collegiality as 'the collaboration of teachers in the same school or in different schools with the sole purpose of improving their teaching practice and the learning taking place in the relevant schools'. Teacher collegiality is an important relationship within school spaces. Conversely, Zimbabwean migrant teachers who participated in this study revealed that teacher collegiality with local South African teachers was adversely affected by their being foreigners. One participant, Munyaradzi, narrated, 'There are times when you feel that you are only a colleague in some situations and an outsider most of the times. When they want my help with a difficult situation, I am their colleague. Once it's done they remember that I am an outsider.' The participant's views suggest that the relationship between him and his colleagues at his school was manipulative. Local teachers only treated him as a colleague when they needed his input or help but immediately switch to treating him as an outsider thereafter. Essentially, the relationship between migrant teachers in South Africa and their peers can be viewed as fluid and fluctuating between being colleagues and at times outsiders. This chapter describes the fluidity and fluctuating relationship between Zimbabwean migrant teachers and their South African counterparts as the 'colleague-outsider' conundrum. The migrant teachers in this study revealed that they were regarded as colleagues when it was convenient for the local South Africa teachers. This writer views this relationship between Zimbabwean migrant teachers and their South African peers as the 'colleague-outsider' conundrum. A study by Sinyolo (2012) viewed this 'colleague-outsider' conundrum as part of the teacher migration paradox. Sinyolo (2012) argues that there are 'love-and-hate' attitudes towards Zimbabwean migrant teachers in South Africa. The 'colleague-outsider' conundrum suggests that teacher collegiality between Zimbabwean migrant teachers and their local South African peers was temporary and largely to the benefit of the later. The relationship between Zimbabwean migrant teachers and South African teachers can be argued to be complex and nuanced due to its fluidity from collegiality to outsider situationally. Central to the colleague-outsider conundrum is the notion that the relationship between migrant teachers and local South African teachers was largely ad hoc. South African teachers were viewed as regarding teachers from outside South Africa as colleagues when it was convenient for them to do so. The ad hoc approach goes against the teacher collegiality that should be prevalent in school spaces.

Another key aspect of the colleague-outsider conundrum is that the relationship between the Zimbabwean migrant teachers and their South African counterparts was situation and context dependent. In addition, another participant, Tawanda, explained, 'You can tell that a local colleague needs help or a favour by the way they address you. If they call you *mfowethu* [isiZulu for colleague/friend/buddy], it means they want a favour. In other contexts, it will be Mr Shumba. You cease to be *mfowethu*.' The verbatim narration by the participant further buttress the view that the relationship between migrant teachers and local South African teachers was ad hoc. Essentially, for the local South African teachers, migrant teachers only became colleagues when it was convenient. Additionally from Tawanda's explanation, it can be noted that the 'colleague-outsider' conundrum is evident in everyday conversations between Zimbabwean migrant teachers and their South African colleagues. Though the 'colleague-outsider' conundrum is subtle the Zimbabwean migrant teachers were convinced that it exists in school spaces. The participants noted that Zimbabwean migrant teachers only become colleagues to their South African colleagues when they need a favour or contribution. Hence, it can be argued that teacher collegiality between Zimbabwean migrant teachers and their South African counterparts was fluid, temporary and at times manipulative to some extent. However, it also emerged from the study that there was greater teacher collegiality among Zimbabwean migrant teachers within South African schools. Mike explained,

> There is genuine friendship and professional relations among our cliques of migrant teachers. I know for certain that I can count on my brothers and sisters from Zimbabwe at our school or neighbouring schools. We share our experiences and challenges in our social media groups. It's really comforting to have people that you can count on when in foreign lands.

The study established that Zimbabwean migrant teachers relied on other migrant teachers to navigate South African school spaces' challenges. Hence, teacher collegiality among migrant teachers was utilized to make up for the skewed relationship with local South African teachers. Thus, the 'colleague-outsider' conundrum provided opportunity for teacher collegiality among Zimbabwean migrant teachers to thrive. Essentially, providing a comfort zone for the migrant teachers in school spaces. Thus, what was lost in teacher collegiality between Zimbabwean migrant teachers and South African teachers was replaced through stronger teacher collegiality among Zimbabwean migrant teachers. Comparatively it can also be noted that teacher collegiality for Zimbabwean migrant teachers was skewed towards their fellow peers who were foreigners as compared to South African teachers. The chapter argues that the relationship between Zimbabwean migrant teachers and their South African counterparts was more nuanced and complex due to the 'colleague-outsider' conundrum. The 'colleague-outsider' conundrum in South African school spaces contributes to a layered teacher collegiality outlook whereby Zimbabwean migrant teachers are colleagues in an ad hoc manner and outsiders as and when necessary. Additionally, it follows from this scenario that Zimbabwean migrant teachers resorted to cluster among themselves leading to the emergence of another layer of teacher collegiality. Thus, there were apparent contradictions in the level of teacher collegiality within South African school spaces as there were layers of teacher collegiality. One layer involved teacher collegiality between Zimbabwean migrant teachers and local South African teachers and the other layer was composed of the relations among migrant teachers. Although outside the purview of this chapter, there could be another layer of teacher collegiality involving the relations among South African teachers only. From the preceding discussion, it can be argued that the colleague-outsider conundrum negatively impacted the teacher collegiality between Zimbabwean migrant teachers and their South African colleagues to a greater extent.

Sense of Belonging

The colleague-outsider conundrum in South African school spaces also affected the Zimbabwean migrant teachers' sense of belonging. A sense of belonging entails 'the experience of personal involvement in a system or environment so that persons feel themselves to be an integral part of that system or environment', according to Hagerty, Lynch-Sauer, Patusky, Bouwsema and Collier (1992: 173 cited in Salami et al. 2019: 29). The participants revealed that the 'colleague-outsider' conundrum impacted on their sense of belonging due to constant reminders that one is an outsider. Tapfumanei revealed, 'It's really difficult for us migrants to feel part of the school. The situation within and outside the classroom always reminds you that you are a foreigner, an outsider.' Tapfumanei revealed that both inside and outside the classroom migrant teachers are constantly reminded that they are outsiders. Essentially, the Zimbabwean teachers' integration within school spaces is curtailed by constant reminders that they are foreigners. Salami et al. (2019: 29) states that 'being valued, needed and accepted' are vital attributes of sense of belonging for migrants in a host country. However, it was evident from the participants that it was difficult for Zimbabwean migrant teachers to be accepted due to the situation inside and outside the classroom. An example of a situation that affected one Zimbabwean migrant teacher's sense of belonging involved maintaining discipline within school spaces.

Chiedza, another Zimbabwean migrant teacher, explained,

> Any misunderstanding or problems with learners is immediately linked with your being a foreigner. Colleagues and the principal rush to conclude that the problem is related to our lack of grounding in the local culture and society. Issues which are supposed to be understood as simply teacher-learner relations are misconstrued as related to being an outsider.

It can be noted that the colleague-outsider conundrum was basically evident in the relationship between some Zimbabwean migrant teachers who participated in this study and learners in South African learning spaces. Additionally, it was also revealed that local South African teachers were quick to link any problems that Zimbabwean migrant teachers had with learners to their outsiderness. Zimbabwean migrant teachers were viewed as outsiders by their colleagues, learners and parents. The linking of problems between learners and Zimbabwean migrant teachers in school spaces confirms the scapegoating theory. The scapegoating theory argues that foreigners are blamed for all social ills in society. Hence, in this case migrant teachers are blamed for contributing to learner indiscipline. Any disciplinary issue involving a migrant teacher and learners is blamed on the former. Migrant teachers are scapegoated as being outsiders and thus fail to understand the learners without due consideration of the circumstances.

Therefore, the findings in this chapter confirm the status of migrants which 'exists in all communities and societies, between those who belong, who are part of "us", and those who may be experienced as foreign or alien' (Crow, Allan and Summers 2001: 30). The curtailment of the sense of belonging of the Zimbabwean migrant teachers is essentially microcosmic of the experiences of migrants in other societies as also established by Crow et al. (2001). Furthermore, school spaces can be argued to be a miniature reflection of the wider society as reflected by the Zimbabwean migrant teachers' experiences in South Africa. This study concurs with the view by Landau (2010) and Nyamnjoh (2010) that the integration of immigrants into host nation communities is restricted as they are regarded as outsiders. Due to these restrictions on the integration of the Zimbabwean migrant teachers, their sense of belonging is hampered despite spending several years teaching in South Africa. Additionally, the colleague-outsider conundrum revealed by the findings from this study aptly resonates with the argument put forward by Ngan and Chan (2013) that an outsider is always an outsider. Therefore, it can be argued that the integration of the Zimbabwean migrant teachers fully into the South African society takes more than living in South Africa for several years. As some Zimbabwean migrant teachers who participated in this study have been in South Africa for more than a decade but they are still regarded as outsiders. Hence, it can be argued that the 'colleague-outsider' conundrum has ramifications on the sense of belonging of Zimbabwean migrant teachers to a greater extent. Resultantly, it can be reasoned that the hindrances in school spaces to the integration of the Zimbabwean migrant teachers are intertwined with the colleague-outsider conundrum.

Indigenous Language and the Colleague-Outsider Conundrum

The chapter further argues that Indigenous languages were weaponized to facilitate the 'colleague-outsider' relationship between Zimbabwean migrant teachers and South African teachers. Indigenous languages were utilized in exclusionary ways that Zimbabwean migrant teachers perceived as targeted on outsiders. Another Zimbabwean migrant teacher working in South Africa, Chiedza, explained,

> Indigenous languages were sometimes used to exclude us migrant teachers from conversations. We try to learn the local languages but the expectation is English which is the medium of instruction would be used in all professional engagements. Unfortunately in some cases to silence a migrant teacher, it's convenient for our local peers to switch to an indigenous language.

The narration by Chiedza reveals that Indigenous languages were utilized in an exclusionary way by South African teachers to silence migrant teachers in school spaces. The medium of instruction in South Africa from Grade 3 is either English or Afrikaans, and this study was carried out in English-speaking schools. Zimbabwean migrant teachers mostly prefer English-speaking schools because the medium of instruction in their home country is English. It can be noted that the use of Indigenous languages in an exclusionary way within South African school spaces buttresses the 'colleague-outsider' conundrum since colleagues strive to communicate in a language that all parties understand to a conversation. Maureen added,

> It is actually surprising that when there is a disagreement or contentious issue, our peers [South African teachers] switch to a local indigenous language. I have noticed that the switching to an indigenous language is done to ensure that you are excluded from the conversation. You end up picking bits and pieces of the conversation which should not be the case in professional spaces. Interesting the same teachers who switch to indigenous languages do not do that when they need help with something.

Fundamentally, Indigenous languages were weaponized in South African school spaces to exclude Zimbabwean migrant teachers from engaging and contributing to some conversations. Priscilla posed the question, 'What other way can you use to eliminate foreigners from a discussion than use an indigenous language? It is not about being fluent in English, but about not wanting us to participate in some conversations.' Hence, it was noted from the Zimbabwean migrant teachers' experiences that the switching to Indigenous languages by some South African teachers was not motivated by the inability to communicate in the medium of instruction but was a way of excluding migrant teachers from the conversation. The effects of the weaponization of local languages on the integration of Zimbabwean migrant teachers established by this study were consistent with other studies. Sinyolo (2012) established that lack of knowledge of local languages affected the integration of migrant teachers in South African school spaces. Therefore, it can be noted that there was exclusion of migrant teachers through the use of Indigenous languages according to findings from this study. Essentially, suggesting that the colleague-outsider conundrum was facilitated by the weaponization of Indigenous languages in school spaces.

Non-recognition of Foreign-Earned Teaching Experience

The chapter further noted that the non-recognition of foreign-earned teaching experience fed into the 'colleague-outsider' conundrum. The non-recognition of foreign-earned teaching experience further essentially strained the relationship between Zimbabwean migrant teachers and their South African counterparts. Most of the Zimbabwean migrant teachers migrated to South Africa after teaching in their home country. A study by Tarisayi and Manik (2019) indicated that poor working conditions were cited as push factors in the migration of Zimbabwean teachers to South Africa. There is consensus among scholars that the majority of teachers migrating from Zimbabwe are experienced and qualified teachers. However, according to the participants in this study their teaching experience in Zimbabwe is not recognized in school spaces in South Africa. Resultantly, less experienced and at times novice teachers get more responsibilities by virtue of only being South African citizens. Brenda narrated,

> It seems my experience prior to teaching in South Africa is considered irrelevant. Before coming to South Africa, I taught in Zimbabwe for eight years. Surprisingly, the school authorities seem oblivious of that experience when assigning responsibilities to teachers. Local teachers with less experience are getting more recognition. I think it has something to do with being a foreigner.

Experienced Zimbabwean migrant teachers were overlooked in assigning responsibilities due to the non-recognition of teaching experience earned outside South Africa. Additionally, another participant, Major, reflected, 'I have been teaching in South Africa for over a decade now. However, I am always treated and viewed like a novice. How long will it take my colleagues to accept me as an experienced and seasoned teacher? Recently qualified South African teachers are treated with more respect as compared to us foreigners.' The Zimbabwean migrant teachers who participated in the study were unanimous that their teaching experience earned before migrating to South Africa was not considered when assigning responsibilities. An example given by one of the participants was the promotion of recently qualified South African teachers. A study by Keevy (2008) noted that migrant teachers were inhibited from pursuing their teaching careers in host countries due to non-recognition of their qualifications. However, this chapter widens the conversation and argues that Zimbabwean migrant teachers' experience outside South Africa was not being recognized. The case of Zimbabwean migrant teachers being denied recognition of their teaching experience gained in Zimbabwe confirms an observation by the Commonwealth on the status of migrant teachers. Additionally, the Commonwealth Secretariat (2011: n.p.) noted that 'there is a lack of recognition of teachers' statuses in host country rules and regulations'. Thus, the non-recognition of the Zimbabwean migrant teachers' teaching experience affected their relationship as it reflected that they were outsiders. The chapter argues that non-recognition of foreign-earned experience was a form of othering of the Zimbabwean migrant teachers.

5. Concluding Remarks

This chapter drew from a multisite study carried out in two selected provinces in South Africa. The concepts of belonging and language as well as teacher collegiality were utilized to unpack the relationship between Zimbabwean migrant teachers and South African teachers in school spaces. The chapter described the relationship between Zimbabwean migrant teachers and South African teachers as a colleague-outsider conundrum. Zimbabwean migrant teachers revealed that they only became colleagues situationally, especially when giving favours to their South African counterparts. The chapter further argued that despite the Zimbabwean migrant teachers spending several years in South Africa they were still outsiders and thus concurring with a study by Ngan and Chan (2013) that an outsider is always an outsider. Additionally, the relationship between Zimbabwean migrant teachers and their South African colleagues was further strained by the non-recognition of foreign-earned teaching experience. The chapter also highlighted the weaponization of Indigenous languages to sustain the colleague-outsider conundrum. It can be concluded from this chapter that scapegoating was influential in shaping the relationship between Zimbabwean migrant teachers and the South African peers in school spaces.

References

Black, R., R. Crush, S. Peberdy, S. Ammassari, L. M. Hilker, S. Mouillesseaux, C. Pooley and R. Rajkotia (2006), 'Migration and Development in Africa: An Overview', *African Migration and Development Series No.1*, Waterloo: Southern African Migration Programme.

Bond, P., B. Amisi, N. Cele and T. Ngwane (2011), 'Xenophobia and Civil Society', *Politikon*, 38 (1): 59–83.

Braun, V. and V. Clarke (2006), 'Using Thematic Analysis in Psychology', *Qualitative Research in Psychology*, 3 (2): 77–101.

Buqa, W. (2015), 'Storying Ubuntu as a Rainbow Nation', *Verbum et Ecclesis*, 36 (2): 1–8.

Claassen, C. (2017), 'Explaining South African Xenophobia. Afrobarometer', *Working Paper*, 173: 1–25.

Cohen, L., L. Manion and K. Morrison (2018), *Research Methods in Education*, 8th edn, London: Routledge.

Commonwealth Secretariat (2011), 'Study Finds Teachers Face Barriers in Refugee Communities', *The Commonwealth*, 6 September. Available online: https://thecommonwealth.org/media/news/study-finds-teachers-face-barriers-refugee-communities (accessed 31 January 2021).

Creswell, J. W. and C. N. Poth (2018), *Qualitative Inquiry and Research Design: Choosing among Five Approaches*, 4th edn, Thousand Oaks: Sage.

Crow, G. P., G. A. Allan and M. Summers (2001), 'Changing Perspectives on the Insider/ Outsider Distinction in Community Sociology', *Community, Work and Family*, 4 (1): 29–48.

Hagerty, B. M., J. Lynch-Sauer, K. L. Patusky, M. Bouwsema and P. Collier (1992), 'Sense of Belonging: A Vital Mental Health Concept', *Archives of Psychiatric Nursing*, 6 (3): 172–7.

Harris, B. (2002), 'Xenophobia: A New Pathology for a New South Africa?', in D. Hookand and G. Eagle (eds), *Psychopathology and Social Prejudice*, 169–84, Cape Town: University of Cape Town Press.

Hickel, J. (2014), 'Xenophobia in South Africa: Order, chaos and the Moral Economy of Witchcraft', *Cultural Anthropology*, 29 (1): 103–27.

Hirsch, A. (2021), 'A Strategic Consideration of the African Union Free Movement of Persons Protocol and Other Initiatives Towards the Freer Movement of People in Africa. South African Institute of International Affairs', *Saiia*, 20 January. Available online: https://saiia.org.za/research/a-strategic-consideration-of-the-african-union-free-movement-of-persons-protocol-and-other-initiatives-towards-the-freer-movement-of-people-in-africa/ (accessed 31 January 2021).

Keevy, J. (2008), 'The Recognition of Teacher Qualifications in the Commonwealth', *Delivering the MDG's: Commonwealth Education Partnerships*, 52–5. Available online: https://www.academia.edu/4391989/The_recognition_of_teacher_qualifications_in_the_Commonwealth (accessed 31 January 2021).

Krumm, H. and Plutzar, V. (2008), *Tailoring Language Provision and Requirements to the Needs and Capacities of Adult Migrants*, Strasbourg: Council of Europe.

Lambert, S. D. and C. G Loiselle (2008), 'Combining Individual Interviews and Focus Groups to Enhance Data Richness', *Journal of Advanced Nursing*, 62 (2): 228–37. doi:10.1111/j.1365-2648.2007.04559.x.

Landau, L. B. (2010), 'Loving the Alien? Citizenship, Law, and the Future in South Africa's Demonic Society', *African Affairs*, 109 (435): 213–30. doi:10.1093/afraf/adq002.

Lim, T. (2010), 'Rethinking Belongingness in Korea: Transnational Migration, "Migrant Marriages" and the Politics of Multiculturalism', *Pacific Affairs*, 83 (1): 51–71.

Ngan, L. L. and K. Chan (2013), 'An Outsider is Always an Outsider: Migration, Social Policy and Social Exclusion in East Asia', *Journal of Comparative Asian Development*, 12 (2): 316–50. doi:10.1080/15339114.2013.801144.

Nieuwboer, C. and R. V. Rood (2016), 'Learning Language that Matters: A Pedagogical Method to Support Migrant Mothers Without Formal Education Experience in Their Social Integration in Western Countries', *International Journal of International Relations*, 51: 29–40. doi:10.1016/j.ijintrel.2016.01.002.

Nyamnjoh, F. B. (2010), 'Racism, Ethnicity and the Media in Africa: Reflections Inspired by Studies of Xenophobia in Cameroon and South Africa', *Africa Spectrum*, 45 (1): 57–93.

Odiaka, N. (2017), 'The Face of Violence: Rethinking the Concept of Xenophobia, Immigration Laws and the Rights of Non-Citizens in South Africa', *BRICS Law Journal*, 4 (2): 40–70.

Okunade, S. (2021), 'Africa Moves Towards Intracontinental Free Movement for its Booming Population', Migration Policy Institute, 21 January. Available online: https://www.migrationpolicy.org/article/africa-intracontinental-free-movement (accessed 31 January 2021).

Rem, D. and D. Gasper (2018), 'The Rhetoric of Dutch Immigrant Integration Policy in 2011', *The International Journal of Social Quality*, 8 (1): 21–48. doi:10.3167/IJSQ.2018.080103.

Ruhlmann, L. and S. McMonagle (2019), 'Germany's Linguistic "Others" and the Racism Taboo', *Anthropological Journal of European Cultures*, 28 (2): 93–100. doi:10.3167/ajec.2019.280209.

Salami, B., J. Salma, K. Hegadoren, S. Meherali, T. Kolawole and E. Diaz (2019), 'Sense of Community Belonging Among Immigrants: Perspective of Immigrant Service Providers', *Public Health*, 167: 28–33.

Sinyolo, D. (2012), 'A Strategy for Managing Teacher Migration in Southern Africa', unpublished PhD Thesis, University of South Africa, Johannesburg.

Tarisayi, K. S. and S. Manik (2019), 'Affirmation and Defamation: Zimbabwean Migrant Teachers' Survival Strategies in South Africa', *Journal of International Migration and Integration*, 22: 183–204. doi:10.1007/s12134-019-00725-5.

Tarisayi, K. S. and S. Manik (2020), 'An Unabating Challenge: Media Portrayal of Xenophobia in South Africa', *Cogent Arts and Humanities*, 7 (1): 1–12. doi:10.1080/23311983.2020.1859074.

Tarisayi, K. S., E. Munyaradzi and M. Chidarikire (2020), 'Micro Commercialisation the New Threat to Teacher Collegiality in Masvingo District', *The Independent Journal of Teaching and Learning*, 15 (1): 91–100.

Tshitereke, C. (1999), 'Xenophobia and Relative Deprivation', *Crossings*, 3 (2): 4–5.

United Nations High Commissioner for Refugees (2021), 'UNHCR and IPU Welcome Council of Europe Parliamentary Resolution in Support of Refugees', UNHCR, 4 June. Available online: https://www.unhcr.org/news/press/2021/6/60ba3ce6b/unhcr-ipu-welcome-council-europe-parliamentary-resolution-support-refugees.html.

9

Heroic Teachers? Understanding the Choices and Strategies of Teachers in a Context in Flux

Ritesh Shah

1. Introduction

In conflict-affected settings, teachers are increasingly positioned as central actors in ensuring the continuity of education, the protection of children and ultimately effective learning and well-being outcomes. They are often labelled 'front line actors' of response in a range of education in emergencies (EiE) and disaster risk reduction (DRR) literature (Burns and Lawrie 2015). As such, there has been growing recognition in recent years to support both the professional development and well-being of these individuals to be able to deliver the type of quality, inclusive education which all learners, but particularly those facing the immediate impacts of conflict, deserve and warrant (see e.g. Mendenhall, Gomez and Varni 2018).

Yet, the personal and professional identities of these teachers, and their (in)capacities and (un)willingness to support such an agenda, are often assumed, rather than carefully explored in such efforts. This is despite a growing body of literature which suggests that understanding teachers' identities and beliefs, and locating their work within broader social-political discourses, may be a fundamental precondition to having any impact on practice.

In this chapter, I put forth the argument, based on prior work developed in this area, that in times of conflict and crisis, teachers' agency and understandings of what it means to be successful in context of adversity warrant much greater attention and focus (Shah 2012; Lopes Cardozo and Shah 2016). Drawing conceptually on Hay's (2002a,b) Strategic Relational Approach (SRA), I seek to highlight how teachers' agency and willingness, and identity as change-makers, is often a product of the mediation between their personal and professional selves in a context shaped and influenced by political, economic and social forces. I explore this within the context of two countries currently affected by the Syrian refugee crisis, Turkey and Jordan. I position teachers' work, and the struggles within the contexts they are currently within, to highlight how their strategies and approaches are shaped by a range of factors that extend beyond that of individual agency and professional expertise alone. I argue that teachers mediate their context based on a combination of personal motivations, community and peer expectations and pre-existing professional values/beliefs. Specifically, I highlight the particular conditions created by the Syrian refugee response in Jordan and Turkey, which render the construction of, reflection on and modification of teacher agency unique. This, in turn, has consequences in regards to the expectations placed upon education personnel to operationalize ambitious agendas of equitable learning, social integration and the protection of students' social and emotional well-being which are often thrust onto their shoulders in such contexts.

In making this argument, I draw on data which I collected from teachers as part of three separate external evaluations I conducted of professional development programmes supporting educational personnel working with Syrian refugee children in Jordan and Turkey (Shah 2017, 2018a,b). A semi-structured, qualitative interview technique known as Most Significant Change (MSC) was used as a primary data collection methodology in all three evaluations. MSC was used to firstly elicit a range of identified changes which educators had experienced, personally and professionally, through the training and support of the programmes. They were then asked to provide greater detail about one of these changes by reconstructing a story of what things were like prior, how the change had unfolded and what things were like for them now. Additionally, interviewees were asked to specify why the change they selected was the most significant one to them (see Shah 2014 for more details about the MSC interview approach). Across these three evaluations, a total of 134 stories of change were collected from both Turkish and Jordanian teachers working with Syrian refugee children, as well as volunteer or temporary Syrian refugee teachers. All stories collected were anonymized to protect the confidentiality of those interviewed, and consent was obtained for use of stories in future publications such as this. Extracts of stories are presented throughout the remainder of the chapter to serve as illustrative examples of the wider themes and issues which surfaced upon undertaking a fuller inductive coding of the data in combination. What these stories reveal is the often intertwined nature of teachers' personal and professional selves, as well as their perceptions of how they locate themselves in contexts that are in flux, uncertain and which oftentimes challenge their capacities for change.

I begin by charting out conceptually one way of understanding and conceptualizing teacher agency and identity in conflict-affected contexts. This then leads to an exploration of the situation in Jordan and Turkey at present time. Both are countries which are hosting sizeable proportions of Syrian refugees following the outbreak of civil war within Syria in 2010. By identifying the differences in the contexts, I then move onto to highlight how this then mediates and influences the ways teacher agency is employed and particularly the opportunities and limitations this might offer for them to act as transformative or even supportive allies for refugee learners.

2. Understanding and Conceptualizing Teacher Agency and Identity

Research from conflict-affected contexts makes clear that teachers' space for manoeuvre (i.e. their personal and professional agency) is bounded and framed by social, political and economic conditions (Vongalis-Macrow 2006; Lopes Cardozo 2009; Pherali 2013). As argued in previous work, the SRA provides a framework to understand teachers as both strategic and political actors and whose agency exists in a dialectical relationship with the broader cultural, political and economic (post-)conflict environment (Shah and Lopes Cardozo 2014, 2016). The SRA, developed by scholars working in the broader field of sociology/political sciences, provides a heuristic tool for exploring the dialectical relationship between structures, agents and agency (Hay 2002b; Jessop 2005).

The basic premise is as follows: the strategically selective context within which actors (such as teachers) operate is based on structural and institutional conditions that can reinforce the motivations, actions or strategies of particular individuals, and work against others, creating both opportunities and constraints for specific courses of action. In response, actors at various scales make conscious and unconscious choices based on the knowledge they hold of this context to realize particular outcomes or objectives. A significant point of SRA is that in any moment the way in which actors understand and respond to their environment can greatly vary, as can their motivations and intentions for action, leading to a plethora of potential outcomes. Thus, both the structured context within which action occurs and the types of agency which actors exhibit have a bearing on the outcomes observed.

This agency, it is argued, is structured in part as well by teachers' own identity both professionally and personally within these contexts. Teacher professional identity should be understood as the ways that teachers, both individually and collectively, view and understand themselves as professionals (Mockler 2011). It is a concept founded on a personal and professional notion of one's work based on sense of self, as well as knowledge and beliefs, dispositions, interests and orientations towards work and change (Drake, Spillane and Hufferd-Ackles 2001). However, a key aspect of identity is that it is not impermeable and is prone to be influenced by the communities and discourses within which teachers live and work (Avalos 2010).

Welmond (2002: 43) suggests that conceptualizing teacher identity is a threefold exploration of:

1) defining what it means to be a teacher in a given context through the voices of the teachers themselves
2) exploring the claims made through policy on how teachers should behave and think (i.e. the 'ideal teacher') and
3) examining the fashion in which teachers navigate this contested terrain.

Research from the Global South has found that teachers often reconcile their own aspirations and wishes with claims coming from outside (whether through policy, political/social or professional discourse) and adopt a flexible identity in response (Schweisfurth 2002; Welmond 2002; McGrath 2008). Hence, teacher identities are not fixed but rather are 'a complex matter of the social and individual, of discourse and practice, of reification and participation, of similarity and difference, of agency and structure, of fixity and transgression, of the singular and the multiple' (Clarke 2009: 189). In conflict-affected settings in which discourses around teachers' work, the nature of the profession and the objectives of schooling tend to shift quite significantly, it can be expected that teachers will face particular constraints and strategically respond in kind. Tensions between new externally introduced or legitimated discourses and extant teacher notions and beliefs about teachers' work can lead to what Jansen (2001: 242) labels an 'identity conflict'. Such conflicts open up possibilities for teachers to draw on and utilize more than one discourse concurrently, as a strategic resource in times of significant change (Jessop and Penny 1998; Osborn et al. 2000; Welmond 2002; Barrett 2008).

In sum, teacher agency should be understood as the way teachers feel about themselves professionally, emotionally and politically, given the conditions of their work and the internal motivations and beliefs they bring to the job. In line with the work of Stuart Hall (2003), the affiliation and role one might have as a teacher should be understood to be in perpetual motion and layered between past and present. Teachers' exercise of agency is based on an interpretation of and reflection on their context, counterbalanced by their own value commitments, personal background and sense of professional expertise. The employment of agency must be understood as strategic and selective in response to specific structural and material constraints. As Lopes Cardozo (2009: 412) contends, while teachers may act according to their reflexivity, rationality and motivations, their actions are embedded in a strategically selective context that creates both opportunities for and constraints to teachers' level of agency and the choices they make. The current time, place and space within which schooling occurs 'selectively reinforces particular forms of action, tactics or strategies' and provides a place within which teachers 'can be reflexive, can reformulate within limits their own identities' (Jessop 2005: 49). The SRA helps to move away from analyses that view teachers' actions as divorced from context or simultaneously limits teachers' agency within tight structural parameters.

The remainder of the chapter now takes these ideas and explores them further in the contexts of Jordan and Turkey, countries which have witnessed hundreds of thousands of Syrian refugee students entering into poorly equipped and resourced education systems in recent years.

3. Finding Agency within a Strategically Selective Context Built on Integration: Turkey

In Turkey, a total of 1.1 million Syrian children and youth reside under temporary protection[1] which grants them access to services such as health care, employment and education.[2] The vast majority (94 per cent) lives outside of camp settings in urban and peri-urban areas.[3] A relatively large proportion of this section of the Syrian refugee population (approximately 23 per cent of the total refugee population) resides in Turkey's three largest cities of Istanbul, Ankara and Izmir.[4]

It is in the large urban settlements, far from the Syrian border, where the refugee population is most vulnerable, according to a recent report by the International Crisis Group. The International Crisis Group (2018: 3) identifies that the refugee community's inability to speak Turkish 'limits opportunities to find and build on shared values and interests' and 'reinforces [Turkish citizens'] convictions that Syrians do not conform to [their] cultural norms'. This is leading to increasing rates of urban violence between Turkish and Syrian communities, self-segregation/ghettoization of Syrian refugees in particular municipalities and locations in major cities and growing perceptions among the Turkish community, particularly the working class, that the Syrian refugees are taking more than they are contributing to society.

For education personnel, who live and work in these communities, these discourses and perceptions about the refugee population also influenced their own beliefs and practices towards them. One counsellor candidly described how 'when Syrian students first started to enrol in our schools, many of us were reluctant to welcome them . . . we had a lot of prejudice against the Syrian population. We thought they were being advantaged in Turkish society, receiving extra money from the government and being given preferences for jobs' (Shah 2018b: 39).

Despite such public sentiment, the government of Turkey has expressed its intention to integrate all Syrian refugees into the Turkish public education system (TPS). This is in line with the Global Compact for Refugees which affirms the importance of integrating refugees within national systems, rather than creating parallel structures as was the case in prior humanitarian crises (UN General Assembly 2018). Such a commitment, however, brings with it a number of challenges for the government of Turkey. One of the most significant, documented in a range of recent reports and studies, are the language skills of incoming Syrian students into the TPS. Many enter with little or no knowledge of Turkish, particularly if they have been out of school or come from informal, non-accredited temporary education centres (TECs) where the language of instruction is Arabic. A range of studies highlight how the lack of appropriate resources, extra support and willingness/capacity of TPS to recognize and accommodate the learning needs of this population leads to Syrian students not able to effectively participate, communicate and succeed in TPS (Tösten, Toprak and Kayan 2017; Mostafa 2018; International Crisis Group 2018). As a result, the risk is that the integration experience becomes one of 'islands of loneliness, disintegration, fear and the idea of them versus us which could further feed feelings of hatred, violence, discrimination and hopelessness' (Tösten, Toprak and Kayan 2017: 1157). For schools in urban areas, concerns also exist about school overcrowding as a result of the influx of Syrian refugee students into TPS, leading to increased tensions between host community and refugee populations and increases in incidences of violence and bullying in schools (Human Rights Watch 2015; International Crisis Group 2018). Finally, the lack of Turkish language also presents significant challenges for the educational personnel and the parents of Syrian refugees to communicate with each other.

In combination, this creates a difficult context for education personnel at present, particularly those with significant years of experience and expertise of working with Turkish students, who now find themselves ill-equipped to deal with a range of new issues and challenges. One teacher recounted how, 'In the education faculty I attended, I was not taught or educated on how to teach refugees or those from other countries. When I came to this school, however, I encountered a number of Syrian students in my classroom, and I was not at all equipped to deal with this challenge' (Shah 2018b: 45).

For many, their sense of professional efficacy was challenged by the new structural and material conditions of their work. While there have been some efforts, on the part of UNICEF, UNHCR and civil society to address these gaps, the challenges at present time remain significant for teachers who are the coalface of managing this commitment to full integration of Syrian refugees into TPS. One counsellor identified that despite attending a thirteen-day training session, at the end: 'I did not feel comfortable at the end of the process to then go and convince the other counsellors and teachers in my district or school about the issue. I was not in a position to be a leader or expert to others on how to support refugee children and their integration' (Shah 2018b: 45).

In times of ambitious reform, such as that which is occurring in Turkey in response to the Syrian refugee crisis, teachers' functions, roles and purpose are often contested and reconceptualized in an attempt at establishing a new institutional order (Tatto 2007, 2011). Such periods often see intense activity at the level of policy discourse towards (re)framing and (re)classifying teachers' labour towards particular outcomes (Bernstein 2000). Yet policy statements and action vary in the degree to which they attempt to frame and/or classify teachers' work throughout such periods of transformation, which is in part mediated by the capacity of the state to regulate these parameters (Connell 2009). Additionally, they are rarely uniform in their voice, message or effect and are instead imbued with competing messages that create tensions and competing strategies (Robertson 2012). Nonetheless, teachers are structured by such classification and framing, whether weak or strong, coherent or not, in ways that lead to residual effects on the agency and practices of individuals and collectives working in schools (Jansen 2001: 245–6).

Hence professional success, for many teachers working in schools with high numbers of Syrian refugee learners, became increasingly focused on whether or not they could effectively teach these students Turkish and integrate them effectively into mainstream education. This was, in turn, shaped by broader political (and educational) discourses that the Syrians should become Turkish and lose their Syrian identity (Hintz and Feehan 2017). As one teacher reflected: 'I see [learning Turkish language and culture] ... as critical for my Syrian students who are now living in this country. It is vital they have access to language so that they can survive and thrive in Turkey as their new home' (Shah 2018b: 20). Agency for transformation was in fact reflected and demonstrated by teacher capacities to transform these Syrian refugees into citizen-subjects of the Turkish state. Whether or not this model of social integration was appropriate or just to the needs of Syrian refugees did not appear questioned or challenged.

4. Varying Agency and Identity: The Case of Jordan

Like Turkey, Jordan has shouldered a large proportion of the Syrian refugee population fleeing conflict within Syria. By early 2018, just over 660,000 Syrian refugees had registered with UNHCR in Jordan.[5] Of the total number of registered refugees, the majority are children and youth with 51 per cent under the age of eighteen.[6] In Jordan, however, the narrative around the Syrian refugees is different. There is less political appetite and willingness within the country to see permanent resettlement as an option, and rather the common expectation is that as soon as practicable, the refugees will return back to Syria. As a result, Jordan has sought to manage the response in a way which frames the refugee population as a security concern and maintain approaches which seek isolation and separation rather than integration (Yahya 2015; Betts, Ali and Memişoğlu 2017; Lenner and Turner 2019). This led to more than half of Syrian refugee children remaining out of school until 2017, with many missing out on several years of schooling. In its place, informal education opportunities in both host community and camp settings took prominence, often operated by national and international NGOs without much state involvement (Human Rights Watch 2016; Carlier 2018).

Following the London Conference in 2016, donors and the Government of Jordan agreed to work together to ensure that Syrians and vulnerable Jordanians living in host community settings would have access to improved living conditions and be able to access basic services like health and education. A number of short-term solutions were employed to achieve this including the establishment of additional double-shift schools to accommodate Syrian students in the afternoon, as well as expediting pre-service teacher training and employing additional contractual teachers for the second shift (Government of Jordan 2018b).

This focus on providing access to all Syrian refugees has worsened overcrowding in schools and placed strain on teachers and existing infrastructure. Schools in Jordan which were already suffering from facilities in need of repair or rehabilitation prior to the crisis have faced increasing strain and damage to their existing infrastructure, with facilities often insufficient to the needs of this increased student population (Government of Jordan 2018a).

Those in schools oftentimes felt the strain between the mandate and moral imperative to enable access to the Syrian refugee population and what was actually feasible. One principal described how:

> Many [refugees] wanted to enrol their children in our school, but we did not have enough space. I tried, as best I could to accommodate about 20 of the students, to the point where we had to put desks and chairs outside the classroom doors to fit the extra students. But there were still about 180 Syrian students who remained on the waiting list and were unable to come to our school. (Shah 2018a: 65)

He told this part of the story with a mixture of remorse and guilt, noting that 'having enough space for our students is a basic need for our community' and that it effects the 'relationship between the school and community and . . . the impression they have our school' (Shah 2018a: 65). For this principal his own reputation, and that of his school, was significantly compromised by the insufficient school infrastructure available to meet community demand.

Additionally, educational quality has also been adversely affected by the significant influx of students into the system. Children in second-shift schools have less contact hours than students in the first-shift. To make up for this, second-shift students are also expected to attend school on Saturdays, but attendance on this extra day remains significantly lower than other days of the week. And, with pre-service teacher training expedited to meet demand, many new teachers in formal schools – particularly in double-shift and camp schools – lack pedagogical skills or experience to be able to effectively address issues arising from overcrowded, disrupted classrooms, children dealing with the effects of trauma and/or violence and bullying within the school. Teachers lack the expertise and support to accommodate the unique demands of a student population who have faced trauma, displacement, interrupted schooling and economic hardship. Often this results in high rates of drop out of Syrian refugee students from the education system and burnout among teachers deployed to support these students (UNICEF and Ministry of Education Jordan 2020;

Sieverding et al. 2018). The facilitation of access prioritized by the international community has not been necessarily backed up by concomitant support from the Government of Jordan to ensure that teachers have the necessary willingness and capacity to enable the learning and well-being outcomes demanded under minimum standards for EiE (INEE 2010).

Similar to Turkey, many of the teachers working in formal schools acknowledged their own shortcomings and the fact that they were not prepared to manage the needs of the learners in their classroom. One counsellor, reflecting on the challenges, noted how:

> because of the refugee population we work with, and the trauma and family issues children live under, the school suffers from many issues with students' misbehaviour. And the teachers, who are less qualified and competent, do not normally have the appropriate skills, knowledge and experience to deal with this ... [teachers do] not appear to understand how some of the issues of behaviour and underachievement were not the fault of the child alone and were instead the result of them being refugees and living in a difficult situation. (Shah 2018a: 80)

She went on to describe how 'teachers resort to using dangerous approaches to dealing with misbehaviour' acknowledging 'their actions would often make the situation worse' (Shah 2018a: 80). The counsellor felt frustrated by being in a context where she observed teachers taking action in ways that were deleterious to student well-being and learning but were likely all they could do to manage. Yet, she perceived herself limited in her capacity to provide 'practical techniques or advice ... as an alternative to what they were doing' (Shah 2018a: 80).

A significant constraint limiting Jordanian educators' agency to move beyond patterns of practice which they acknowledged as deleterious to student well-being was one of knowledge and skills. As a result, they consciously chose strategic actions which they knew were *wrong* but which enabled them to survive the challenges of managing overcrowded classrooms with a range of learning needs. To fault these teachers as apathetic, or unconsciously reproducing violence, may perhaps be too simplistic.

Within the refugee camps of Jordan, and particularly informal education programmes set up to support refugee learners who are either out of school or needing additional learning support, the role and nature of the teacher is rendered somewhat different. There, and unlike the formal education system where teachers may only be Jordanian nationals, the majority of individuals staffing such programmes are Syrian refugees. Because they are Syrian refugees, they are not officially allowed to be paid a salary but can be offered stipends or transportation allowances that are often significantly below the minimum wage. Yet, in the camp setting, working as a teacher is often one of the better roles available and is one highly sought after. This is because often NGOs offer up to these volunteer teachers initial training as well as ongoing professional development and support (Magee and Pherali 2019; Kraft and Smith 2019).

In some literature, it has been contended that these *accidental* teachers[7] may lack the necessary inculcation into a set of shared professional values and beliefs to maintain strong conviction or vocation for the work they do (Bennell and Akyeampong 2007; Mpokosa et al. 2008). However, such arguments have been countered by ethnographic accounts of teachers in conflict-affected contexts which document a sense of a strong moral purpose – or the desire to do good or make a difference – in their communities or broader society (Shriberg, Kirk and Winthrop 2007; Kirk and Winthrop 2008). For example, Kirk and Winthrop (2008: 877), in a study of Afghan community-based teachers, remark that 'although not necessarily qualified or experienced, [they] have important attributes for the critical work they do' with a 'strong sense of their roles in the community, especially with respect to promoting children's moral and ethical character and well-being'.

Such was the case in the refugee camps of Jordan as well, with many of the Syrian volunteer teachers discussed ways in which having the responsibility of a teacher had instilled or restored such a moral purpose. For example, one teacher described how he had 'blossomed as a teacher . . . and [felt] more confident to support the students in my community to learn in the best possible way – whether in Azraq or in Syria when I return' (Shah 2017: 97). This individual, who left Syria halfway through completing his teaching degree, felt that as a result of his experiences both as a refugee herself and through the experiences he had gained as a teacher in Jordan, he would remain committed to supporting her community wherever he was in the future. Importantly, as Kirk and Winthrop (2008: 877) identify, such vocation are 'significant assets to be acknowledged by communities, education authorities and their [external] partners supporting education' despite the fact that officially, this individually might be classified as unqualified. In other words, it is because of the context of the camps, which affords opportunities for non-traditional teachers to assume such a role, that such individuals' agency for transformation can be inculcated, supported and strengthened. Unfortunately, outside the camp settings, this agency is often hindered by a different set of strategically selective conditions which perceive Syrian refugees as stealing jobs and opportunities from host community populations.

Alongside this, taking on the role and identity of a teacher also serves an important role in helping individuals to navigate a sense of purpose and hope in the midst of displacement and uncertainty. One Syrian volunteer specified how working as a teacher in the informal learning centres 'reminded me of my roles and responsibility as a teacher [and] . . . restored some of the hope and professional identify I lost when I left Syria' (Shah 2017: 99). Another noted: 'we lost hope, and working here at the centre is where I have found it again' (Shah 2017: 103). In this respect, the narratives of the Syrian refugee teachers stand in contrast to those of the Jordanian and Turkish educators presented earlier. It signals that the varying times, places and spaces within which education occurs in both countries appears to 'selectively reinforces particular forms of action, tactics or strategies' and provides a place within which teachers 'can be reflexive, can reformulate within limits their own identities' (Jessop 2005: 49).

5. Conclusion

These narratives from Jordan and Turkey highlight the myriad of ways in which individual teacher agency and capacity alone may not be enough to overcome the significant structural barriers which the profession faces at present in supporting quality and well-being for all, but particularly the most vulnerable. At the same time, it suggests that such conditions can also instil agency, particularly for those who have come into the system from a different vantage and often seeking a sense of purpose in a time of personal or professional struggle.

Seemingly, many of the teachers working in both countries at present, and across both formal and informal systems, do not see their work without meaning and do in fact hold a strong conviction and will for change.

What they understand this change to mean, however, is not always focused on a notion of transformation which promotes social justice or equity and may in fact reproduce prevalent hegemonic forces which act to maintain a social hierarchy between refugee and host community populations. Such is the case in Turkey, where political discourses of integration have become intertwined with notions of what effective teaching and learning in Turkish should look like. Or alternatively, in the case of Jordan, where the government has signalled that the Syrian refugees are only present in the country temporarily and remain outsiders, many teachers and counsellors approached their work with refugee populations with a sense of tentativeness. In other words, the strategically selective national context shapes teachers' conscious and unconscious strategies towards refugee learners and leads to actions against principles of inclusion and equity which many of them espouse. As noted by Dryden-Peterson et al. (2019: 347), the ways in which national-level actors position refugees' futures within policies, 'when enacted at school levels, variably enable or constrain opportunities'. As the frontline actors at a school level, they are often reconciling their own personal and professional identities against national discourses around refugee futures.

In other words, teachers' strategic actions cannot be understood as divorced from but rather mutually constitutive of the strategically selective context in which they operate. Specifically, teachers may have intentions and preferences, but these are not fixed but actively formed and reformed in processes of structured coupling with current cultural, political and economic realities (Jones 2010: 29–30). Miller Marsh (2003: 8) notes, teachers are 'continually in the process of fashioning and refashioning [agency] by patching together fragments of the discourses to which [they] are exposed'. Revealing the reconciliation of roles, and of the context within which their work is framed and reframed, has been a key focus of this chapter. In doing so it highlights the choices and strategies which teachers articulate of operating in strategically selective contexts which may not always afford or share a vision of transformation – and at the same time how even in seemingly unconducive contexts for transformative teacher agency, opportunities are found for this to be established.

Notes

1 http://www.goc.gov.tr/icerik6/temporary-protection_915_1024_4748_icerik.
2 Law on Foreigners and International Protection, April 2014.
3 UNHCR (2018), August 2018 Operational Update. Available online: https://data2.unhcr.org/en/documents/download/67065.
4 International Crisis Group (2018), Turkey's Syrian Refugees: Defusing Metropolitan Tensions.
5 UNHCR 2 January 2018 Syria Regional Refugee Response Interagency Information Sharing Portal. Available online: http://data.unhcr.org/syrianrefugees/country.php?id=107.
6 Ibid.
7 'Accidental teachers' is a term commonly used for paraprofessional, volunteer or emergency teachers who end up in permanent positions as society transitions from the emergency to post-conflict phases.

References

Avalos, B. (2010), 'Teacher Identity Construction in Reform Driven Contexts', *Journal of All India Association for Educational Research*, 22 (2): 1–13. Available online: http://www.ejournal.aiaer.net.

Barrett, A. (2008), 'Capturing the Difference: Primary School Teacher Identity in Tanzania', *International Journal of Educational Development*, 28 (5): 496–507.

Bennell, P. and K. Akyeampong (2007), 'Teacher Motivation in Sub-Saharan Africa and South Asia', Educational Papers, 71, London: DFID. Available online: https://assets.publishing.service.gov.uk/media/57a08be640f0b652dd000f9a/ResearchingtheI ssuesNo71.pdf (accessed 10 February 2021).

Bernstein, B. (2000), *Pedagogy, Symbolic Control and Identity: Theory, Research, Critique*, Oxford: Rowman &Littlefield Publishers.

Betts, A., A. Aliand and F. Memişoğlu (2017), 'Local Politics and the Syrian Refugee Crisis', Refugee Studies Centre, 24 November. Available online: https://www.rsc.ox.ac.uk/publications/local-politics-and-the-syrian-refugee-crisis-exploring-responses-in-turkey-lebanon-and-jordan (accessed 2 February 2021).

Burns, M., and J. Lawrie, eds (2015), *Where it's Needed Most: Quality Professional Development for All Teachers*, New York: Inter-Agency Network for Education in Emergencies. Available online: https://inee.org/resources/where-its-needed-most-quality-professional-development-all-teachers (accessed 30 Nov 2020).

Carlier, W. (2018), 'Background Report: The Widening Educational Gap for Syrian Refugee Children', *KidsRights Report 2018*, Amsterdam: KidsRights. Available online: https://reliefweb.int/sites/reliefweb.int/files/resources/Background Report 2018 - The Widening Educational Gap for Syrian Refugee Children_0.pdf (accessed 30 October 2020).

Clarke, M. (2009), 'The Ethico-Politics of Teacher Identity', *Educational Philosophy and Theory*, 41 (2): 185–200.

Connell, R. (2009), 'Good Teachers on Dangerous Ground: Toward a New View of Teacher Quality and Professionalism', *Critical Studies in Education*, 50 (3): 213–29.

Drake, C., J. Spillane and K. Hufferd-Ackles (2001), 'Storied Identities: Teacher Learning and Subject-Matter Context', *Journal of Curriculum Studies*, 33 (2): 1–24.

Dryden-Peterson, S., E. Adelman, M. J. Bellino and V. Chopra (2019), 'The Purposes of Refugee Education: Policy and Practice of Including Refugees in National Education Systems', *Sociology of Education*, 92 (4): 346–66. doi:10.1177/0038040719863054.

Government of Jordan (2018a), 'Education Strategic Plan 2018–2022', Ministry of Education, Amman. Available online: https://planipolis.iiep.unesco.org/sites/default/files/ressources/jordan_esp_2018-2022.pdf (accessed 2 November 2020).

Government of Jordan (2018b), 'Jordan Response Plan 2018–2020 for the Syria Crisis', Ministry of Education, Amman. Available online: http://www.jrp.gov.jo/Files/JRP%202020-2022%20web.pdf (accessed 2 November 2020).

Hall, S. (2003), 'Cultural Identity and Diaspora', in J. E. Braziel and A. Mannur (eds), *Theorizing Diaspora: A Reader*, 233–46, Oxford: Blackwell.

Hay, C. (2002a), 'Globalisation as a Problem of Political Analysis: Restoring Agents to a "Process Without Subject" and Politica to a Logic of Economic Compulsion', *Cambridge Review of International Affairs*, 15 (3): 379–92.

Hay, C. (2002b), *Political Analysis: A Critical Introduction*, ed. B. G. Peters, J. Pierre and G. Stoker, New York: Palgrave Macmillan.

Hintz, L. C. Feehan (2017), 'Burden or Boon? Turkey's Tactical Treatment of the Syrian Refugee Crisis', Middle East Institute Essay Series, 10 January. Available online: https://www.mei.edu/publications/burden-or-boon-turkeys-tactical-treatment-syrian-refugee-crisis (accessed 1 October 2021).

Human Rights Watch (2015), '"When I Picture My Future I See Nothing": Barriers to Education for Syrian Refugee Children in Turkey', Human Rights Watch, 8 November. Available online: https://www.hrw.org/report/2015/11/08/when-i-picture-my-future-i-see-nothing/barriers-education-syrian-refugee-children (accessed 5 November 2020).

Human Rights Watch (2016), '"We're Afraid for Their Future": Barriers to Education for Syrian Refugee Children in Jordan', Human Rights Watch, 16 August. Available online: https://www.hrw.org/report/2016/08/16/were-afraid-their-future/barriers-education-syrian-refugee-children-jordan (accessed 5 November 2020).

INEE (2010), *Minimum Standards for Education: Preparedness, Response, Recovery*, 2nd edn, New York: INEE.

International Crisis Group (2018), 'Turkeys Syrian Refugees: Defusing Metropolitan Tensions', *Europe Report 248*, 29 January. Available online: https://www.crisisgroup.org/europe-central-asia/western-europemediterranean/turkey/248-turkeys-syrian-refugees-defusing-metropolitan-tensions (accessed 5 May 2020).

Jansen, J. (2001), 'Image-Ining Teachers: Policy Images and Teacher Identity in South African Classrooms', *South African Journal of Education*, 21 (4): 242–6.

Jessop, B. (2005), 'Critical Realism and the Strategic-Relational Approach', *New Formations*, 56: 40–53.

Jessop, T. and A. Penny (1998), 'A Study of Teacher Voice and Vision in the Narratives of Rural South African and Gambian Primary School Teachers', *International Journal of Educational Development*, 18 (5): 393–403.

Jones, P. (2010), 'Cultural Political Economy and the International Governance of Education: A Theoretical Framework', *International Educational Governance*, 12: 19–56.

Kirk, J. and R. Winthrop (2008), 'Home-Based School Teachers in Afghanistan: Teaching for Tarbia and Student Well-Being', *Teaching and Teacher Education*, 24 (4): 876–88.

Kraft, K. and J. D. Smith (2019), 'Between International Donors and Local Faith Communities: Intermediaries in Humanitarian Assistance to Syrian Refugees in Jordan and Lebanon', *Disasters*, 43 (1): 24–45. doi:10.1111/disa.12301.

Lenner, K. and L. Turner (2019), 'Making Refugees Work? The Politics of Integrating Syrian Refugees into the Labour Market in Jordan', *Middle East Critique*, 28 (1): 65–95. doi:10.1080/19436149.2018.1462601.

Lopes Cardozo, M. T. A. and R. Shah (2016), 'A Conceptual Framework to Analyse the Multiscalar Politics of Education for Sustainable Peacebuilding', *Comparative Education*, 52 (4): 516–37. doi:10.1080/03050068.2016.1220144.

Lopes Cardozo, M. T. A. (2009), 'Teachers in a Bolivian Context of Conflict: Potential Actors for or against Change?', *Globalisation, Societies and Education*, 7 (4): 409–32.

Magee, A. and T. Pherali (2019), 'Freirean Critical Consciousness in a Refugee Context: A Case Study of Syrian Refugees in Jordan', *Compare: A Journal of Comparative and International Education*, 49 (2): 266–82. doi:10.1080/03057925.2017.1403312.

McGrath, S. (2008), 'Caught Between Different Worlds: Teachers and Educational Change', *International Journal of Educational Development*, 28 (5): 493–95.

Mendenhall, M., S. Gomez and E. Varni (2018), 'Teaching Amidst Conflict and Displacement: Persistent Challenges and Promising Practices for Refugee, Internally Displaced and National Teachers'. Available online: https://inee.org/system/files/resources/266060eng.pdf (accessed 5 November 2020).

Miller Marsh, M. (2003), *The Social Fashioning of Teacher Identities*. New York: Peter Lang Publishing.

Mockler, N. (2011), 'Beyond "what works": Understanding Teacher Identity as a Practical and Political Tool', *Teachers and Teaching: Theory and Practice*, 17 (5): 517–28.

Mostafa, B. (2018), 'Moving Beyond Access: Integration of Syrian Refugee Students into Turkish Public Schools in the Bursa Province', *Colombia Academic Commons*, 26 June. doi:10.7916/D8KP9JM9.

Mpokosa, C., S. Ndaruhutse, C. McBride, S. Nock and J. Penson (2008), *Managing Teachers: The Centrality of Teacher Management to Quality Education*. Lessons from developing countries, London: CfBT and VSO.

Osborn, M., E. McNess, P. Broadfoot and A. Pollard (2000), *What Teachers Do: Changing Policy and Practice in Primary Education*, London: Continuum.

Pherali, T. J. (2013), 'Schooling in Violent Situations: The Politicization of Education in Nepal, before and after the 2006 Peace Agreement', *Prospects*, 43: 49–67. doi:10.1007/s11125-012-9255-5.

Robertson, S. (2012), '"Placing" Teachers in Global Governance Agendas', *Comparative Education Review*, 56 (4): 584–607.

Schweisfurth, M. (2002), 'Democracy and Teacher Education: Negotiating Practice in the Gambia', *Comparative Education*, 38 (3): 303–14.

Shah, R. (2012), 'Goodbye Conflict, Hello Development? Curriculum Reform in Timor-Leste', *International Journal of Educational Development*, 32 (1): 31–8.

Shah, R. (2014), 'Assessing the "true Impact" of Development Assistance in the Gaza Strip and Tokelau: "Most Significant Change" as an Evaluation Technique', *Asia Pacific Viewpoint*, 55 (3): 262–76. doi:10.1111/apv.12062.

Shah, R. (2017), 'Evaluation of NRC's Education Programming in the Camps of Jordan', Norwegian Refugee Council. Available online: https://www.flyktninghjelpen.no/globalassets/pdf/evaluations/camps-education-clean.pdf (accessed 1 October 2021).

Shah, R. (2018a), 'Evaluation of NRC's Host Community Education Programme in Jordan', Norwegian Refugee Council. Available online: https://www.nrc.no/globalassets/pdf/evaluations/nrc-hc-evaluation-final.pdf (accessed 1 October 2021).

Shah, R. (2018b), 'Evaluation of ODGEDER's Welcoming Schools Project 2017–2018', Auckland, NZ.

Shah, R. and M. T. A. Lopes Cardozo (2014), 'Education and Social Change in Post-Conflict and Post-Disaster Aceh, Indonesia', *International Journal of Educational Development*, 38: 2–12.

Shriberg, J., J. Kirk and R. Winthrop (2007), *Teaching Well? Educational Reconstruction Efforts and Support to Teachers in Postwar Liberia*, New York: International Rescue Committee, Child and Youth Protection and Development Unit. Available online: https://inee.org/system/files/resources/doc_1_Teaching_Well_IRC_Liberia_Report.pdf (accessed 1 October 2021).

Sieverding, M., C. Krafft, N. Berri, C. Keo and M. Sharpless (2018), 'Education Interrupted: Enrollment, Attainment, and Dropout of Syrian Refugees in Jordan', *IDEAS Working Paper Series from RePEc*. Available online: https://erf.org.eg/app/uploads/2018/12/1261-...-larger-size.pdf (accessed 1 October 2021).

Tatto, M. T. (2007), 'Reforming Teachers Globally', in *Oxford Studies in Comparative Education*, Oxford: Symposium Books.

Tatto, M. T. (2011), 'Reimagining the Education of Teachers: The Role of Comparative and International Research', *Comparative Education Review*, 55 (4): 495–516.

Tösten, R., M. Toprak and M. S. Kayan (2017), 'An Investigation of Forcibly Migrated Syrian Refugee Students at Turkish Public Schools', *Universal Journal of Educational Research*, 5 (7): 1149–60. doi:10.13189/ujer.2017.050709.

UN General Assembly (2018), *Global Compact for Refugees*, New York: United Nations.

UNICEF and Ministry of Education Jordan (2020), 'Jordan Country Report on out of School Children', UNICEF Jordan. Available online: https://www.unicef.org/jordan/reports/jordan-country-report-out-school-children (accessed 1 October 2021).

Vongalis-Macrow, A. (2006), 'Rebuilding Regimes or Rebuilding Community? Teachers Agency for Social Reconstruction in Iraq', *Journal of Peace Education*, 3 (1): 99–113.

Welmond, M. (2002), 'Globalization Viewed from the Periphery: The Dynamics of Teacher Identity in the Republic of Benin', *Comparative Education Review*, 46 (1): 37–65.

Yahya, M. (2015), *Refugees in the Making of an Arab Regional Disorder*, Washington, DC: Carnegie Endowment for International Peace. Available online: https://www.jstor.org/stable/resrep12989?seq=4#metadata_info_tab_contents (accessed 1 October 2021).

Part III

Critical Reframing in an Age of Migration

10

Migrant Teachers Filling the Gap

Required but Not Revered

Sadhana Manik

1. Introduction

Teaching, like many other professions comprising of highly skilled individuals, has become a global profession (Manik 2005; Bense 2016), with selected teachers from particular contexts being extremely mobile, crossing national boundaries without restraint to provide educational services which are in demand. The shortage of qualified teachers globally and in particular in developed (Maylor et al. 2006; Reid and Collins 2012; Datta-Roy and Lavery 2017) or rapidly developing countries has been documented. This gap in the global teaching market has created immense opportunities for teachers to travel abroad to particular destinations to meet this demand. While there are policies in place to attract migrant teachers, sometimes referred to as international teachers (Fimyar 2018) or overseas trained teachers (Edwards 2014) in the literature, to destination countries in the north, the nuances of their lived experiences in host schools in many countries (apart from the language barrier which is frequently reported) and the formidable challenges teachers face in their socio-professional integration are not adequately reported.

This chapter is an attempt to contribute to filling that gap in the scholarship on South African (SA) migrant teachers' unsettling experiences in the Global North, which troubles their integration into the profession in two country contexts. The empirical data draws from two studies with data across a period of more than fifteen years, collected in the UK and the United Arab Emirates, where migrant teachers are positioned as temporary, at times cheap labour open to exploitation and discrimination in host schools and countries. I argue that despite one study being in 2005 and the other more current, the 'disturbances' to migrant teachers' socio-professional integration are rooted in the same narrative of migrant teachers from the Global South as 'temporary and deficit'. This chapter is thus a scholarly contribution to migrant teachers' socio-professional identity constructions and their status in destination countries and schools. I conclude by arguing for the need for greater migrant teacher support initiatives (induction and mentorship) in schools and for workplace equality with policies to ensure that migrants' rights are protected in line with the suggested principles espoused in the Commonwealth Teacher recruitment Protocol (2004).

2. Insights from the International Literature

Niyubahwe et al. (2013) undertook a review of the literature on migrant teachers in a few developed countries (Australia, Canada and Israel), and they reported that international studies on the integration of migrant teachers into host environments have generally used a community of practice framework, with concepts of adaptation and integration as key constructs. Their findings highlight three main areas (namely that of employment, professional integration and a lack of recognition of skills acquired in source countries) which are explored in this chapter as expressed by migrant teachers across the two studies. Datta-Roy and Lavery (2017) draw attention to most migrant teachers' experiences of a culture shock in respect of culture, communication and climate. The literature also reveals that teacher preparation in terms of migrants' socialization into a new environment appears to be inadequate with inconsistent induction efforts in many countries such as Australia (Reid and Collins 2012). Discrimination appears to be a common finding experienced by immigrant teachers, as Datta-Roy and Lavery (2017: 723) cite Reid, Collins and Singh (2010) who found 'perception amongst some immigrant teachers that overseas trained teachers were discriminated against, especially in terms of promotional opportunities, access to professional development and many other aspects of school life'.

3. South Africa and Migrant Teachers

South Africa is an attractive country for migrant teachers from the African continent, and there have been several studies which have explored immigrant teachers' experiences in South Africa since 2011, particularly that of Zimbabwean teachers (Manik 2013, 2014; Anganoo 2020 Weda and de Villers 2019;

Tarisayi and Manik 2019). The researchers have reported on challenges facing migrant teachers in several domains of their lives: professional, economic and sociocultural.

Qualified SA teachers have long been attracted to several destinations outside of the continent. Despite this, there is a distinct dearth of scholarship focusing on SA migrant teachers' experiences in destinations abroad, particularly in host schools. SA teachers (White, Indian and coloured, but not African) who were native English speakers emigrated en masse, after 1994 when South Africa became a democracy, to the UK. Recruitment agencies working on behalf of schools presented highly profitable packages to teachers to fulfil the labour needs in British schools (primary and secondary) (Manik 2005; de Villers 2007). It is documented that SA teachers were the highest number of foreign teachers in the UK (Miller, Mulvaney and Ochs 2007 and cherished by UK principals for their work ethic and commitment to quality teaching. In 2008, UK immigration legislation changed marking an end to the youth mobility scheme and only South Africans with British ancestry could be recruited to teach abroad. This curtailed the continuous voluminous outward flow of teachers to the UK. Soon thereafter, a migration corridor opened to the Middle East, in particular the United Arab Emirates for SA teachers and this expanded substantially with more attractive packages (socio-economic) than in the UK with multiple visa options (from single-entry to family visas) leading to throngs of SA teachers (again with the same racial profiles as the UK trend) emigrating to several destinations in the UAE (mostly Dubai, Abu Dhabi and Al Ain). This corridor remains open currently, and even British teachers have been exiting their country in large numbers to teach in the UAE (Ferguson 2018; Adams 2019). Thus, it is common knowledge that the two major destinations for SA migrant teachers since the early 2000s have been the UK followed by the UAE.

The limited available literature on teacher emigration from South Africa (Manik 2005, 2014; Anganoo 2020) revealed positive experiences abroad in host societies but these studies also demonstrated that there is a plethora of unsettling challenges facing migrant teachers abroad which they have to navigate on a regular basis from their arrival. Anganoo's study (2020) on SA primary school teachers migrating to Arab Gulf countries outlines their early school-based experiences. The majority of her sample were Indian female teachers located in the emirate of Abu Dhabi. She found that 'The professional identities of migrant teachers were clearly not fixed' and 'for those migrant teachers who endured unpleasant experiences such as racial and professional discrimination, they felt excluded and marginalised, and harboured thoughts of returning to South Africa' (Anganoo 2020: 14).

4. Theoretical Fibres of Migrant Teacher Identities and Work Environments

In this chapter, I conflate the personal and professional identities of SA migrant teachers, showing how they are interwoven and thus difficult to separate. I thus refer to socio-professional identities, which take cognizance of the migrant teachers' social histories and identities in South Africa and how that influences their professional identity constructions in the host schools. A study by Maylor et al. (2006: n.p.) on migrant teachers in the UK (including a few SA teachers) also merges teachers' identities and cultural aspects with the professional. They argue that cultural and professional identities develop over time and migrant teachers' 'identity(ies) are differentiated by country of origin, gender, race, ethnicity, class, age, teacher training and teaching experience'.

Kostogriz and Peeler (2004, 2007: 2) draw attention to migrant teachers' professional identities in Australian classrooms (favouring the concept of 'spaces') by highlighting the numerous 'spatial struggles' in the 'pedagogical spaces' that migrant teachers occupy. Arguing for the need for 'equitable work place spaces', they problematize the use of the concept 'community' generally used to describe the professional space occupied by teachers. They draw attention to professional spaces being characterized by 'relative homogeneity of teachers' and how this is 'contaminated by the arrival of migrant teachers in host schools' (2007, 2004: 5). I borrow from their theoretical framing of migrant teachers' challenges being 'deeply rooted in the politics of workplace' and how this space is 'a site for the negotiation of professional identity and the professionalism' for migrant teachers in the UK and in the UAE. They use concepts of 'assimilation, hybridization' and draw attention to places where 'power manifests' itself (2007, 2004: 11, 13). In another paper by Kooy and de Feitas, on the narratives of three Asian migrant teachers in Canada, they also hone in on migrant teachers' belonging and their 'membership in the teaching profession' (Kooy and de Feitas 2007: 868). They similarly draw on migrant teachers occupying a 'hybrid space of contested authorit . . . between their institution and their lived history' (Kooy and de Feitas 2007: 867). These teachers are teaching in English, their second language, and speak of 'betrayal by language' of 'struggles, hardships and survival' and English as a 'foreign language' (Kooy and de Feitas 2007: 872–3). The authors articulate 'navigations and negotiations' in 'evolving teacher identities' (Kooy and de Feitas 2007: 872–7) contending that 'The English language . . . interferes with each of the migrant teachers' "sense of belonging"'. This does not apply to the SA teachers in either the UK or the UAE as English is their first language; nevertheless, the SA migrant teachers lack a sense of 'belonging' in foreign school environments due to several hurdles, experiences which I call 'disturbances' to their anticipated seamless socio-professional integration.

5. The Studies

The epistemological orientation for both studies which form the foundation for this chapter was constructivist and aligned to an interpretivist paradigm (Cohen, Manion and Morrison 2018). The UK study (2005) was an ethnographic mixed methods study where data was generated over a three-year period. While the total sample was 120 SA migrant teachers, the data used in this chapter is extracted from data sets comprising fifteen teachers who were currently teaching in the UK and twelve who had returned to South Africa, one focus group discussion with SA teachers in London (with four teachers) and one diary with entries that commenced from the day of emigration onwards. SA migrant teachers were migrating to a society where English is the medium of instruction and the language most spoken in society. The religion which dominates in the UK is Christianity.

The UAE study is part of an ongoing SA teacher migration study from 2011 due for renewal in 2021, and it chronicles SA migrant teachers' motivations, trajectories, experiences and return across several years. The UAE data set of nine teachers (interviews, emails, WhatsApp messaging and a focus group discussion) is used. The data is generated from an ongoing longitudinal teacher migration study which commenced in 2011, tracking teachers from their exit (interviews) and regularly communicating with them while they are abroad (through a focus group, emails and WhatsApp messages) and when they return to South Africa (interviews). SA migrant teachers, proficient in the English language, were migrating to a society where English is not widely spoken by the locals and the dominant language is Islam. The UAE has been working towards internationalizing its education by introducing English as a subject and as a medium of instruction in some subjects (Vester 2018).

SA Migrant Teachers and the Challenge of Qualification Recognition

The first professional disturbance for SA migrant teachers in the UK occurred when they were informed that they are not recognized as qualified teachers in the UK despite having their qualifications verified in South Africa before their recruitment. Teachers were informed of this on arrival in the UK by school principals. They would need to study further and write an examination for the recognition of their qualifications to obtain qualified teacher status (QTS). A teacher's comment in the questionnaire revealed the extent of annoyance upon finding this out: 'the fact that you've got a teaching degree and you're still seen as an unqualified teacher – absolute bollocks'. Qualification recognition appears to be used as a 'gatekeeping mechanism' to 'deskill' and devalue SA migrant teachers, and this was also evident in another study of Asian migrant teachers in Australia (Kostogriz and Peeler 2007: 111). Qualification recognition is also important as it points to an act of discrimination, and it does have monetary implications in terms of migrant teachers' daily earnings and their benefits. Studies on teacher migration have indicated that SA teachers migrate primarily for financial gains (Manik 2007; Morgan Sives and Appleton 2006; Vester 2018) as post level one teachers earn an average of R280,000 in South Africa (Mlambo 2020). Currently unqualified teachers in the UK earn an annual salary of £20,800 (R380,800), while qualified teachers and equivalent earn £22,243 (407,200 SA rand) (BusinessTech 2019). The silver lining for SA migrant teachers was their acceptance by school principals in the UK who attempted to compensate them with an offering of additional duties with financial implications (tuition or ground duty). Upon remaining as a teacher in the UK, there was eventually a route to residency and citizenship in the UK if teachers chose to remain and continue teaching abroad. More recently after 2008, immigration rules have become stringent with the introduction of a points-based five-tier system and majority of SA migrant teachers, who are non-White (without British ancestry), are ineligible to migrate to teach in the UK unless they teach STEM subjects (prerequisite is to be a native English speaker). Currently, secondary school teachers are in high demand in the UK and can thus be recruited under Tier 2 of the skills shortage of labour (SOL).

In the UAE, SA migrant teachers are recognized as qualified teachers (there are no discriminatory legislation with financial implications like the QTS in England, to label them as unqualified with lower salaries because their training is outside of the UAE). Teachers are further informed that if they study further, they will receive a salary increase; thus, there are no policy mechanisms in place to deskill and purposefully devalue teachers' qualifications after they have been vetted by the recruitment agencies. Michele (interview, 2016) explained that she will receive a R5000 (SA rand) monthly salary increase after completion of her postgraduate studies. However, in the UAE, despite this affirming policy, numerous benefits (fee accommodation, tax free earnings, etc.) and a higher salary than in the UK, discrimination is evident because migrant teachers, regardless of their qualifications, can never displace an Emirati citizen. Thus, the gatekeeping mechanism in place is that citizenship options do not exist for any migrant workers (they are the '*other*') including the much-needed teachers in the UAE.

SA Migrant Teachers as Temporary Workers

Migrant teachers are a temporary stopgap measure for the UAE until local teachers are adequately trained. Hence in the UAE, all migrant teachers are given two- or three-year contracts which can be renewed (more recently only two-year contracts as there are claims by participants of a surplus of international teachers in the UAE at present) with no option of ever remaining indefinitely. Ashraf and his wife are teachers (interview, 2019) and he explained that 'it will be for as long as they need us'. Tanielle (interview, 2015) had earlier stated that 'permanency is not an option for teachers'. In addition, the contracts clearly stipulate that your services can be terminated immediately, and I describe her specific case to elucidate the harshness of this clause. Tanielle's narrative is instructive here as she was one of those teachers whose future in the UAE was destroyed in the blink of an eye. She was on her second migration to the UAE and her contract was still valid; she was considered a valuable resource to her school and enjoying this second migration with her family (as she was now on a family package and not a single-entry visa as her previous contract) when she encountered an unexpected disturbance at school which plunged her into a whirlwind of professional confusion, destabilized her life in the UAE and forced her to return to South Africa and assess her future as a migrant teacher.

In a focus group discussion in 2015, Tanielle and Nadia both affirmed religious tolerance in the UAE, a Muslim country, but four years later, Tanielle lost her job in the UAE despite her commendable work at the school which led to her being selected to train teachers: 'I have been selected to roll out a project which I am excited about . . . I was asked to assist with the training of teachers'. After a colleague left Christian religious books on her table (for Tanielle's child) that were mistakenly distributed to learners ('My colleague gave me some religious books and these were mistakenly placed'), her contract was immediately terminated without her being allowed to provide an explanation to the education department. Tanielle (WhatsApp message) stated that she quickly collected the few books when she realized the error. However, a learner informed her parent of the mistake and the parent reported Tanielle to the local education department. There were several statements taken at school but she was never asked to explain herself to authorities outside of the school who made the decision to end her employment. 'I . . . told her (the principal) what happened . . . I was so disappointed that my name was mentioned in a negative way at such a level.' Then the principal 'informed me that my contract was terminated with immediate effect . . . I have 30 days to secure new employment.' Tanielle chose to return to South Africa temporarily before migrating elsewhere to teach. It is evident that migrant teachers have no rights in the UAE and they can be deported without a proper investigation (Impact International 2021), similar to the UK where if there are learner complaints, teachers could face deportation. Migrant teachers in Abu Dhabi were recently transferred to being under the helm of the Ministry of Education and there was a new fear of job loss that was growing as Tanielle's close friend informs her, 'now under MoE. There is still talk about it (changing contracts) but no change as yet . . . They terminated many contracts at the end of the previous academic year'.

In the UK, SA teachers occupied either short-term positions or longer-term positions if they were directly recruited by a school or supplied by an agency for a particular post. Teachers can be given a year or longer contracts depending on the schools and these can be renewed. Teachers can write the local exam to become recognized as qualified teachers but that is time-consuming (can take up to four years). Another key disturbance for migrant teachers' existing professional identities presented itself in respect of the short-term positions, a construct labelled as 'supply' teachers, meaning that their positions were temporary and lacked stability (Manik 2005). The unequal level of employment afforded to some migrant teachers was deeply worrying. These teachers were recruited by agencies on behalf of schools and they would thus 'belong' to the agency (and not the school unless the school sponsored their migration) and they could be used to temporarily fill in a gap in any school if a teacher was absent. For the longer-term positions, another disturbance destabilizing migrant teachers, demeaning them, occurred when the recruitment agency 'sold' the teacher to the school for a longer-term contract and this had the effect of a bitter taste of 'slavery' for migrant teachers' professional identities (Manik 2005). Rene, SA teacher (focus group discussion, 2003) who was very proud of her teaching abilities and professional standing in South Africa as a Grade 12 teacher (final exit grade at school), explained the loss of power and professional status she felt: 'They (recruitment agency) charge a fee to the school and you feel so cheap, it's so terrible.'

It is evident that Rene realizes that a migrant teacher is perceived as 'a commodity' to be sold but this has implications as she feels devalued. This aspect of her tenure at the school diminishes her own perception of her professional status as a valuable teacher.

Sociocultural Disturbances Impacting on Professional Experiences

Both studies referred to in this chapter have shown that during the recruitment process, prospective migrant teachers are assured of support in the form of induction and mentorship on arrival in destination countries. They thus feel satisfied that they would be able to not only easily acclimatize to society but also adapt to school life. It appears that migrant teacher socialization into the professional space is foregrounded as necessary by recruitment agencies and schools. Thus, while there are efforts by recruitment agencies and schools to support the migrant teachers, their supposed seamless integration into schools does not unfold due to a myriad of reasons. Migrant teachers from South Africa, across a fifteen-year span, reveal in both studies (one undertaken between 2002 and 2005 and the other between 2011 and 2020) that their professional integration is disrupted in several ways (what many scholars have termed a 'culture shock', cf. Manik 2005; Maylor et al. 2006) by sociocultural disturbances at school. For Nadia in the UAE, adjustment was not easy as she occupied the position of a subject advisor for the department of education in South Africa before her recruitment to the UAE, and she therefore had not been a teacher in a classroom for some time. Nevertheless, she commented that 'I will wait out the rest of the year and get used to the transition'. However, that time was inadequate and a year later she was still commenting: 'I have been trying to find myself in this foreign country and getting used to being in the classroom again.' Other teachers in the UAE had been teaching in South Africa, and they also commented on the need for greater efforts to induct and mentor migrant teachers. By far, the UK appeared to offer the greatest 'cultural shock' to migrant teachers due to learner behaviour and school location; however, this chapter does not explore this immense disturbance due to chapter constraints.

Staff and the Staffroom: Professional Isolation

Being temporary had repercussions for staff at the schools apart from the SA migrant teachers. In the UK, the staff did not acknowledge their presence in the staffroom nor build any relationships with the migrant teachers because of their transitory status at school. In some UAE schools, the Arab teachers are perceived by the migrant teachers as unaccepting, being worlds apart from them and distant. Nadia (2014) explained her feelings of the staff at the school, 'Well I have been here for 4 months and realised a massive chasm between the English medium Teachers and the Arabic staff . . . so many discrepancies. Just this morning I had an experience that shows my training makes me different from the Arab teachers . . . they lack integrity, professionalism, so much more.'

Two years later in 2016, Nadia chose not to renew her contract:

> I have no energy or inclination to continue. I am demotivated and constantly tired. Teaching drains the last little bit of motivation I have to try and work on something other than school work . . . In the previous term, I taught Grade 12 which took a while to get used to the curriculum. Then at the end of the last few days of the term, I was called into the principal's office and asked if I could change to teach Grade 10.

She was then transferred to co-teach another class and 'in a meeting, immigrant teachers were informed that co teaching is a way of saving them from having their services terminated'.

Nadia's (email) realization reveals several strands of 'workplace politics' in this 'hybrid' pedagogical space (Kooy and de Freitas 2007; Kostogriz and Peeler 2004). She is not adapting and making a positive difference in the UAE. The idea that migrant teachers are perceived as professionally incompetent and Nadia not being affirmed for her professional contributions in teaching at the school demotivates and angers her: 'I was so angry at the change, I offered my name to be given to . . . for a transfer. I am really "gatvol" (an Afrikaans expression meaning "fed-up") of how things are run at the school and how we get treated like we know nothing. The expats are never recognised as doing anything good.' She later writes about how being in Abu Dhabi was a 'soul destroying experience'. Her final comment points to her total capitulation. She later emigrated to China to teach. SA migrant teachers who experience professional devaluation (such as Nadia) also exhibit 'spatial marginalization' but somewhat different to Kostogriz and Peeler's (2007) articulation of it. In the UK and the UAE, they self-isolated (preferring to interact with other international teachers rather than local colleagues). Nadia did not mingle, further entrenching her separation. Thus, belonging to a local teaching community (Kostogriz and Peeler 2004, 2007; Niyubahwe et al. 2013), sharing ideas and thoughts about teaching and learning in the same school environment were absent.

Racism and xenophobia were evidently perpetrated by colleagues in the UK and return-migrant from the UK Rajen (2003) remarked, 'every staff has 1 or 2 racists but they are in the minority so as a teacher you ignore it.' Vis (2003), also a return-migrant from the UK, believed that the local White teachers in school could be perceived as behaving with arrogance but he acknowledged that perhaps given his own identity as a SA having emerged from deep-rooted distrust of the 'other' based on apartheid racial classifications prior to 1994, he could be misjudging the situation because he was feeling out of place and self-isolating: 'I was one dark skinned person sitting in the staffroom ... maybe they accepted me but I didn't accept them!'

Lyn (diary, 2003) also spoke of the value of a professional community and belonging to it in England: having colleagues and the comfort that they offer in being able to overcome the stresses posed by learners: 'We are off to Newquay with a group of teachers. The support amongst the staff is fantastic! Only thing that keeps me going.'

In the UAE, Tanielle explains that there is a preference that migrant teachers must be recruited from Western countries to teach subjects in English but more so, there is a preference for the identity of migrant teachers to be 'White'. Nadia (Coloured) shared a story about a SA Indian migrant teacher who was dark skinned and recruited to the same school and her treatment by a female Arab member of staff who blatantly discriminated: she refused to shake her hand when introduced, and repeated incidents by the colleagues to alienate the migrant teacher indicated racism. Eventually, the staff was informed after a short while that the migrant teacher had become a 'runner' (packed her belongings overnight and fled the UAE). Nadia explained that Indians from India and not South Africa work in predominantly low-skilled jobs in the UAE and many families have Indian maids, thus to have learners also treat an Indian teacher poorly is not uncommon. That their minds have been 'contaminated' (Kostogriz and Peeler 2004) with racial links and power is revealed in the actions of learners, who don't associate Indian teachers with South Africa but with their low-skilled workers from India. It is evident that this 'spatial struggle' in the 'pedagogical space' (Kostogriz and Peeler 2004) had resulted in migrant teacher flight from the UAE.

6. Some Concluding Theoretical Insights and Recommendations

Despite the time difference between the two case studies (one being in 2005 and the other from 2011 to 2020), there are some enduring theoretical insights for research into teacher migration from South Africa. There are several factors, at the confluence of which lies the narrative of migrant teachers from the south as deficit and temporary. Thus, there is socio-professional exploitation and the separation of migrant teachers whether it is intentional or not by members of staff and policies in host contexts. The knock-on effect is that school spaces for migrant teachers can become places of pernicious behaviour, paranoia and persecution unless there is a commitment by government and school with initiatives to provide ongoing support ensuring the integration of migrant teachers.

Migrant teachers' experiences in the UK and the UAE have demonstrated a key difference in policy orientation based on their treatment and an acknowledgement of their value in schools. In the UK, there is a 'recruit, reduce and retain' principle evident in foreign teachers' recruitment. They are recruited to the UK and once abroad, they experience a 'reduction' in their status by being labelled as unqualified and temporary. They are then urged to study to obtain QTS so that they can be retained as teachers. There are some discriminatory caveats to the concept of recognition. In the UK, SA teachers' qualifications are not being recognized despite wide acceptance by principals across England that SA teachers are of high quality. Matimba (2015) drew attention to migrant teachers from Australia, Canada, New Zealand and the United States who can apply for QTS without having to study towards it, this despite SA migrant teachers being the largest number of immigrant teachers in the UK in the early 2000s (before 2008 and the end of the youth mobility scheme). Miller, Mulvaney and Ochs (2007) present statistics that between July 2001 and July 2004, recruited teachers to England in descending order of quantity recruited were as follows: South Africa (6,722), Australia (4,484), New Zealand (2,515), Jamaica (1,671) and Canada (1,591). Shajimon, Bartley and Beddoe (2019) strongly argue that the discrimination is evident that there is preferential treatment in the recognition mechanism which favours migrant teachers from particular countries. SA migrant teachers have always been adequately qualified (see Keevy and Jansen's teachers' qualifications comparability table 2010). National Academic Recognition Information Centre (NARIC), the recognition-awarding institution, will need to account for this blatant ongoing discrimination targeting

SA migrant teachers. In the UK, being labelled as unqualified and having the temporary status of filling in for absent teachers (supply teaching) is grounds for immediately being relegated to the professional fringes in the staffroom.

In the UAE, the principle is to 'recruit and use' migrant teachers, thus while the SA qualification is recognized, migrant teachers are not recognized at the interpersonal level for their professional contributions at school despite monetary gratification through policy imperatives, rewarding salaries and benefits. In the UAE, all migrant teachers, not just SA migrant teachers, are temporary and thus harbour fear of complaints that can lead to an immediate termination of their contracts.

Teacher retention in host and home countries takes on renewed significance in this era of globalized professions of highly skilled staff. The deskilling, devaluing and exploitation of migrant teachers (lower pay scales than local teachers) is unfair and it impacts on teachers' socio- professional identities and diminishes their professional status. Local teachers are privileged while migrant teachers suffer a loss of professional power, yet it is the services of the latter which are in demand. It is clear that migrant teachers were not afforded adequate rights to protect them despite the development of a Commonwealth Teacher recruitment protocol in 2004 which was designed to protect migrant teachers, source and host countries. Miller, Mulvaney and Ochs (2007: 159) had long admonished the country stating that 'the UK government needs to safeguard the rights and civil liberties of overseas trained teachers against rogue teacher recruitment agencies, individual schools and head teachers whose practices border on exploitation, colonialism and slavery'. Of course, the UAE is currently at the helm of discrimination in the services of SA migrant teachers, and since this is the latest migration trend, it needs to be equally addressed. Another theoretical insight is evident in the mechanisms for the integration of migrant teachers, as this is critical to their sense of belonging in host schools. Socializing teachers into the profession in both countries is valuable in ensuring that they understand the nature of their work and the culture in host schools. Key tools in managing their professional integration are induction and mentorship (Shajimon et al. 2019). In both the studies, migrant teachers' integration was unique given each teacher's history, and thus the adjustment to the classroom was tempered by their professional experiences and identities (racial and professional) in South Africa. Migrant teachers underestimated or did not anticipate certain obstacles to their integration, such as learner behaviour. They navigated a host of disturbances in their effort to be recognized and accepted as professionals by their peers. Interestingly, management in most schools was presented by migrant teachers as being very supportive and keen to initiate constructive efforts to assist migrant teachers but this aligns with the need to retain teachers in host schools. Their development of a sense of belonging to the local teaching fraternity in host countries then (UK) and now (UAE) remains elusive.

7. Conclusion

Teaching will continue to be a mobile profession as teachers are in need across the world with local teachers not fulfilling local needs and a need for migrant teachers to respond to this demand. SA migrant teachers' thoughts about their experiences are critical for their professional integration, their sense of belonging to a global teaching fraternity and teacher retention. Despite the expanse of time between the two case studies on SA migrant teachers in host countries abroad, the disturbances which trouble and unhinge them remain deeply rooted in a narrative of discriminatory practices in the profession, namely that of migrant teachers from the south being deficit and temporary workers. The 'troubling' experiences of migrant teachers on their arrival, persist in host schools leading to their feelings of dissatisfaction is important for ensuring the equal treatment of migrant teachers in their work environment and protecting their rights so that they are not devalued professionally.

References

Adams, R. (2019), 'Teachers in England Have "unmanageable job"', *The Guardian*, 19 June. Available online: https://www.theguardian.com/education/2019/jun/19/teachers-in-england-have-unmanageable- job-global-survey.

Anganoo, L. D. (2020), 'South African Primary School Migrant Teachers' School-based Experiences in Arab Gulf Countries', PhD Thesis, University of KwaZulu-Natal, South Africa.

Appleton, S., A. Sives and W. J. Morgan (2006), 'Should Teachers Stay at Home? The Impact of International Teacher Mobility', *Journal of International Development*, 18: 771–86.

Bense, K. (2016), 'International Teacher Migration: The Exploration of a Global Phenomenon', PhD Thesis, University of Western Australia, Australia.

Cohen, L., L. Manion, and K. Morrison (2018), *Research Methods in Education*, London: Routledge.

Collins, J. and C. Reid (2012), 'Immigrant Teachers in Australia', *Cosmopolitan Civil Societies Journal*, 4 (2): 38–61.

Datta-Roy, S. and S. Lavery (2017), 'Experiences of Overseas Trained Teachers Seeking Public School Positions in Western Australia and South Australia', *Issues in Educational Research*, 27 (4): 720–35.

De Villiers, R. (2007), 'Migration from Developing Countries: The Case of South African Teachers to the United Kingdom', *Perspectives in Education*, 25 (2): 67–76.

Edwards, D. (2014), 'Migrant Teachers: A Case Study', PhD thesis, Faculty of the Graduate School, University of Maryland. Available online: https://www.researchgate.net/publication/274079800_MIGRANT_TEACHERS_A_CASE_STU DY.

Ferguson, D. (2018), 'I Will Never Return to Teach in England: UK Teachers Finding Refuge Abroad', *The Guardian*, 2 October. Available online: https://www.theguardian.com/education/2018/oct/02/never-return-teach-england-refuge- abroad.

Fimyar, O. (2018), 'We Have a Window Seat': A Baktinian Analysis of International Teachers' Identity in Nazarbayev Intellectual Schools in Kazakhstan',. *European Education*, 50: 301–19.

ImpACTt International (2021), 'They Told us They Hated Black-Africans: UAE Authorities Detain, Torture and Deport Over 800 Migrant Workers'. Available online: https://impactpolicies.org/en/news/235/they-told-us-they-hated-black-africans-uae-authorities- detain-torture-and-deport-over-800-migrants.

Keevy, J. and J. Jansen (2010), *Fair Trade for Teachers: Transferability of Teacher Qualifications in the Commonwealth*, London: Commonwealth Secretariat.

Kooy, M. and E. de Feitas (2007), 'The Diaspora Sensibility in Teacher Identity: Locating Self Through Story', *Canadian Journal of Education*, 30(3): 865–80.

Kostogriz, A. and E. Peeler (2004), 'Professional Identity and Pedagogical Space', *Australian Association for Research in Education (AARE)*, Coldstream: 1–16. Available online: http://hdl.handle.net/10536/DRO/DU:30024277.

Kostogriz, A. and E. Peeler (2007), 'Professional Identity and Pedagogical Space', *Teaching Education*, 18 (2): 107–22.

Manik, S. (2005), 'Trials, Tribulations and Triumphs of Transnational Teachers: Teacher Migration Between South Africa and the United Kingdom', unpublished PhD Thesis, University of KwaZulu-Natal, South Africa.

Manik, S. (2007), 'To Greener Pastures: Transnational Teacher Migration from South Africa', *Perspectives in Education*, 25 (2): 55–65.

Manik, S. (2013), 'Zimbabwean Immigrant Teachers in Kwa-Zulu Natal Count the Cost of Going Under the Hammer', *Alternation*, 7: 67–87.

Manik, S. (2014), 'South African Migrant Teachers' Decision-Making: Levels of Influence and "Relative Deprivation"', *Journal of Southern African Studies*, 40 (10): 151–65.

Maylor, U., M. Hutchings, K. James, I. Menter and S. Smart (2006), 'Culture Clash: The Experiences of Overseas-Trained Supply Teachers in English Schools', Paper presented at the British Educational Research Association Annual Conference,

University of Warwick, 6–9 September 2006. Available online: http://www.leeds.ac.uk/educol/documents/161422.htm.

Miller, P. W., G. Mulvaney and K. Ochs (2007), 'The Commonwealth Teacher Recruitment Protocol: Its Impacts and Implications for the Global Teaching Profession', *Research in Comparative and International Education*, 2 (2): 151–62.

Niyubahwe, A., J. Mukamurera and F. Jutras (2013), 'Professional integration of immigrant teachers in the school system: A literature review', *McGill Journal of Education/Revue des sciences de l'éducation de McGill*, 48 (2): 279–96.

Mlambo, S. (2020), 'Do SA Teachers Really Earn R460k per Annum on Average?', *IOL*, 27 February. Available online: https://www.iol.co.za/news/south-africa/do-sa-teachers-really-earn-r460k-per-annum-on- average-43609215.

Reid, C., J. Collins and M. Singh (2010), *Globalisation and Teacher Movements Into and out of Multicultural Australia: Final Report*, Sydney: Western Sydney University. Available online: http://handle.uws.edu.au:8081/1959.7/560932.

Shajimon, P., A. Bartley, and L. Beddoe (2019), 'What Lessons Can be Learned from Nursing and Teaching?', *European Journal of Social Work*, 22: 16–29.

Tarisayi, K. S. and S. Manik (2019), 'Affirmation and Defamation: Zimbabwean Migrant Teachers' Survival Strategies in a Xenophobic South Africa',. *Journal of International Migration and Integration*, 22 (1): 1–22.

Vester, T. M. (2018), 'Teacher Migration: A Case Study of South African Teachers Migrating to Abu Dhabi', MA diss., University of KwaZulu-Natal, South Africa.

Weda, Z. and R. de Villiers (2019), 'Migrant Zimbabwean Teachers in South Africa: Challenging and Rewarding Issues', *Journal of International Migration and Integration*, 20 (4): 1013–28.

The Subtle Work of Whiteness in Canadian Teacher Education

Lilach Marom

1. Introduction

Many studies have shown the importance of diversifying the teaching force and argue that in order to answer the needs of the highly diverse student population, the teaching force should 'better reflect the backgrounds, worldviews, cultures, and languages of the students' (Schmidt 2010: 2). Yet, although Canadian educational policies and public discourses promote diversity as a central tenant of Canadian society (Fleras and Elliott 2002; Joshee 2004), the Canadian teaching force is still highly homogenous, composed mainly of White, middle-class women who speak English with a Canadian accent (Janzen and Cranston 2016; Ryan, Pollock and Antonelli 2009; Li et al. 2021). This chapter explores the mismatch between diversity discourses and the homogeneity of the teaching profession at the entry point to the profession – teacher education.

This study emerged from a research project in which I examined the recertification process of immigrant teachers – or internationally educated teachers (IETs) – in British Columbia (BC) (Marom 2015, 2017a, 2019a). One concern that emerged from this project and drove the current study was that teacher education in Canada, in spite of its claim to foster diversity, often becomes a site for social reproduction (Fleras and Elliott 2002; Haig-Brown 2011). IETs were expected to morph into 'good Canadian teachers', yet prevalent conceptions of the 'good teacher' were grounded in 'Canadian normativity'. This normativity entailed not only pedagogical and professional norms but also broader assumptions about what is core (and thus what is not core) to teaching in Canada (Marom 2017b, 2019a).

Building on this previous work, this study sought to explore whether the need to adapt to a certain model of 'Canadian normativity' operated only in the case of IETs (who often belong to racialized groups) or also in the wider context of minoritized groups. I wondered whether Canadian-born teachers, or first- and second-generation immigrants who do not fit the prototypical image of Canadian teachers, were similarly marginalized during their teacher education. Teacher education is a good site for such an examination since faculties of education are particularly inclined to have a gap between the rhetoric and the practice of diversity (Ahmed 2007; Cochran-Smith 2003; Li et al. 2021). While diversity is often prevalent on paper, the reality of the programs (e.g. admissions, structures and pedagogies) often convey 'assimilationist assumptions and employ linguistic tools that privilege White cultural norms and values' (Bell and Hartmann 2007: 907). I employ the theoretical frame of Critical Race Theory (CRT) (Ladson-Billings 1998, 2005) and the concept of racial microaggressions (Solórzano, Ceja and Yosso 2000) in order to focus on White normativity that might otherwise remain hidden behind the appealing term 'diversity'.

2. Critical Race Theory in Teacher Education

Diversity in Canada is constitutionalized under the policy of multiculturalism (Bedard 2000), which is promoted as a pillar of Canadian society. Canadian prime minister Justin Trudeau famously said: 'There is no core identity, no mainstream in Canada', and that he sees Canada as 'the first post-national state' (cited in Malcolm 2016: para. 2). Simpson, James and Mack (2011), however, claim that discourses on racism and colonialism are neutered and diminished under the multicultural umbrella. They argue that Canada is utilizing its claim to multiculturalism as a mechanism to ignore the operations of racism and colonialism at the structural and institutional level. Since in Canada racial issues are diffused under the prevalence of multicultural terminology, CRT is a useful frame to demonstrate that race remains a key element in the Canadian social outlook.

CRT is a theoretical perspective committed to social justice that attempts to expose the racial assumptions underpinning the core structures of Western societies (particularly in the US context). As such, it challenges notions of neutrality, colour blindness and meritocracy that are embedded within educational systems and in other public institutions and aims to expose the racial factors that circulate and operate within liberal discourses (Delgado and Stefancic 2000; Ladson-Billings 1999; Tate and Ladson-Billings 1995; Yosso 2005).

Through the frame of CRT, racism is analysed not just by its manifestation in visible acts (such as hate crimes) but more importantly via its subtle, hidden, structural operations that have led to the disadvantages experienced by minoritized groups. The focus of CRT is not on intentions but on outcomes, especially because in institutions such as universities, racism operates in much subtler ways (Henry and Tator 2009a). CRT scholars call these subtle forms of racism 'microaggressions', that is, covert manifestations of racism in daily life and in social and educational institutions. Racial microaggressions are 'subtle insults (verbal, nonverbal, and/or visual) directed toward people of colour, often automatically or unconsciously' (Solórzano, Ceja and Yosso 2000: 60).

> In the field of teacher education, CRT aims for radical changes, claiming that teacher education programs have remained 'rooted in traditional ways of preparing teachers peppered with some discussion of race or culture . . . The language of the programs includes social justice and multiculturalism and diversity while the ideology, values and practices are assuredly re-inscribing white privilege, power, and racism.' (Cross 2005: 266)

Cross (2005) claims that this is a form of new racism that operates through an invisible system of powers and privileges at the institutional level and serves the same cultural agents and power relations even when a program is redesigned to promote social justice. White normativity is so ingrained in education institutions that unless it is constantly put under scrutiny and pushed against, it will continue to be reproduced.

3. Methodology and Data Sources

The methodological design of this study is grounded in in-depth, semi-structured interviews with ten racialized teacher candidates near the end of their BEd program. I use (interchangeably) the terms 'racialized' and 'minoritized' (Dowd 2008) instead of racial and/or minority groups, as it highlights the social construction of marginalization experienced by racial and ethnic minority groups even if they become the numerical majority (which is the case in some urban areas in BC).

Qualitative interviews are rooted in the understanding that individual stories are of worth (Kvale 1996; Seidman 2005). Interviews are particularly revealing when exploring the effects of complex institutional structures on individual experiences. As Seidman (2005: 10) argues, 'Social abstractions like "education" are best understood through the experiences of the individuals whose work and lives are the stuff upon which the abstractions are built.'

My focus on interviews is consistent with the CRT frame, which uses counter-stories as a means to highlight voices that have traditionally been marginalized in Western institutions and that can shed light on the complex ways in which racism works. The counter-story is a tool for 'exposing, analyzing, and challenging the majoritarian stories of racial privilege' (Solórzano and Yosso 2002: 32). This is pertinent to teacher education as most teacher education programs 'are designed mainly with traditional-age White students in mind, a reality that may be invisible to those in such programs but is visible to those who sense not belonging' (Sleeter and Milner 2011: 88).

The selection process of the participants aimed to create a purposive sample (Etikan, Musa and Alkassim 2016) that conveys the local diversity in BC; for that reason, I interviewed five Indigenous, three East Asian Canadian and two South Asian Canadian teacher candidates. The non-Indigenous participants were first- or second-generation immigrants. While the number of interviewees does not represent their relative percentage of the BC population, all these groups are central to discourses on diversity in BC.

This methodological design is important in light of the theoretical divide in studying Indigenous and immigrant populations (Lawrence and Dua 2011). The divide is partly due to Indigenous scholars' critique against '[erasing] the specific and unique location of Aboriginal peoples as Indigenous to this land by equating them with multicultural and immigrant groups' (St. Denis 2011: 311). However, as Lawrence and Dua (2011: 254) argue, 'there is a need for scholarship that ends practices of segregation, and attempts to explore the complex histories of interactions between peoples of colour and Aboriginal peoples'. While both groups are positioned in contested ways in relation to each other, they both might be affected by overlapping but distinct mechanisms of reproduction that underlie teacher education in Canada. As Indigenous and immigrant are the two fastest growing populations in Canada, increasing their integration into the teaching force is of importance to Canada as a multicultural country (Statistics Canada 2021) aiming for reconciliation with Indigenous peoples (The Truth and Reconciliation Commission 2015).

In this chapter I share data from interviews with five teacher candidates. All participants were women in their mid-twenties to early thirties, which is consistent with the high concentration of females in the teaching profession.

This is not surprising as teaching is associated with the notion of care, which in turn is associated with a motherly figure. Yet it's important to note that care in teaching is criticized as conveying a 'prototypical' mother-child model that assumes White privilege (Thompson 1998), whereas women of colour often display caring differently to both protect and support their kids (Gomez, Allen and Clinton 2004).

In research that draws heavily on interviews, particularly with a relatively small sample size, it is important to discuss the limitations of the findings. This study does not aim for objective validity but rather relies on the intersubjectivity of the researcher and the participants (Ferrarotti 1981) as a means to access and acknowledge experiential knowledge that might otherwise remain hidden in teacher education.

4. Findings

In the interviews, the participants shared several episodes where they felt targeted, othered or excluded during the teacher education program. For them, these experiences were not divided into neat categories but rather constituted an accumulative process that resulted in feelings of being out of place. However, in order to capture this accumulative process, I have organized the data in three layers:

1. The gap between the rhetoric of diversity and the participants' experiences in the program.
2. The transmission of institutionalized Whiteness through subtle, racial microaggressions.
3. The emotional and professional toll racialized teacher candidates pay when confronting Whiteness in teacher education.

Talking Diversity, Reproducing Whiteness

The terms 'diversity' and 'inclusion' were prevalent in documents and policies in the teacher education program, as well as in course titles and syllabus descriptions. In the mission statement of the teacher education program it is stated that the program 'is committed to preparing educators who will be knowledgeable, capable, flexible, and compassionate members of the profession guided by a sense of social and ethical responsibility in relation to their students and the wider society'.[1] It further states that 'to achieve this mission, teacher educators [in the program] are aware that enacting global citizenship necessitates a dialogical approach to issues of social justice, equity, sustainability and social action'.

However, the participants shared many examples of gaps between the prevalence of diversity discourses and their experiences in the program. For example, when I asked Tamam, a first-generation immigrant from South Asia, if she felt that she could incorporate her cultural and religious traditions into the program, she shared,

> There is a big gap between the theory and the practice. Maybe I haven't tried, but I was so overwhelmed with the things I had to learn that I wasn't thinking about what I can bring. I'm in a different level of thinking, the adjustment level, not at the initiating level. This is how intimidated I am.

As Tamam explained, she was so preoccupied with adjusting to the program she did not have the means to share her knowledge and experiences. The feeling of being overwhelmed or intimidated is not unique to immigrant and racialized students and can be experienced by new students and those unfamiliar with higher education. Yet one must keep in mind that teacher education programs in Canada are typically post-baccalaureate programs; hence, its students are not new to academic culture. Tamam felt that even if she had tried to share her knowledge, it would not have been appreciated in the program:

> I have not even thought about connecting my teaching to my heritage and culture because where is the place for it in the system? There is no place, even if I wanted to. I feel like everything is so predominantly based on the White population. Even if I want to bring something from my culture, will it be welcomed? Even if they say it will be, in reality, I don't think so.

Similarly, Jenny, a second-generation immigrant from East Asia, shared, 'Other teaching perspectives, like Asian perspectives, were definitely missing or ignored. We also talked about Aboriginal education, but incorporating it is a whole different thing. Talking about it is not really putting it to use.' This example points not only to what is missing from the curriculum but also to the gap between prescribed and lived curriculum. Talking about diversity or Aboriginal education on a theoretical level or including it in syllabi is not synonymous with creating inclusive learning spaces. In order to really allow for diverse knowledges and perspectives to be manifested, there is a need to move beyond the rhetoric of the importance of diversity to the embodiment of diversity in praxis.

The gap between discourses and practice was even more explicit during the practicum, as Willow, an Indigenous teacher candidate, shared:

> At a staff meeting they were talking about the district priority areas. One of them was improving Indigenous education, and the principal said, 'well, we only have 2-3 Indigenous students and they are all doing pretty well, so we don't need to be worrying about that one, so don't spend any time discussing this topic. That is not important.' I remember feeling that it was like a slap in the face. It is not about how many Indigenous students you have; it is about the fact that you are a school in Canada. Just hearing this from an admin in a huge school – it was heartbreaking ... That's when I realised that nobody was getting it ... It made me think, 'Why do I want to be a teacher? I'm not going to be able to fit in.'

As this example shows, although Indigenous education is a declared priority in BC (BC Government 2017), it is not necessarily implemented in a meaningful way at the school level. Indigenous education is often treated as an add-on or a policy to put a checkmark beside. While reconciliation is embraced in educational institutions on the superficial level, there is often pushback or watering down attempts to engage deeply with decolonizing processes (Donald 2012; Kerr and Parent 2018).

Racialized teacher candidates described similar patterns of exclusion of non-Western cultures and knowledge that were constructed as outside the Canadian mainstream. For example, Tamam shared her experience as a Muslim in the practicum:

> Some of my Muslim friends don't want to have any music for their kids in school, but what are [schools] doing for these kids? Are they just sitting in the library or are they doing something with them? Are there any alternatives? The system is supposed to be secular, [yet] Christmas, Halloween, and Easter are still celebrated. All these things are based in specific cultural traditions, and if you don't agree with them, then you still have to ... because everybody is doing it and [you] want to fit in the system. So, they say it's a multicultural system, but is it really?

While the Canadian public education system is constitutionalized as secular (Canada Department of Justice 1982), it is embedded in particular Anglo-Christian cultural and religious preferences that are set as the norm (Henry and Tator 2009a). The outcome is that teacher candidates who do not fit neatly into the norm constantly need to negotiate their place in the system. This is also reflected in the Canadian school calendar that is set by Christian holidays (with 'patched' solutions such as teachers' professional development day on Chinese New Year), although many Canadian families celebrate different holidays.

Christian cultural domination was further followed by English linguistic domination, as Tamam, who spoke English as a second language, experienced:

> My school advisor (SA) told me that she is very worried about the English language, that because of the way the Chinese and other immigrants are speaking it, it is going to be ruined. The impression that I got is that I need to have native English-speaking abilities in order for me to better fit. And I think now I have internalized it . . . So, although I'm done with the program and I'm certified, I'm too scared to apply for jobs.

This example exposes a problematic understanding of 'correct' language. First, English has become an official language in many countries and, therefore, equating 'true English speakers' with certain Western accents and figures of speech is flawed (Mufwene 1998). Second, there is often an unspoken connection between language – especially accent – and racism and discrimination based on skin colour and ethnicity (Kubota 2015; Lippi-Green 2012).

White Normativity as Racial Microaggressions

Henry and Tator (2009b: 29) argue that race should be central to any critical analysis since Whiteness is a main property of institutional privilege, a colourless colour that defines the standards through 'organizational policies and practices that, regardless of intent, are directly or indirectly disadvantageous to racial minorities'. Satzewich and Liodakis (2010: 194) call it 'White institutional power', that is, the way Whiteness is ingrained in social institutions as an organizing category by which the 'normative' is defined (Thompson 2003). The participants in this study differ in their backgrounds, race, ethnicity and religious affiliation, but they all shared various experiences of being pushed into a White normative model of teaching.

Most of the participants' counter-stories did not reflect overt racism but rather subtle, racial microaggressions. It is important to note that subtle does not mean insignificant but, rather, mundane. Research demonstrates that exposure to daily forms of microaggressions has an accumulative and long-lasting impact on both academic success and the general well-being of racialized people (Solórzano, Ceja and Yosso 2000; Sue et al. 2007).

One repeated expression of microaggressions that emerged from the participants' reflections was a push to assimilate to the White normativity of the program. Some participants described this as 'Whitewashing'. Whitewashing is a term coined to describe the attempts of the media to appeal to a White audience by making ethnic characters 'look Whiter'. It is now used as an umbrella term for many things, including the expectations from members of minoritized groups to 'act White' (Brown 2003). Celeste, a second-generation Chinese Canadian, shared her experience of Whitewashing in the program:

> The goal for me and for my minority friends was always to be as Whitewashed as we can and to prove that we are not different. It was always a bad thing to be part of your own culture. If you are very, very Whitewashed, you could bring a little bit of your culture in and people would say, 'cool.' But if you were deep in your culture, people would think, 'This is too much. This is too different,' and they don't want to talk to you.

As Celeste describes, Whiteness was the norm to which minoritized teacher candidates were expected to conform. This aligns with Brown's (2014: 336) findings that 'in contrast to images of teacher education as race neutral in their cultural orientation, the literature on preservice teachers of colour in mainstream teacher education programs are defined by Whiteness'. As emerges from this example, if you were 'White enough', sharing some cultural knowledge would be perceived as a positive thing, but it should not be too much. This is consistent with an add-on multicultural approach that acknowledges diversity on the superficial level without challenging racial inequalities in society (Gorski 2008).

Jenny shared her family's reaction to the transformation she went through during the teacher education program:

> When I talk, my family and my friends, they would be like, 'why are you suddenly all polite and Whitewashed?' But if you are White and you grew up [in White culture], then you naturally fit in, because this is how you were brought up.

In this example, Jenny referred to interaction styles that might differ between Asian Canadians and White Anglo-Canadians. As she explains, what is considered a 'normative' interaction is actually a particular norm of the dominant culture. The normative professional space is not always noticeable to people who fit the mainstream, but it is noticeable to those on the margins. While institutional marginalization can target students based on diverse social positions (such as race, ethnicity, class, gender and their intersection), in the North American context Whiteness is a key societal force. As Picower (2009: 198) argues, 'Whiteness remains masked from everyday consciousness, allowing [Whites] to be blind not only to their own privileges but also to their group membership.'

Racialized teacher candidates who were not born with this 'group membership' tended to have more challenges in the program, as Celeste further commented:

> No one really explicitly talks about it, but you can definitely feel that most people who struggled in the practicum are from minority groups or less conforming to that professional attitude. I felt that the program is Westernized. I don't know how [you can] change it, because all of us [from minority groups] are becoming Whitewashed to be able to be here.

As Celeste describes, 'Whiteness was embedded in the professional norms of teacher education' (Marom 2019b), and 'acting White' served as an 'admission fee' (Bourdieu and Wacquant 1992: 107) racialized teacher candidates had to pay in order to be successful in the program. Yet paying this fee invoked feelings of self-doubt and disconnect from their culture.

White normativity was also exerted in relations with peers, as Daria, an Indigenous teacher candidate, described:

> Many of my fellow peers didn't want to take the Aboriginal education course . . . and I felt like that somehow was held against me. Which made me really upset, because I was so excited about this course. I thought, 'This is my opportunity. People are going to learn what I know . . .' And then everyone in the hallways were, 'Why are we taking this? This is so stupid. I'm going to be a music teacher. I don't need it.'

As emerged from this example, although an Aboriginal education[2] course is now mandatory in teacher education programs in BC (British Columbia Ministry of Education 2015) in the 'hallway talk' it was conceived as an unnecessary add-on that is not central to being a teacher. What made this experience difficult for Daria was not only that Indigenous education was not deemed important by many teacher candidates but also that she felt she had to educate her peers, as racialized students are often expected to (Chinnery 2008). Daria explained further:

> I had to say things like, 'No! Indigenous education is an important thing. It can be done well. I'm sorry if it is not being done well in your class.' That was probably one of the biggest challenges I had in the program – having to be the person that is validating why Indigenous education is an important thing for teachers in Canada.

While Daria felt that she was expected to educate her peers, her peers could maintain the position of the 'perfect stranger' (Dion 2007) who claims distance and disconnect from the colonial legacy of Canada. Such a position can be understood as a tool of Whiteness (Picower 2009) that White teacher candidates use as a way of avoiding, undermining and diverting issues of race and privilege.

The Emotional and Professional Toll of Confronting Whiteness

Interactions and experiences such as the ones described above led the participants to realize that they either had to conform to the construction of the program or be exposed to othering and marginalization. Jenny shared, 'It felt like if you want to be certified here, you need to be like us.' Willow added, 'I wasn't comfortable teaching considering that I wasn't allowed to do it the way I wanted to do it. It all just felt so backward.' Similarly, Tamam explained, 'Whatever it is, you just have to suck it up, especially being an immigrant and a visible minority. I didn't feel confident to stand up to the system. Whatever was going on I just had to adjust to it, you see, because I wanted to pass.' All the participants, although diverse in their backgrounds, race and ethnicity, faced similar challenges as an outcome of the White normative construction of the teacher education program. While the participants in this study graduated the program, their journey to become teachers was not easy, and they needed to overcome numerous barriers in order to graduate, particularly if they wanted to stand up to the system and to stay connected to their cultural heritage. These challenges were not limited to professional aspects of their experience but to their self-identification. For example, Tamam shared:

> I felt that all my experiences and my ethics and everything were, like, good for nothing. I didn't feel that I had anything valuable . . . I always felt that I have nothing to offer – although I have lots to offer – because of all these psychological pressures. I felt intimidated; I thought I could never work in education because, 'What's the point?' . . . I felt that it is only for the White population, like only they have the right to become teachers.

Similarly, Daria shared:

> I remember just going home and crying after every school day in the practicum, [feeling] that I wasn't good enough. But actually, I wasn't good enough through their eyes, and I had to remind myself of that. Today I still feel surprised by how well I'm doing in my career because I was so convinced that I was going to be a bad teacher.

The thing that connects the diverse participants is that none fits the White normativity of the program. This commonality is important in illuminating the, often unspoken, Whiteness underpinning teacher education. Furthermore, it demonstrates that subtle forms of microaggressions can thrive even in a teacher education program that self-proclaims orientation towards inclusivity and diversity. Racial microaggressions accumulate during the program in a way that negatively affects the experiences of racialized teacher candidates in teacher education as well as their career trajectories.

5. Concluding Thoughts

This chapter suggests that while the Canadian education system declares itself a promoter of multiculturalism and inclusivity, it is underlined by subtle forms of racism and White normativity. The increase in the 'language of diversity' in discourse and policies does not deeply challenge the colonial and racial structures framing educational institutions in Canada (Ahmed 2012; Coulthard 2014; Thobani 2007). While diversity rhetoric is used, and the diversity of the student body increases, Whiteness remains 'ingrained and institutionalized' (Cochran-Smith 2003) in teacher education. Since Whiteness operates in subtle ways and underlies professional discourses (Marom and Ruitenberg 2018), it is harder to detect and confront. Microaggressions can flourish even when an institution has a declared commitment to diversity and when its instructors are well intentioned.

The burning question is whether teacher education can change or whether it is inherently flawed? Similar questions are being asked today in the North American context about other social institutions, such as law enforcement (Maynard 2017). Some critics argue that we need to abolish discriminating social institutions and start anew; others argue that an education paradigm shift is still possible (Stein 2019, 2021). What is clear is that in order to dismantle White institutional power (Satzewich and Liodakis 2010) change cannot be superficial but rather needs to be made at all levels of teacher education programs (e.g. hiring, scheduling, tuition and programming).

Some steps towards inclusivity in teacher education could include the creation of initiatives (e.g. R/EQUAL) for individuals and institutions to collaborate and create networks that support change since, as Ahmed (2012: 26) explains, individuals often come up against 'brick walls' when attempting to implement inclusion in their institutions. Since microaggressions can be hidden in the cracks of a program (e.g. in 'hallway talk', during the practicum, in cultural events), a collaborative, international approach to naming and identifying similar patterns in diverse settings is needed.

Furthermore, since many teacher education programs in Canada and elsewhere are becoming shorter and increasingly fragmented due to market demands and the changing structure of hiring in the university (Grimmett and Young 2012; Marom and Ruitenberg 2018), discourses on diversity must be tied to discourses on immigration, markets and internationalization in education. These are not disconnected phenomena, and one is dependent on the other.

Within teacher education programs, creating an online, anonymous system for students to document incidents of overt and covert racism could be useful in increasing institutional awareness. Such a system should not be intended to shame individuals but rather to gather data that might be hidden from the institutional view.

Lastly, it is crucial to create a stronger connection between the off- and on-campus pieces of teacher education programs (e.g. course instructors, administrators and practicum schools) as well as to implement a careful process for selecting and training school and faculty mentors. Having diverse school advisors and diverse faculty members could lead to a dramatic change in the experiences of racialized teacher candidates.

Unless such systemic changes are made, the struggles of racialized teacher candidates and internationally educated teachers will continue to be misunderstood as individual problems instead of as overarching phenomena that underlie Western teacher education and, therefore, need to be accounted for on a policy and institutional level.

Notes

1 I omit the reference to avoid identifying the institution.
2 I use 'Indigenous' and 'Aboriginal' interchangeably.

References

Ahmed, S. (2007), 'The Language of Diversity', *Ethnic and Racial Studies*, 30 (2): 235–56.

Ahmed, S. (2012), *On Being Included: Racism and Diversity in Institutional Life*, Durham: Duke University Press.

BC Government (2017), 'Aboriginal Education in British Columbia'. Available online: http://www2.gov.bc.ca/gov/content/education-training/ways-to-learn/aboriginal-education.

BC Ministry of Education (2015), 'Introduction to British Columbia's Redesigned Curriculum'. Available online: https://curriculum.gov.bc.ca/sites/curriculum.gov.bc.ca/files/pdf/curriculum_intro.pdf.

Bedard, G. (2000), 'Deconstructing Whiteness: Pedagogical Implications for Anti-racism Education', in G. J. Dei and A. Calliste (eds), *Power, Knowledge and Anti-racism Education: A Critical Reader*, 41–56, Halifax: Fernwood.

Bell, J. M. and D. Hartmann (2007), 'Diversity in Everyday Discourse: The Cultural Ambiguities and Consequences of "happy Talk"', *American Sociological Review*, 72 (6): 895–914. doi:10.2307/25472502.

Bourdieu, P. and L. J. D. Wacquant (1992), *An Invitation to Reflexive Sociology*, Chicago: University of Chicago Press.

Brown, K. D. (2014), 'Teaching in Colour: A Critical Race Theory in education Analysis of the Literature on Preservice Teachers of Colour and teacher Education in the US', Race Ethnicity and Education, 17 (3): 326–45.

Brown, M. K., M. Carnoy, E. Currie, T. Duster, D. B. Oppenheimer, M. M. Shultz and D. Wellman (2003), *Whitewashing Race: The Myth of a Colour-blind Society*, Oakland: University of California Press.

Canada Department of Justice (1982), *Canadian Charter of Rights and Freedoms*. Available online: http://laws-lois.justice.gc.ca/eng/Const/page-15.html (accessed 15 October 2021).

Chinnery, A. (2008), 'Revisiting "The Master's Tools": Challenging Common Sense in Cross-cultural Teacher Education', *Equity and Excellence in Education*, 41 (4): 395–404.

Cochran-Smith, M. (2003), 'Standing at the Crossroads: Multicultural Teacher Education at the Beginning of the 21st Century', *Multicultural Perspectives*, 5 (3): 3–11.

Coulthard, G. S. (2014), *Red Skin, White Masks: Rejecting the Colonial Politics of Recognition*, Minneapolis: University of Minnesota Press.

Cross, B. E. (2005), 'New Racism, Reformed Teacher Education, and the Same ole' Oppression', *Educational Studies: Journal of the American Educational Studies Association*, 38 (3): 263–74. doi:10.1207/s15326993es3803_6.

Delgado, R. and J. Stefancic (2000), *Critical Race Theory: The Cutting Edge*, Philadelphia: Temple University Press.

Dion, S. (2007), 'Disrupting Molded Images: Identities, Responsibilities and Relationships -teachers and Indigenous Subject Material', *Teaching Education*, 18 (4): 329–42. doi:10.1080/10476210701687625.

Donald, D. (2012), 'Forts, Colonial Frontier Logics, and Aboriginal-Canadian Relations: Imagining Decolonizing Educational Philosophies in Canadian Contexts', in A. A. Abdi (ed.), *Decolonizing Philosophies of Education*, 91–111, Rotterdam: Sense Publishers.

Dowd, A. C. (2008), 'The Community College as Gateway and Gatekeeper: Moving Beyond the Access "Saga" to Outcome Equity', *Harvard Educational Review*, 77 (4): 407–19.

Etikan, I., S. A. Musa and R. S. Alkassim (2016), 'Comparison of Convenience Sampling and Purposive Sampling', *American Journal of Theoretical and Applied Statistics*, 5 (1): 1–4. doi:10.11648/j.ajtas.20160501.11.

Ferrarotti, F. (1981), 'On the Autonomy of the Biographical Method', in B. Bertraux (ed.), *Biography and society: The Life History Approach in the Social Sciences*, 19–27, Beverly-Hills: Sage.

Fleras, A. and J. H. L. Elliott (2002), *Engaging Diversity: Multiculturalism in Canada*, Toronto: Nelson Thomson Learning.

Gorski, P. C. (2008), 'What we're Teaching Teachers: An Analysis of Multicultural Teacher Education Coursework Syllabi', *Teaching and Teacher Education*, 25 (2): 309–18. doi:10.1016/j.tate.2008.07.008.

Grimmett, P. P. and J. C. Young (2012), *Teacher Certification and the Professional Status of Teaching in North America: The new Battleground for Public Education*, Charlotte: Information Age Publishers.

Gomez, M. L., A. R. Allen and L. Clinton (2004), 'Cultural Models of Care in Teaching: A Case Study of one pre-service Secondary Teacher', *Teaching and Teacher Education*, 20 (5): 473–88.

Haig-Brown, C. (2011), 'Decolonizing Diaspora', in A. A. Abdi (ed.), *Decolonizing Philosophies of Education*, 73–90, Rotterdam: Sense Publishers.

Henry, F. and C. Tator (2009a), 'Introduction: Racism in the Canadian University', in F. Henry and C. Tator (eds), *Racism in The Canadian University: Demanding Social Justice, Inclusion, and Equity*, 3–21, Toronto: University of Toronto Press.

Henry, F. and C. Tator (2009b), 'Theoretical Perspectives and Manifestations of Racism in The Academy', in F. Henry and C. Tator (eds), *Racism in The Canadian University: Demanding Social Justice, Inclusion, and Equity*, 22–59, Toronto: University of Toronto Press.

Janzen, M. and J. Cranston (2016), 'The Challenges of Implementing a Diversity Admission Policy', *University Affairs*, 27 June. Available online: http://www.universityaffairs.ca/opinion/in-my-opinion/challenges-implementing-diversity-admissions-policy/ (accessed 15 October 2021).

Joshee, R. (2004), 'Citizenship and Multicultural Education in Canada: From Assimilation to Social Cohesion', in J. Banks (ed.), *Diversity and Citizenship Education: Global Perspectives*, 127–56, San Francisco: Jossey-Bass.

Kerr, J. and A. Parent (2018), 'The First Peoples' Principles of Learning in Teacher Education: Responding to the Truth and Reconciliation Commission's Calls to Action', *Canadian Journal of Native Education*, 40 (1): 36–53.

Kubota, R. (2015), 'Race and Language Learning in Multicultural Canada: Towards Critical Antiracism', *Journal of Multilingual and Multicultural Development*, 36 (1): 3–12.

Kvale, S. (1996), *Interviews: An Introduction to Qualitative research Interviewing*, Thousand Oaks: Sage.

Ladson-Billings, G. (1998), 'Just What is Critical Race Theory and What's it Doing in a Nice Field Like Education?', *International Journal of Qualitative Studies in Education*, 11 (1): 7–24. doi:10.1080/095183998236863.

Ladson-Billings, G. (1999), 'Preparing Teachers for Diverse Student Populations: A Critical Race Theory Perspective', *Review of Research in Education*, 24: 211–47. doi:10.2307/1167271.

Ladson-Billings, G. (2005), 'The Evolving Role of Critical Race Theory in Educational Scholarship', *Race Ethnicity and Education*, 8 (1): 115–19. doi:10.1080/1361332052000341024.

Lawrence, B. and E. Dua (2011), 'Decolonizing Anti-racism', in A. Mathur, J. Dewar and M. DeGagné (eds), *Cultivating Canada: Reconciliation Through the Lens of Cultural Diversity*, 233–63, Ottawa: Aboriginal Healing Foundation.

Li, G., J. Anderson, J. Hare and M. McTavish, eds (2021), *Superdiversity and Teacher Education: Supporting Teachers in Working With Culturally, Linguistically, and Racially Diverse Students, Families, and Communities*, New York: Routledge.

Lippi-Green, R. (2012), *English With an Accent: Language, Ideology, and Discrimination in the United States*, 2nd edn, New York: Routledge.

Malcolm, C. (2016), 'Trudeau Says Canada has no "Core Identity"', *Toronto Sun*, 14 September. Available online: http://www.torontosun.com/2016/09/14/trudeau-says-canada-has-no-core-identity (accessed 15 October 2021).

Marom, L. (2015), 'Contradicting Trajectories of Diversity and Exclusion in Policies Related to Internationally Educated Teachers in British Columbia', *International Journal of Interdisciplinary Civic and Political Studies*, 10 (2): 1–12.

Marom, L. (2017a), 'Mapping the Field: Examining the Recertification of Internationally Educated Teachers', *Canadian Journal of Education*, 40 (3): 2–34.

Marom, L. (2017b), 'Eastern/Western Conceptions of the "Good Teacher" and the Construction of Difference in Teacher Education', *Asia-Pacific Journal of Teacher Education*, 45 (6): 1–17. doi:10.1080/1359866X.2017.1399982.

Marom, L. (2019a), 'From Experienced Teachers to Newcomers to the Profession: The Capital Conversion of Internationally Educated Teachers in Canada', *Journal of Teaching and Teacher Education*, 78 (2): 85–96. doi:10.1016/j.tate.2018.11.006.

Marom, L. (2019b), 'Under the Cloak of Professionalism: Covert Racism in Teacher Education', *Race Ethnicity and Education*, 22 (3): 319–37. doi:10.1080/13613324.2018.1468748.

Marom, L. and C. Ruitenberg (2018), 'Professionalism Discourses and Neoliberalism in Teacher Education', *Alberta Journal of Educational Research*, 64 (4): 364–77.

Maynard, R. (2017), *Policing Black Lives: State Violence in Canada From Slavery to the Present*, Halifax: Fernwood Publishing.

Mufwene, S. (1998), 'Native Speaker, Proficient Speaker and Norms', in R. Singh (ed.), *The Native Speaker: Multilingual Perspectives*, 111–23, New Delhi: Sage.

Picower, B. (2009), 'The Unexamined Whiteness of Teaching: How White Teachers Maintain and Enact Dominant Racial Ideologies', *Race, Ethnicity and Education*, 12 (2): 197–215.

Ryan, J., K. Pollock and F. Antonelli (2009), 'Teacher Diversity in Canada: Leaky Pipelines, Bottlenecks, and Glass Ceilings', *Canadian Journal of Education*, 32 (3): 591–617.

Satzewich, V. and N. Liodakis (2010), *'Race' and Ethnicity in Canada: A Critical Introduction*, 2nd edn, Don Mills: Oxford University Press.

Schmidt, C. (2010), 'Introduction: Moving From the Personal to the Political in IET Scholarship', *Canadian Journal of Educational Administration and Policy*, 100: 1–4.

Seidman, I. (2005), *Interviewing as a Qualitative research*, 2nd edn, New York: Teacher College Press.

Simpson, J. S., C. E. James and J. Mack (2011), 'Multiculturalism, Colonialism, and Racialization: Conceptual Starting Points', *Review of Education, Pedagogy, and Cultural Studies*, 33 (4): 285–305. doi:10.1080/10714413.2011.597637.

Sleeter, C. E. and H. R. Milner (2011), 'Researching Successful Efforts in Teacher Education to Diversify Teachers', in A. F. Ball and C. A. Tyson (eds), *Studying Diversity in Teacher Education*, 81–104, Lanham: Rowman and Littlefield.

Solórzano, D. G., M. Ceja and T. Yosso (2000), 'Critical Race Theory, Racial Microaggressions, and Campus Racial Climate: The Experiences of African American College Students', *Journal of Negro Education*, 69 (1/2): 60–73.

Solórzano, D. G., and T. J. Yosso (2002), 'Critical Race Methodology: Counter-storytelling as an Analytical Framework for Education Research', *Qualitative Inquiry*, 8 (1): 23–44.

St. Denis, V. (2011), 'Silencing Aboriginal Curricular Content and Perspectives Through Multiculturalism: "There are Other Children Here"', *Review of Education, Pedagogy and Cultural Studies*, 33 (4): 306–17. doi:10.1080/10714413.2011.597638.

Statistics Canada (2021), *Population Growth and Demography*. Available online: https://www.statcan.gc.ca/eng/subjects-start/population_and_demography (accessed 15 October 2021).

Stein, S. (2019), 'Navigating Different Theories of Change for Higher Education in Volatile Times', *Educational Studies*, 55 (6): 667688. doi:10.1080/00131946.2019.1666717.

Stein, S. (2021), 'What can Decolonial and Abolitionist Critiques Teach the Field of Higher Education?', *The Review of Higher Education*, 44 (3): 387–414. doi:10.1353/rhe.2021.0000.

Sue, D. W., J. Bucceri, A. I. Lin, K. L. Nadal and G. C. Torino (2007), 'Racial Microaggressions and the Asian American Experience', *Cultural Diversity and Ethnic Minority Psychology*, 13 (1): 72–81.

Tate, W. F. and G. Ladson-Billings (1995), 'Toward a Critical Race Theory of Education', *Teachers College Record*, 97 (1): 47–68.

Thobani, S. (2007), *Exalted Subjects: Studies in the Making of Race and Nation in Canada*, Toronto: University of Toronto Press.

Thompson, A. (1998), 'Not the Colour Purple: Black Feminist Lessons for Educational Caring', *Harvard Educational Review*, 68 (4): 522–54.

Thompson, A. (2003), 'Tiffany, Friend of People of Colour: White Investments in Antiracism', *International Journal of Qualitative Studies in Education*, 16 (1): 7–29.

Truth and Reconciliation Commission of Canada (2015), 'Honouring the Truth, Reconciling for the Future: Summary of the Final Report of The Truth and Reconciliation Commission of Canada', 23 July. Available online: http://www.trc.ca/websites/trcinstitution/File/2015/Honouring_the_Truth_Reconciling_for_the_Future_July_23_2015.pdf.

Yosso, T. J. (2005), 'Whose Culture has Capital? A Critical Race Theory Discussion of Community Cultural Wealth', *Race Ethnicity and Education*, 8 (1): 69–91. doi:10.1080/1361332052000341006.

12

A Two-Tiered System of Teacher Preparation

Kerry Kretchmar

1. Neoliberalism and Education

A global proliferation of neoliberalism has been underway since the 1970s and is evident in policies, governance, the ways we understand and talk about society and what is valued (Harvey 2006). Neoliberalism prioritizes freedom and individualism over the collective, both of which are defined in consumer terms. Neoliberal policies promote the free market, personal responsibility, choice and private enterprise and view government as ineffective and bureaucratic. This has led to increased privatization and deregulation and decreased state intervention, coupled with the defunding of public services, such as higher education, libraries and health care (Apple 2006; Burch 2009; Harvey 2006). Finally, neoliberal capitalism is inextricably linked to racism and both are deeply intertwined to frame American society (Kelley 2017; Kendi 2019; Robinson 2000). In a society in which policies, institutions and practices are racist (e.g. segregated, unequal neighbourhoods and schools, the impact of the carceral state of Black Americans and voter suppression among communities of colour), the 'free market' upholds those inequities and further perpetuates White supremacy (Kelly 2017; Kendi 2019; Robinson 2000).

Shifts towards neoliberalism are evident in many spheres of life but are especially profound in American education, which has experienced trends towards choice, accountability and efficiency. This is illustrated through policies such as the dramatic expansion of school choice, school evaluation and ranking based on standardized tests scores as mandated by the 2001 No Child Left Behind Act and its 2015 reauthorization (The Every Student Succeeds Act), merit pay initiatives for teachers and the deregulation of teacher education (Apple 2006; Ball 2012; Burch 2009; Ravitch 2010). The focus on bureaucratic problems and managerial solutions, rather than resource neglect and racist public policy, obscures the racist structural, systemic and historical root causes of an increasingly stratified society. Education reforms often avoid a racial and economic analysis in order to persuade the general public that we do not have to alleviate poverty or dismantle racism to work towards equity (Apple 2006; Lipman 2013).

Yet as Apple (2011: 224) wrote in a critical analysis of teacher preparation and globalization, '[n]one of this can be understood without also recognizing the ways in which the realities of the United States are influenced and often shaped by our connections with economic, political, and cultural policies, movements, and struggles outside our official borders'. Neoliberalism is a global phenomenon and, in a broad sense, it has caused a shift towards an understanding of education as a commodity whose main purpose is producing workers (Friedrich 2016). Globally, phrases such as knowledge-based economy and human capital education are commonly used in the public narrative and within policy to articulate the shared purposes of schooling (Spring 2008). Yet, this uniform approach is contested and often comes into conflict with local culture and values for schooling (Spring 2008). Policies, pedagogies and the politics of a globalized neoliberal education system have 'involved major conflicts, contradictions, and compromises among groups with competing visions of "legitimate" knowledge, what counts as "good" teaching and learning, and what is a "just" nation-state and world order connected to globalization' (Singh, Kenway and Apple 2005: 10). Despite those tensions, an overarching notion that education can become borderless to serve our globalized economy prevails and often fails to account for the ways this approach can also perpetuate systemic inequities (Apple 2011; Hursh and Martina 2003).

2. Schooling in the United States

Amid a global context that is attempting to define education's purpose and values in a uniform way as the production of workers, the United States offers an example of the complexities and inequities that arise amid a neoliberal educational system. The US two-tiered teacher education system is a product of a stratified and diverse school system, in which state and local governments are primarily responsible for funding, policy, school decision-making and teacher certification and education. Ninety per cent of school funding comes from state and local sources (Epstein 2011).[1] Although education funding formulas are complex, local property taxes play a key role in how schools receive funding and typically lead to students living in upper-middle-class areas attending schools with more resources, while schools serving students of colour living in poor areas are less resourced (Epstein 2011: 3). In addition, local and state school control results in significant variations in terms of curriculum, organization of the classroom, teacher certification requirements and how effective teaching is defined and evaluated. An illuminating example of this is the ways textbook companies create different versions of American history texts for states with different political leanings (Chick and Altoona 2006). Throughout the history of American schools, tensions around conflicting views on the purpose, values and curriculum have been a constant (Tyack and Cuban 1995).

As a result of a diverse system, teachers' working conditions vary by school and district. Teachers working in schools that serve low-income families and families of colour often face lower salaries and challenging work conditions, including more intense accountability cultures that lead to less autonomy and result in high teacher turnover (Darling-Hammond 2016: 51). Sutcher, Darling-Hammond and Carver-Thomas (2016: 51) write, 'The United States lacks a systematic approach to recruiting, preparing, and retaining teachers, or for using the skills of accomplished teachers to help improve schools'. Teaching conditions in the United States are framed by unequal resources, limited government supports, dramatically different levels of training, low salaries and little time for collaboration of professional learning. Teachers work 'under radically different teaching conditions – with those in the most affluent communities benefiting from small classes and a cornucopia of materials, equipment, specialists, and supports, while those in the poorest communities teach classes of 30 or more without adequate books and supplies' (Sutcher, Darling-Hammond and Carver-Thomas 2016: 53). Thus, teacher preparation in the United States cannot be separated from the varied conditions of teaching and the larger inequities that shape the American school system and society including poverty (Berliner 2013; Rothstein 2004) and racism (Ladson-Billings 2014; Love 2019).

3. The Current State of Teacher Education

Teacher preparation programmes have historically struggled to produce both enough teachers and effective educators (Fraser 2007). Teacher shortages are a persistent problem in low-income areas due to high teacher turnover, among other factors (Ingersoll and Smith 2003). The quality of university-based teacher preparation programmes has varied significantly with some excellent teacher preparation programmes that interconnect theory, clinical practice and communities to prepare effective educators (Darling-Hammond 2006) as well as ineffective and poor teacher preparation programmes (Levine 2006). Strong university-based teacher preparation programmes view teachers as professionals, focus on learner and learning-cantered pedagogy, evaluate effectiveness using holistic performance assessments and develop complex and varied and adaptive knowledge, skills and dispositions in educators (Darling-Hammond 2006; Darling-Hammond and Bransford 2007). Successful programmes equip educators with the theory and tools to resist a racist and classist system in their classrooms (Delpit 2006; Gorski 2006). While that is the model of strong programmes, not all university-based teacher preparation programmes include these components and many programmes fail to balance theory and practice effectively (Levine 2006) or position the teacher as a saviour who frame their work through a deficit view in which they must save children in poverty (Delpit 2006; Gorski 2006).

Over the last twenty-five years, the United States has experienced a proliferation of fast-track, non-university-based teacher preparation programmes supported by policies and funding seeking to deregulate teacher education (Zeichner 2010). This is fuelled by the overarching narrative that public institutions in the United States are failing and must be privatized and reformed through neoliberal policies, including initiatives such as charter school expansion, voucher programmes, merit pay for teachers and mayoral control in large districts that primarily target and impact low-income communities of colour (Apple 2006 Berliner and Glass 2014; Chubb and Moe 1990). In recent years, teachers and teacher education have been a frequent target of blame for educational inequities. In his book *Bad Teacher*, Kevin Kumashiro (2015) describes the common narrative that if teachers and students 'simply try hard enough' learning will occur and the 'success or failure of an educational system gets placed on the shoulders of the most visible individuals in the educational landscape'(Kumashiro 2015: 18) despite the contextual factors such as unequal funding and resources that frame the system. Public perception of school success in the United States often focuses on the individual teacher and moves attention away from the broader systemic issues (Kumashiro 2015: 21).

At the same time teachers and teacher preparation are blamed for school inequities, 70–80 per cent of the nation's teachers are still prepared in public colleges and universities, yet these programmes have been impacted by dramatic budget cuts to higher education (Newfield 2018). University-based teacher education programme's ability to innovate and improve has been constrained by budget cuts (Zeichner 2011). Between 2008 and 2013, states cut $16 billion from higher education budgets (Hiltonsmith and Draut 2014). Covid-19 led to even more drastic cuts to already lean budgets. Higher education in California alone faced a $1.7 billion reduction in Governor Newsom's 2020 budget (Murakami 2020). At the same time, significant funding and policy support has poured into the expansion of fast-track preparation programmes that operate independently from Universities, like *Teach For America* and Relay Graduate School of Education (GSE). Even amid the pandemic, the number of incoming *Teach For America* corps members in 2020 remained relatively stable from 2019 (Teach For America 2020).

As budgets are cut for higher education programmes, increased accountability demands have influenced the operation and structure of teacher education programmes (Gatti 2016; Sleeter 2008;Zeichner 2010). Zeichner (2010) argued that an increase in reporting and measuring all aspects of teacher preparation to state departments of education detracts from quality teacher preparation, as teacher educators are forced to focus their energy and effort on rationalizing and documenting every element of their work and programme.

4. Fast-Track Teacher Preparation

As resources for universities and colleges diminish and accountability demands increase, focused philanthropic and federal funding has led to the proliferation of teacher certification programmes that function independently from universities. Different variations of programmes exist under this umbrella, yet fast-track teacher preparation programmes that construct teaching through a narrow neoliberal lens, including a technocratic focus on teaching and an exacting focus on standardized test scores, constitute the largest type and they have experienced significant funding and policy support. These programmes prepare teachers primarily for schools that serve high proportions of low-income students of colour and conceptualize the teacher as a technician, use test scores as the primary indicators of a teacher's success and approach teacher preparation through a prescriptive and teacher-centric model (Kretchmar and Zeichner 2016).

Teach For America (TFA)[2] is the most well-known of these programmes. Each year, TFA places the 'best and the brightest' recent college graduates, the vast majority of whom have not studied education, in classrooms in 'under-resourced urban and rural' schools (Teach For America website 2015).[3] TFA teachers are trained in a five-week summer institute before being hired by school districts across the country for a limited two-year commitment (Heilig and Jez 2010, 2014). In its inception, TFA purportedly ameliorated a teacher shortage in low-income areas. As the organization grew and teacher shortages were no longer occurring in many partner districts, TFA began to argue their teachers were more effective than traditionally trained teacher and created contracts that privileged TFA teachers over university-based teachers (Brewer et al. 2016). This is a stark contrast to most university-based programmes that are two to four years and provide a full semester of student teaching field placement and attempt to prepare teachers for a long professional career.

TFA and other fast-track programmes typically share a number of characteristics grounded in neoliberal ideologies. Teaching is approached in a technocratic way. Effective teaching is evaluated and defined as standardized tests and measurable metrics, and teachers are viewed as solely responsible for student achievement or failure (Brewer 2014). Programmes such as Relay proudly present themselves in opposition to teacher education programmes' focus on theory (Kretchmar and Zeichner 2016). Preparation is devoid of attention to the relational and sociocultural elements that impact teaching and learning. A curricular analysis from three representative fast-track programmes, *Teach For America, Relay* and *MATCH*, found that training materials were narrowly focused on strategies. The strategies themselves included practices such as learning stations and wait time which are widely accepted, yet these were presented in prescriptive and teacher-directed ways, like a checklist of technical skills to accomplish without the tools or theory to help educators analyse individual learner's needs and make differentiated decisions in a dynamic classroom. Further the materials lacked a depth of analysis related to race, power, poverty or sociocultural theory, although they are preparing teachers to work with low-income populations of colour (Kretchmar and Zeichner 2016) despite a long body of research that contends that this sort of understanding of race, privilege and class is critical to being a culturally relevant educator (Delpit 2006; Ladson-Billings 2014). This view of teaching as a technocratic practice that defines learning through measurable metrics reflects neoliberal conceptions of teacher preparation (Kumashiro 2015).

The growth of fast-track teacher preparation models can be partially attributed to TFA (Kretchmar, Sondel and Ferrare 2016). Research on TFA alumni demonstrated that they understand educational change through managerial terms, believing that inequity is a result of resource mismanagement and a lack of accountability and that solutions lie rest with individuals and can be found in ideas such as merit pay for teachers, increased autonomy for leadership, standardization and an end to teachers unions' ability to collective bargain over working conditions and wages (Trujillo and Scott 2014). Research has illuminated TFA's connection to broader efforts to reform education through neoliberal initiatives and the ways TFA alumni serve as key connectors in a wide-ranging and varied network that has promoted policies including charter district reform and the deregulation of teacher education (Kretchmar, Sondel and Ferrare 2014; Lahann and Reagan 2011). TFA alumni frequently serve as founders, leaders and workers in organizations that are expanding of charter schools, fast-track teacher preparation programmes and other related neoliberal educational ventures (Kretchmar, Sondel and Ferrare 2014, 2016; Higgins, Hess, Weiner and Robison 2011).

Teach For America and other fast-track programmes frequently teach in 'no-excuses' charter school networks like KIPP[4] and Uncommon Schools[5] that serve low-income students of colour and focus on an extended school day and year, a strict and rigid environment and with the main goal and indicator of effective education as standardized test scores. 'No-excuses' charter schools have faced significant critiques for their use of direct instruction (Goodman 2013), narrow focus on raising standardized test scores (Sondel 2015) and racist hiring practices, discipline policies and school cultures (Sondel, Kretchmar and Dunn 2019).

Both 'no-excuse' charter school and the fast-track teacher preparation training model have grown due to focused and strategic funding (Grossman and Loeb 2008). The federal government has increased funding to fast-track routes to teacher preparation and decreased funds to university-based teacher preparation programmes. Venture philanthropists, in particular the Walton, Gates, Dell and Fischer Foundations, have promoted neoliberal educational policies through unprecedented and strategic contributions to shape the current urban educational system (Colvin 2005; Scott 2009). These foundations operate under the assumption that educational reform will benefit from the same principles and strategies that have proven successful in the business world, particularly a focus on competition, accountability and efficiency (Scott 2009). For instance, through an analysis of grant data from the fifteen largest K-12 grantmakers in 2000, 2005 and 2010, Reckhow and Snyder (2014) found that most major education foundations supported neoliberal initiatives such as fast-track teacher preparation programmes, charter management organizations (CMOs) and management training programmes. In addition, they found an increasing convergence in donations; the top fifteen funders tend to give money to the same organizations, indicating overlap in their agenda and policy goals. The greatest example of this convergence is TFA, which received a total of $44.5 million from thirteen of the top fifteen funders in 2010.

In addition to supporting the expansion of fast-track programmes, foundations and the federal government have specifically promoted the growth of charter schools of education that operate independently from university systems financially and through policy. While many similar programmes exist and the number is growing, the largest among these is Relay GSE, an independent, masters-granting institution that currently has eighteen locations and was created in partnership with KIPP, Achievement First, Uncommon CMOs and TFA (Relay 2020). These programmes prepare and licence teachers in a variety forms but typically use accelerated models that approach teacher preparation through a teacher as technician model.

As noted in the discussion of the general state of teacher preparation, the neoliberalization of the American educational system has come with increased and narrow accountability measures for teacher preparation programmes. Fast-track programmes such as TFA and Relay GSE are centred and designed around intensive accountability metrics, which primarily measure teaching effectiveness through standardized assessment data (Brewer 2014; Foote 2009). For example, Relay GSE requires that all graduates show at least a year's worth of growth in their students using measurable metrics. TFA requires corps members to set yearly significant gains goals in their classes, often defined as 80 per cent of students achieving a year and a half of growth on standardized test scores (Brewer 2014). These programmes rely heavily on standardized proof points to secure philanthropic and federal funding.

Many critics of university-based teacher education have used the growth and ostensible success of these fast-track and charter programmes to promote further deregulation of teacher education (Mehta and Teles 2012; Zeichner and Pena-Sandoval 2015). Think tanks and advocacy organizations such as the American Enterprise Institute and National Council on Teacher Quality (NCTQ), among others, have long contended that teacher education would benefit from neoliberal reforms and alternative pathways into the profession, to increase competition among providers and recruit different candidates into the profession (Hess 2001). Alternative pathways to teaching are growing as a result and some require even less training than fast-track programmes. In fact, the American Board for Certification in Teacher Excellence (ABCTE), which requires only a bachelor's degree, background check and certification test, is an approved pathway to becoming a teacher in fourteen states (American Board for the Certification in Teacher Excellence 2020).

While the current landscape of teacher preparation is more complex and variable by state than I can fully describe in the scope of this chapter, the context presented above presents a neoliberal system where the expansion of fast-track preparation programmes and charter schools of education are providing preparation of teachers for low-income schools that primarily serve students of colour, while schools in middle-class and wealthy communities continue to be staffed by teachers prepared through university-based programmes (Kretchmar and Zeichner 2016). This increasingly bifurcated model of teacher preparation is constructing teachers differently with significant implications for equity. Teachers who are primarily working with students of colour in low-income areas are being constructed to view teaching as a short-term, prescriptive job and their training is devoid of many of the theoretical understandings needed to develop adaptive, dynamic educators. This is in contrast to the preparation of many teachers working with middle-class and wealthy communities, who are prepared to translate theory into practice in the classroom in service of meeting the needs of all learners and a sustained career as an educator. The quality of university-based teacher preparation varies widely, and this is not an attempt to claim that all teachers in middle-class and upper-class communities are effective. Instead, the intention is to note glaring inequities in a system in which students in higher-income, whiter areas receive teachers prepared with a more robust conception of teaching and learning, while teachers prepared to work in lower-income areas with higher proportions of students of colour are offered a narrow and neoliberal view of teaching and learning via fast-track programmes.

5. The Global Construction of Teachers

The neoliberal model of education has a global reach both through the exportation of the TFA model and through the ways international educators are recruited and trained in the United States.

Teach For America's fast-track preparation model, leadership training and ideology have been exported to fifty-eight other countries through *Teach For All*, a programme started by TFA's founder, Wendy Kopp (Teach For All 2020). Like TFA, *Teach For All* offers a two-pronged mission that focuses on preparing teachers in fast-track programmes and developing leaders who will look to managerial, neoliberal reforms and solutions for education. *Teach For All*'s 'common theory of change is situated in ideologies of equality, accountability, and measurable impact' (La Londe, Brewer and Lubienski 2015: 3). Partnering with Teach For All is an attractive proposition in many countries as explained by Friedrich (2016: 163):

> They promise to deliver teacher education in a cost-effective manner (public monies cover only a portion, if any, of the service), providing high-needs schools with quality educators in a matter of weeks. As opposed to State-provided teacher education, Teach For All follows the market logic of supply and demand to manage growth, contraction and closure. In exchange for providing this service, the only thing *Teach For All* seems to be asking of the State is a seat at the table where educational policy is decided.

Like TFA, Teach For All's influence extends far beyond teacher preparation and it impacts educational policy and reform by promoting neoliberal initiatives grounded in the belief that teachers are the 'root cause for student achievement or failure instead of the plethora of contextual out-of-school factors that actually inform student achievement' (La Londe, Brewer and Lubienski 2015: 18). Despite some brief references to understanding local traditions, Teach For All generally approaches teacher preparation and educational policy as borderless and unified around the same narrow, managerial vision of teaching and learning as Teach For America (La Londe, Brewer and Lubienski 2015: 18).

The same neoliberal ideologies of TFA and *Teach For All* are present in the way international teachers are recruited, trained and treated in the United States with a focus on efficiency and a narrow, metric-based vision of teaching and learning. Teachers come to the United States from other countries for a variety of reasons, but due to the deregulated environment a lack of oversight or policies related to international teachers often results in exploitation. International teachers are frequently charged 'ongoing, exorbitant fees for everything from placement to transportation to one's own insurance' (Dunn 2016: 10). As Dunn explains (2016: 1):

> [a]lmost 20,000 international teachers on temporary visas pay $5,000–$6,500 each to enter and work in the United States, and districts pay finders' fees of up to $11,500 per teacher. As a result, educators are literally 'sold' as both a solution to the staffing shortage and, in the words of the recruiters, as 'cultural ambassadors' for urban youth.

Often, international teachers who are recruited to come to the United States face challenges including no training in American culture and schools, policies and a lack of preparation or support for teaching students of colour or students in poverty (Dunn 2013; 2016). Dunn (2013: 188) writes:

So are teachers without borders a reality or a possibility? I would counter the neoliberal globalizing rhetoric that claims that there are no borders; such claims only fortify the cultural borders experienced between teachers and students. By pretending that cultures and nations do not matter, we are only making them matter more. If we were more serious in our consideration of the borders that do exist, we could actually develop teachers who transcend them and start to break them down. That requires a commitment to challenging the political spectacle of neoliberal globalization and the master narrative of urban school reform that teaching is easy and that culture does not matter.

International teachers have the potential to be effective educators who offer unique insights and perspectives, but when they are recruited and onboarded into a neoliberal system in a way that is devoid of attention to context or culture, they are often unable to fulfil that potential (Dunn 2013). We cannot presume international teachers understand US schools because they have been teachers in another context. They need unique supports in order to merge their backgrounds and strengths effectively into the US context (Dunn 2013: 171). Teacher educators should have a role in the preparation of international teachers through specific professional development, coaching and preparing American teachers to collaborate successfully with international teachers (Dunn 2013: 171).

6. Vision for Teacher Preparation

To capture the complexities of the profession and build on the assets educators from a variety of backgrounds can bring to the system, a new vision for teacher preparation must exist outside of the current limited neoliberal framework examined above. We must view teachers and teacher preparation as one important component of an educational system that is shaped by larger societal forces including poverty and racism (Berliner 2013; Rothstein 2004). Teachers and teacher educators need to understand the way society outside of the classroom impacts student learning, and they need theory and skills that can support them to navigate their context and work relationally with students, communities and families (Darling-Hammond 2006; Apple 2011). Simply put, a new vision for teacher preparation and teaching cannot solely be centred on teachers but must include broader struggles for economic and racial justice. Schools and teacher preparation alone cannot solve the challenges of poverty (Duncan and Murnane 2011) in a system where a majority of American public school students live in poverty (Suitts 2015).

A new vision for teacher preparation must emphasize the development of future citizens as much the production of workers. This requires teacher preparation programmes to serve as a model of democracy with authentic community engagement built into their structures. Community members and parents can play key roles in developing programmes and defining and evaluating effective teachers. These spaces of teacher preparation must do more than develop the tools for teachers to critique structural inequities and racism; instead, these programmes must shift power in practice and develop new structures for teacher preparation that strive to be anti-racist and powered by the community (Zeichner, Payne and Brayko 2015). Examples of a more democratic approach exist. For example, such teacher education programmes at University of Washington that hired community organizers to mentor pre-service teachers (Zeichner, Payne and Brayko 2015) and the Grow Your Own Illinois[6] programme recruits community members, parents and organizers to become teachers (Skinner, Garreton and Schultz 2011). Rather than neoliberal ideas informing what constitutes effective education, communities, parents and teachers must work together to determine what they value and how to shape students and teaching.

This vision would strive to create community teachers described by Murrell (2001: 4) as 'Community teachers have a clear sense of their own cultural, political, and racial identities in relation to the children and families they hope to serve. This sense allows themes to play a central role in the successful development and education of their students.'

US and international educators have the potential to become community teachers through support and preparation that develops a depth of understanding of the community and culture they are teaching in, as well as how their experiences and cultural background can inform and bolster their connection to teaching.

Teachers have to learn in context and find a way to merge their own background and experience with the language, culture and history of their school's community/communities. Community teachers are able to draw on the cultural capital of students to effectively engage them in authentic learning (Gay 2010) and teach in ways that are informed by community knowledge (Darling-Hammond 2006). Learning must be contextualized and relevant and meaningful (Darling-Hammond 2006; Delpit 2006; Ladson-Billings 2014). Drawing on community knowledge helps students learn and can disrupt negative perceptions of families and communities, particularly in high poverty areas (Murrell 2001). Learning from and about families and the communities of students allows teachers to develop a perspective of working alongside communities in solidarity versus trying to fix them or save students from communities.

This approach offers uniquely powerful possibilities for international teachers but it requires strategic support, mentorship and orientation in order to help international teachers develop a rich and complex understanding of US schools (Dunn 2013: 187). As noted by Singh Kenway and Apple (2005: 23), 'Teachers engaged in responsive educational policies, pedagogies, and politics provide a source of hope in the struggles against complacency of neoliberal globalism and the resentment engendered by globalization from above.' Teachers cannot be isolated as the sole determinant in student achievement and yet educators hold important agency and hope for creating something new.

7. Conclusion

The two-tiered educational system in the United States offers a glimpse into the limitations of a neoliberal system and the ways this can exacerbate inequities. At the same time that we critique and question the practices within this system, we must imagine and vision something new and look to build models for teacher preparation and support that embody the sort of world we want to live in.

Notes

1. Approximately 10 per cent of K-12 students in the United States attend private schools. Private schools in the United States range in focus, quality and teaching conditions (Council for American Private Education 2021).
2. Available online: https://www.teachforamerica.org/ (accessed 8 November 2021).
3. Some language at the TFA website was updated since 2015 due to critique. The updated language disguises the problem addressed.
4. Available online: https://www.kipp.org/ (accessed 8 November 2021).
5. Available online: https://uncommonschools.org/ (accessed 8 November 2021).
6. Available online: https://growyourownteachers.org/ (accessed 8 November 2021).

References

Apple, M. W. (2011), 'Global Crises, Social Justice, and Teacher Education', *Journal of Teacher Education*, 62 (2): 222–34.

Apple, M. (2006), *Educating the 'Right' way: Markets, Standards, God, and Inequality*, New York and London: Routledge.

Ball, S. (2012), *Global Education Inc.: New Policy Networks and the neo-liberal Imaginary*, London: Routledge.

Berliner, D. C. (2013), 'Effects of Inequality and Poverty vs. Teachers and Schooling on America's Youth', *Teachers College Record*, 115 (12): 1–26.

Berliner, D. C. and G. V. Glass, eds (2014), *50 Myths and Lies That Threaten America's Public Schools: The Real Crisis in Education*, New York: Teachers College Press.

Brewer, T. J. (2014), 'Accelerated Burnout: How Teach For America's Academic Impact Model and Theoretical Culture of Accountability Can Foster Disillusionment Among its Corps Members', *Educational Studies*, 50 (3): 246–63.

Brewer, T. J., K. Kretchmar, B. Sondel, S. Ishmael, and M. M. Manfra (2016), 'Teach for America's Preferential Treatment: School District Contracts, Hiring Decisions, and Employment Practices', *Education Policy Analysis Archives*, 24 (15): n15.

Burch, P. (2009), *Hidden Markets: The new Education Privatization*, New York: Routledge.

CAPE, Council for American Private Education (2021), Available online: https://www.capenet.org/facts.html (accessed 8 November 2021).

Chick, K. A. and S. Altoona (2006), 'Gender Balance in K-12 American History Textbooks', *Social Studies Research and Practice*, 1 (3): 284–90.

Chubb, J. E. and T. M. Moe (1990), *Politics, Markets, and America's Schools*, Washington, DC: Brookings Institution Press.

Colvin, R. L. (2005), 'A new Generation of Philanthropists and Their Great Ambitions', in F. M. Hess (ed.), *With the Best of Intentions: How Philanthropy is Reshaping K-12 Education*, 21–48, Cambridge, MA: Harvard Education Press.

Darling-Hammond, L. (2006), *Powerful Teacher Education: Lessons From Exemplary Programs*, San Francisco: Jossey-Bass.

Darling-Hammond, L. and J. Bransford, eds (2007), *Preparing Teachers for a Changing World: What Teachers Should Learn and be Able to do*, San Francisco: Jossey-Bass.

Delpit, L. (2006), *Other People's Children: Cultural Conflict in the Classroom*, New York: The New Press.

Duncan, G. J. and R. J. Murnane, eds (2011), *Whither Opportunity?: Rising Inequality, Schools, and Children's Life Chances*, New York: Russell Sage Foundation.

Dunn, A. H. (2013), *Teachers Without Borders?: The Hidden Consequences of International Teachers in U.S. Schools*, New York: Teachers College Press.

Dunn, A. H. (2016), 'Trafficked Teachers: Sucking Educator Labor Across Borders', *Journal of Curriculum and Pedagogy*, 13 (1): 30–3.

Epstein, D. (2011), 'Measuring Inequity in School Funding', Center for American Progress, 3 August. Available online: https://www.americanprogress.org/issues/education-k-12/reports/2011/08/03/10122/measuring-inequity-in-school-funding/ (accessed 8 November 2021).

Foote, D. (2009), *Relentless Pursuit: A Year in the Trenches With Teach for America*, New York: Vintage Press.

Fraser, J. W. (2007), *Preparing America's Teachers: A History*, New York: Teachers College Press.

Friedrich, D. (2016), 'Teach for all, Public–private Partnerships, and the Erosion of the Public in Education', in A. Verger, C. Lubienski and G. Steiner-Khamsi (eds), *World Yearbook of Education 2016: The Global Education Industry*, 160–74, London: Routledge.

Gay, G. (2010), *Culturally Responsive Teaching: Theory, Research, and Practice*, New York and London: Teachers College Press.

Gatti, L. (2016), *Toward a Framework of Resources for Learning to Teach: Rethinking US Teacher Preparation*, New York: Springer.

Goodman, J. F. (2013), 'Charter Management Organizations and the Regulated Environment: Is it Worth the Price?', *Educational Researcher*, 42 (2): 89–96.

Gorski, P. C. (2006), 'Complicity With Conservatism: The de-politicizing of Multicultural and Intercultural Education', *Intercultural Education*, 17 (2): 163–77.

Grossman, P. and S. Loeb, eds (2008), *Taking Stock: An Examination of Alternative Certification*, Cambridge, MA: Harvard Education Press.

Harvey, D. (2006), *A Brief History of Neoliberalism*, Oxford: Oxford University Press.

Heilig, J. V. and S. J. Jez (2010), 'Teach for America: A Review of the Evidence', *National Education Policy Center*, 9 June. Available online: https://nepc.colorado.edu/publication/teach-for-america (accessed 8 November 2021).

Heilig, J. V. and S. J. Jez (2014), 'Teach for America: A Return to the Evidence', *National Education Policy Center*, 7 January. Available online: https://nepc.colorado.edu/publication/teach-for-america-return (accessed 8 November 2021).

Hess, F. M. (2001). *Tear Down the Wall: The Case for a Radical Overhaul of Teacher Certification*, Washington, DC: The Progressive Policy Institute.

Higgins, M., F. M. Hess, J. Weiner, and W. Robison (2011), 'Creating a Corps of Change Agents: What Explains the Success of Teach for America?', *Education Next*, 11 (3): 18–26.

Hiltonsmith, R., & Draut, W. (2014). The great cost shift continues: State higher education funding after the recession. Dēmos.

Hursh, D. and C. A. Martina (2003), 'Neoliberalism and Schooling in the US: How State and Federal Government Education Policies Perpetuate Inequality', *Journal for Critical Education Policy Studies*, 1 (2): 1–13.

Ingersoll, R. M. and T. M. Smith (2003), 'The Wrong Solution to the Teacher Shortage', *Educational Leadership*, 60 (8): 30–3.

Kelley, R. D. (2017), 'What did Cedric Robinson Mean by Racial Capitalism', *Boston Review*, 12 January. Available online: http://bostonreview.net/race/robin-d-g-kelley-what-did-cedric-robinson-mean-racial-capitalism (accessed 8 November 2021).

Kendi, I. X. (2019), *How to be an Antiracist*, New York: One World/Ballantine.

Kumashiro, K. K. (2015), *Bad Teacher! How Blaming Teachers Distorts the Bigger Picture*, New York: Teachers College Press.

Kretchmar, K. and K. Zeichner (2016), 'Teacher Prep 3.0: A Vision for Teacher Education to Impact Social Transformation', *Journal of Education for Teaching*, 42 (4): 417–33.

Kretchmar, K., B. Sondel and J. J. Ferrare (2014), 'Mapping the Terrain: Teach for America, Charter School Reform, and Corporate Sponsorship', *Journal of Education Policy*, 29 (6): 742–59.

Ladson-Billings, G. (2014), 'Culturally Relevant Pedagogy 2.0: Aka The Remix', *Harvard Educational Review*, 84 (1): 74–84.

Lahann, R. and E. M. Reagan (2011), 'Teach for America and the Politics of Progressive Neoliberalism', *Teacher Education Quarterly*, 38 (1): 7–27.

La Londe, P. G., T. J. Brewer and C. A. Lubienski (2015), 'Teach for America and Teach for all: Creating an Intermediary Organization Network for Global Education Reform', *Education Policy Analysis Archives*, 23 (47): 1–25.

Levine, A. (2006), *Educating School Teachers*. Washington, DC: Education Schools Project.

Lipman, P. (2013), *The new Political Economy of Urban Education: Neoliberalism, Race, and the Right to the City*, New York: Routledge.

Love, B. L. (2019), *We Want to do More Than Survive: Abolitionist Teaching and the Pursuit of Educational Freedom*, Boston: Beacon Press.

McShane, M. Q. and Hess, F. M. (2014), 'The Politics of Entrepreneurship and Innovation', in B. S. Cooper, J. G. Cibulka and L. D. Fusarelli (eds), *Handbook of Education Politics and Policy*, 2nd edn, 304–21, New York: Routledge.

Mehta, J. and S. Teles (2012), 'Jurisdictional Politics: A new Federal Role in Education', in F. M. Hess and A. Kelly (eds), *Carrots, Sticks, and the Bully Pulpit: Lessons From a Half-century of Federal Efforts to Improve America's Schools*, 197–216, Cambridge, MA: Harvard Education Press.

Murakami, K. (2020), 'State Cuts Grow Deep', *Inside Higher ED*, 15 May. Available online: https://www.insidehighered.com/news/2020/05/15/size-state-budget-cuts-becomes-clearer (accessed 8 November 2021).

Murrell, C. Jr (2001), *The Community Teacher: A new Framework for Effective Urban Teaching*, New York: Teachers College Press.

Newfield, C. (2018), *The Great Mistake: How we Wrecked Public Universities and How We Can Fix Them*, Baltimore, MD: Johns Hopkins University Press.

Ravitch, D. (2010), *The Death and Life of the Great American School System: How Testing and Choice are Undermining Education*, New York: Basic Books.

Relay Graduate School of Education (2020), Available online: https://www.relay.edu/about-relay-history (accessed 8 November 2021).

Robinson, C. J. (2000), *Black Marxism: The Making of the Black Radical Tradition*, Chapel Hill/London: The University of North Carolina Press.

Rothstein, R. (2004), *Class and Schools: Using Social, Economic, and Educational Reform to Close the Black-white Achievement gap*, New York: Teachers College Press.

Scott, J. (2009), 'The Politics of Venture Philanthropy in Charter School Policy and Advocacy', *Educational Policy*, 23 (1): 106–36.

Singh, M., J. Kenway and M. W. Apple (2005), 'Globalizing Education: Perspectives From Above and Below', *Counterpoints*, 280: 1–29.

Skinner, E. A., M. T. Garreton and B. D. Schultz (2011), *Grow Your own Teachers: Grassroots Change for Teacher Education. Teaching for Social Justice*, New York: Teachers College Press.

Sleeter, C. E. (2008), 'Equity, Democracy, and Neoliberal Assaults on Teacher Education', *Teaching and Teacher Education*, 54: 1947–57.

Sondel, B. (2015), 'Raising Citizens or Raising Test Scores? Teach for America, "No Excuses" Charters, and the Development of the Neoliberal Citizen', *Theory & Research in Social Education*, 43 (3): 289–313.

Sondel, B., K. Kretchmar and A. Hadley Dunn (2019), '"Who do These People Want Teaching Their Children?" White Saviorism, Colorblind Racism, and Anti-blackness in "No Excuses" Charter Schools', *Urban Education*, 23 April. doi:10.1177/0042085919842618.

Spring, J. (2008), 'Research on Globalization and Education', *Review of Educational Research*, 78 (2): 330–63.

Suitts, S. (2015), 'A new Majority Research Bulletin: Low Income Students now a Majority in the Nation's Public Schools', *Southern Education Foundation*, January.

Sutcher, L., L. Darling-Hammond and D. Carver-Thomas (2016), 'A Coming Crisis in Teaching? Teacher Supply, Demand, and Shortages in the U.S.', *Learning Policy Institute*, 15 September.

Teach For All (2020), *What we do*. Available online: https://teachforall.org/what-we-do (accessed 8 November 2021).

Teach For America (2015), *About us*. Available online: https://www.teachforamerica.org/about (accessed 19 October 2015).

Teach For America (2020), *What we do*. Available online: https://www.teachforamerica.org/what-we-do (accessed 8 November 2021).

Trujillo, T. and J. Scott (2014), 'Superheroes and Transformers: Rethinking Teach For America's Leadership Models', *Phi Delta Kappan*, 95 (8).

Tyack, D. B. and L. Cuban (1995), *Tinkering Toward Utopia: A Century of Public School Reform*, Cambridge, MA: Harvard University Press.

Zeichner, K. (2010), 'Competition, Economic Rationalization, Increased Surveillance, and Attacks on Diversity: Neo-liberalism and the Transformation of Teacher Education in the US', *Teaching and Teacher Education*, 26: 1544–52.

Zeichner, K. (2011), 'Improving Teacher Education is the United States', American Educational Research Association. Available online: https://www.aera.net/Portals/38/docs/Annual_Meeting/Zeichner_AERA_essay-1b.pdf (accessed 12 November 2021).

Zeichner, K. and C. Pena-Sandoval (2015), 'Venture Philanthropy and Teacher Education Policy in the U.S: The Role of the new Schools Venture Fund', *Teachers College Record*, 117 (6): 1–44.

Zeichner, K., K. A. Payne and K. Brayko (2015), 'Democratizing Teacher Education', *Journal of Teacher Education*, 66 (2): 122–35.

13

Teacher Migration and Education in the (Post)colonial Context

Lessons from the Global South

Phillip D. Th. Knobloch

Immigration is the key to prosperity and education. At least in the nineteenth century, this was a powerful political motto in Argentina. The country was large, extremely sparsely populated and, as it was later called, underdeveloped. Moreover, large parts of today's national territory were still largely under the control of Indigenous peoples. Against this background, it seemed only logical for the liberal intellectual elite of the young nation to attract immigrants to the country in order to settle, cultivate, develop and civilize it, as it was called at the time.

In this context, a slogan by the Argentine writer Juan Bautista Alberdi (1810–1884) became famous: 'gobernar es poblar', to govern means to populate. He then tried to explain exactly what he meant by this in a text he wrote in Paris in 1879: 'To govern is to populate in the sense that to populate is to educate, improve, civilize, enrich and aggrandize spontaneously and rapidly, as has happened in the United States' (Alberdi 1915). Thus, to populate also means to educate.

Even though it seems quite plausible in this case that to govern means to populate, and to populate means to educate, the question arises at this point as to who is educating or is supposed to educate whom here. Should the immigrants educate the locals? Or should the local people educate the immigrants? Should they educate each other? Or should both groups be educated by a third entity, such as the state?

While the issue of immigration and (teacher) education has long dominated and shaped political and educational debates in Argentina, as well as in other so-called classic immigration countries, this topic has only recently come to the fore in many European countries. This is mainly due to the massive immigration that at least some European countries, such as Germany, have been facing in recent years and decades. Immigration movements and the associated political and pedagogical discussions have gained momentum in recent years, especially due to the arrival of many people who have fled the civil war in Syria or come from other countries outside the European Union and are applying for political asylum here. And among the refugees and immigrants are also teachers who worked and were trained in their home countries. Some of these teachers may now also want to work as teachers here again, and perhaps the local society also has an interest in recruiting qualified teachers from this group.

Since a large number of refugees and migrants coming to Europe come from countries that are usually described as *non-Western*, one can ask whether this specific background plays or should play a role with regard to the recognition of teacher training and the qualification of teacher candidates. Therefore, in a first step, we will take a look at an example of how the recognition of teacher training programmes from abroad is currently regulated in one of the German federal states. In a second step, we will then take a closer look at the distinction between Western and non-Western countries. This seems particularly interesting against the background of Latin American educational history, as this distinction has long played a central role there in discussions about immigration and (teacher) education. An in-depth examination of the concepts of the West and non-West seems particularly necessary with regard to contemporary teacher education, as this distinction still shapes our thinking and actions in many respects. This becomes clear not least in the fact that according to the common understanding, pedagogical thinking and action should be modern and critical; modernity and critical thinking, in turn, are considered to be characteristic of the West. Therefore, the question arises whether, especially in view of the current mass immigration from non-Western countries, a comprehensive, historically informed and theoretically sophisticated examination of the concept of the West or non-West is necessary for contemporary teacher education.

1. Teacher in the Age of Migration: Recognition of Educational Qualifications

There are specific rules and regulations in each country for the recognition of educational qualifications obtained abroad. In the Federal Republic of Germany, the school system is under the responsibility of the federal states, which is why the conditions for the recognition of teaching qualifications obtained abroad are regulated by the respective federal state. In the federal state of North Rhine-Westphalia, for example, the recognition procedures are carried out by certain district governments. A distinction is made here between 'teaching qualifications, teaching examinations and university degree examinations' (MKFFI NRW n.d.: 5) (1) from the area of the EU or the European Economic Area as well as from Switzerland and (2) degrees from other countries. However, not only qualifications from abroad must be recognized but also those that were acquired (3) in the former GDR or (4) in other federal states of Germany.

The recognition procedures for educational qualifications acquired in other countries outside the EU are carried out in the federal state of North Rhine-Westphalia by the Detmold District Office. The basic requirements for successful recognition (cf. Bezirksregierung Detmold n.d.: 2) include (1) proof of a completed teaching degree at an academic university; (2) at least two teaching subjects must have been studied, as well as educational sciences; (3) for the primary school teaching profession, the subjects mathematics and German as well as another approved teaching subject must have been studied in addition to the study in educational sciences. (4) For the teaching profession at special schools, two subjects as well as two special needs education subjects must have been studied in addition to the study in educational sciences. In addition, all subjects must be approved in accordance with the North Rhine-Westphalia Ordinance on the Admission of Teachers. If the degree is recognized, (5) additional proof of the required German language skills must be provided. A corresponding test can be taken free of charge at the State Examination Office for Teaching Qualifications at Schools in North Rhine-Westphalia. Alternatively, it is also possible to prove the language skills by means of the 'Goethe-Zertifikat C2: Großes Deutsches Sprachdiplom', which is subject to a fee.

Ultimately, the recognition of teaching degrees obtained abroad is about ensuring that they are more or less equivalent to the degrees obtained in Germany. As seen, this applies not only to degrees from abroad but even to those that were acquired in Germany but in another federal state. There is therefore nothing to argue against the fact that teachers who have fled war in a non-European country, for example, and are therefore currently in Europe or Germany, should also have their degrees recognized – like all other teacher trainees – or have to acquire the qualifications they do not yet have.

Even though it certainly makes sense that all teacher trainees have comparable *formal* qualifications, the question also arises whether it matters in terms of *content* with regard to the required qualification if teachers come from so-called non-Western countries, were educated and socialized there. Therefore, with regard to the content of teacher education, the question arises whether the pedagogical significance of the distinction between the West and the non-West should be comprehensively addressed. In order to get a closer look at this pedagogical significance, we first deal with Stewart Hall's distinction between 'the West and the Rest' in the following section.

2. The West and the Rest

When we speak of Western and non-Western countries or cultures, we do so in the sense in which Stuart Hall (2019) used the term 'the West and the Rest' in an essay first published in 1992. Hall emphasizes that the term 'the West' is not a geographical but rather a historical construct that refers to a certain type of society. 'By "Western" we mean the type of society that is developed, industrialized, urbanized, capitalist, secular, and modern. Such societies arose at a particular historical period – roughly, during the sixteenth century, after the Middle Ages and the breakup of feudalism. They were the result of a specific set of historical processes – economic, political, social, and cultural' (Hall 2019: 142). In his essay, Hall tries to show that this image of the West or of modernity could only be gained in demarcation from that which was not Western, that is, from the so-called Rest. The modern European self-image or the understanding of Western modernity thus developed in the confrontation with the non-European world. And in the course of the development of this conception of the West, a conception of the non-West developed in parallel. Hall traces the development of these ideas and justifies this with the fact that these concepts are a 'system of representation', a 'particular pattern of thought and language' (Hall 2019: 143), which is still significant and effective today.

Hall's reflections are revealing in that modernity is usually associated with the Enlightenment, and this in turn is considered a European or intra-European achievement that was developed independently of the Rest of the world. 'The emergence of an idea of "the West" was central to the Enlightenment. The Enlightenment was a very European affair. European society, it assumed, was the most advanced type of society on earth, European man the pinnacle of human achievement. It treated the West as the result of forces largely internal to Europe's history and formation' (Hall 2019: 144).

Hall now suggests that modernity or the West should no longer be identified only with the Enlightenment and the increasingly developing Europe since then but should begin with the early so-called European discoveries and the subsequent so-called European expansion in order to trace the emergence of the modern idea of 'the West and the Rest'. These 'discovered' and often conquered and colonized countries and peoples served the formation of modern European identity insofar as they represented what Europe or modernity was not, or did not want to be, or could not be.

According to Hall, the understanding of the West that developed in the course of European discoveries and expansion has various functions, whereby he distinguishes between four functions. First, the idea of the West serves to classify and categorize different societies. In this sense, the concept of the West is a 'tool to think with' (Hall 2019: 142). Furthermore, the ideas of Western and non-Western societies are also linked to certain images, which is why Hall speaks of a language and a 'system of representation' (Hall 2019: 143). Hall sees a third function in using the concept of the West as a yardstick for comparing different societies, as these can be closer or further away from Western societies. Hall sees a fourth function in using the concept of the West to evaluate societies. This is the case, for example, when Western societies are described and perceived as developed and in the end good, while non-Western societies are described as underdeveloped and bad.

Although it is certainly true that the distinction between 'the West and the Rest' was usually used to emphasize the superiority of the West over the Rest of the world, Hall also points out that non-Western cultures were not always devalued by Europeans. Rather, they were often even idealized: 'In these images and metaphors of the New World as an Earthly Paradise, a Golden Age, or Utopia, we can see a powerful fantasy being constructed' (Hall 2019: 165).

Hall therefore considers it important to differentiate between two distinctions: On the first level, a simplifying and stereotyping distinction between the West and the Rest takes place. 'By this strategy, the Rest becomes defined as everything that the West is not – its mirror image' (Hall 2019: 171). In a second step, a distinction is then made between the good and bad sides of the Rest. The Rest or this 'Other is then itself split into two "camps": friendly/hostile, Arawak/Carib, innocent/depraved, noble/ignoble' (Hall 2019: 171).

3. Discourse and Ideology

Stuart Hall's reflections on the meaning of the West are initially revealing because he shows how the concept of the West developed in the course of the so-called European expansion in distinction to foreign non-European societies and how this concept is or can be used. The thesis that this developing concept of the West was closely linked to historical and social developments is also convincing; after all, the progressiveness, modernity and superiority of Western societies justified European expansion, European colonialism and, overall, the rise of Europe or the West to a dominant world power.

It remains largely unclear in Hall's text, however, what conclusions can be drawn from these considerations regarding the present. This is due to the fact that the concept of the West can be used in very different ways, as Hall has convincingly shown with regard to the four functions. For, as we have seen, the non-Western is not always evaluated negatively, nor is the Western always evaluated positively – just think of Rousseau, mentioned by Hall, and his critique of society.

However, if one goes back even further in historical observation, it becomes apparent that Western Europe was not always counted as the West as a whole either. This is because the concept of the West was developed not only in distinction to non-European societies but also to certain European societies. In this context, the Latin American semiotician Walter Mignolo (2012: 121) speaks of the invention of tradition, since modern Europe also distinguished itself from its pre-modern history during the Enlightenment in order to give contour to its own identity and the concept of modernity. France, England and Germany in particular were now considered the centres of modernity, while from this perspective Southern Europe was perceived as traditional and backward. With regard to the development of the concept of 'the West and the Rest', it is certainly important to point out that the backwardness attributed to Spain – to which the term *leyenda negra* refers – was above all also tied to the atrocities and acts of violence that occurred in the course of Spanish colonialism in America. Thus, while Spain was initially still one of the essential motors of European expansion and the conquest of the Rest of the world, the protagonists of the Enlightenment, in processes of internal demarcation, later assigned it to the Rest themselves. One can certainly say that the term Southern Europe is still sometimes used pejoratively today and associated with tradition and backwardness.

Since the West can also be located outside and the Rest inside Europe, it is instructive to distinguish, with Mignolo (2000), between an *inner outside* and an *outer outside* with regard to the construction of the idea of the West – Mignolo (2012: 122) also speaks of the 'creation of an own inside' in this context. Analogously, one could of course also distinguish between an *inner inside*, that is, Europe, and, for instance with regard to developed and democratic former European colonies such as Canada or Australia, an *outer inside*.

Against the background of these diverse possible uses of the term 'the West', the question arises, as I said, as to what conclusions can be drawn from this analysis for the present. It is therefore important to point out in this context that Hall analyses the development of the concept of the West in relation to the emergence of discourses, referring to Foucault's concept of discourse. 'A discourse is similar to what sociologists call an "ideology": a set of statements or beliefs which produce knowledge that serves the interests of a particular group or class' (Hall 2019: 156). While the concept of ideology goes hand in hand with the assumption that there are 'true statements about the world (science) and false statements (ideology)' (Hall 2019: 156), Foucault emphasizes that 'statements about the social, political, or moral world [...] are rarely ever simply true or false' (Hall 2019: 156). This is because '"the facts" do not enable us to decide definitely about their truth or falsehood, partly because "facts" can be constructed in different ways. The very language we use to describe the so-called facts interferes in this process of finally deciding what is true, and what false' (Hall 2019: 156–7). Powerful discourses, which in the sense described dispose to a very specific perception of the world, are therefore dependent on power, since they would otherwise, of course, not be powerful. Accordingly, one can only speak of a discourse if one ascribes to it the power to figure the idea of truth and reality in a very specific and contingent way. Accordingly, the analysis of the concept of the West is particularly revealing in such contexts in which specific groups develop a specific idea of the West and the Rest, which becomes a truth, so to speak, and thereby primarily serves their own group interests, but in turn also harms others. This does not mean, however, as Hall points out, that discourses are necessarily developed with strategic and egoistic motives. In summary, Hall therefore states:

> Discourses are ways of talking, thinking, or representing a particular subject or topic. They produce meaningful knowledge about the subject. This knowledge influences social practices, and so has real consequences and effects. Discourses are not reducible to class interests but always operate in relation to power – they are part of the way power circulates and is contested. The question of whether a discourse is true or false is less important than whether it is effective in practice. When it is effective – organizing and regulating relations of power (say, between the West and the Rest) – it is called a 'regime of truth'. (Hall 2019: 160)

4. Coloniality and Colonialism

The Latin American critical theory based on the concept of decoloniality also emphasizes that the examination of the concept of the West and its emergence is primarily required in connection with the critique and analysis of power relations. This is already evident in the concept of *coloniality of power* (Quijano 2000), which occupies a central position in decolonial theory. Analogous to the expression of 'the West and the Rest', the concepts of modernity and coloniality are at the centre of considerations here, whereby, as already seen with Hall, the concept of the West is associated with modernity; the concept of coloniality is used here as a counter-concept to the concept of modernity.

Just as Hall speaks of the 'West and the Rest becoming two sides of a single coin' (Hall 2019: 144), Mignolo says: 'modernity and coloniality are two sides of the same coin' (Mignolo 2009: 42). Both authors also agree that the Rest or coloniality is the dark or darker side of the Enlightenment or modernity: '"The Other" was the "dark" side-forgotten, repressed, and denied, and the reverse image of the enlightenment and modernity' (Hall 2019: 177); and a relevant article by Mignolo (2009: 39) is entitled: 'Coloniality: The Darker Side of Modernity'.

However, the concept of coloniality is not only a counter-concept to that of modernity but above all is used to describe a 'colonial matrix of power' (Mignolo 2012: 49), which is why the term 'coloniality of power' (Mignolo 2012: 50) is also used synonymously. This power relationship designated by the term coloniality, which extends to various levels, goes back to European colonialism but continues to have an effect into the present. Originally, this power relationship referred to the asymmetrical relationship between the European colonizers and the American colonized, and to all forms of oppression, exploitation and control that occurred in the process. This refers primarily to the areas of economy, politics, nature, culture and knowledge (cf. Mignolo 2012: 49–51).

According to Mignolo, one can speak of a coloniality of knowledge insofar as thinking was also colonized in the course of European colonialism, and indeed worldwide. This means that in the course of European colonialism, a world view spread among both the colonized and the colonizers that largely corresponds to the previously discussed understanding of 'the West and the Rest' – in its respective historical form. The spread of this world view in the colonies should not only be understood as a consequence of colonialism but rather as an instrument of colonization. For with this understanding of the West and the Rest, not only was a Western view disseminated in the colonies; rather, colonialism as a whole was also legitimized through the idea of the cultural superiority of the West that was transmitted in this way.

One can speak of a legitimization of colonialism insofar as the described concept of the West or modernity (as I said: always in its respective historical form) served to present the colonial project as a whole as, in retrospect, a mission of education. At first, in the Spanish colonies in America, of course, it was not yet called an educational mission but a religious mission aimed at evangelizing or Christianizing the colonized. In this way, it could be argued that colonialism served to save the souls of the colonized people and not – as was criticized very early on – their exploitation and oppression. Later, after the political independence of the Latin American states, it was no longer the reference to religion but to the Enlightenment that was used to justify post- and neocolonial asymmetrical power relations – that is, the coloniality of power.

If one compares Hall's concept of 'the West and the Rest' with Mignolo's concept of modernity and coloniality, it seems to me that an essential difference lies in the fact that in Hall's figure of thought a strict (one could also say essentialist) distinction is made between the West and the Rest, and thus between different societies, cultures or groups; accordingly, as seen, Hall describes, for example, different countries or regions as Western or non-Western. In contrast, with Mignolo's concept of modernity and coloniality, specific societies, cultures, countries or other groups can certainly be described as modern and also as colonial – and this is precisely where the key to understanding this concept lies.

The point of Mignolo's concept of modernity is that this term always has a positive connotation and is associated with the achievements of modernity, that is, democracy, human rights, emancipation and so on. The concept of coloniality, on the other hand, always has a negative connotation and not only stands for pre-modern European and non-European traditions and lifestyles but is also used to describe those acts of (modern) Europeans (or of people who identify themselves with modernity) that stand in opposition to the positive achievements of modernity.

In this context, Mignolo speaks of a *rhetoric of modernity* that always strictly distinguishes between (positive) modern and (negative) colonial deeds and events. For example, the increase in world knowledge gained in the course of the European discovery of the world can be chalked up to modernity, while the acts of violence and atrocity committed by the colonizers are attributed to coloniality. This rhetoric of modernity thus leads to keeping the image of modernity pure and outsourcing everything negative to the side of coloniality.

Mignolo speaks of a *logic of coloniality* insofar as the understanding of modernity marked by the rhetoric of modernity can be used to criticize and at the same time legitimize coloniality. This logic comes into play, for example, when there is an asymmetrical power relationship between two groups that is legitimized with the cultural superiority of the dominant group – which identifies with modernity. If violent or atrocious acts are committed against the dominated group from the dominant group, this can be criticized by referring to the incompatibility of these acts with the ideals of modernity.

At the same time, however, this critique strengthens and legitimizes the asymmetrical power relationship, since the critique invokes modernity, with which in turn the dominant group identifies itself. It is thus precisely the ability to criticize that makes the dominance of modern culture and intellectual attitudes plausible and clarifies why the ideals of enlightenment and civilization should continue to be spread throughout the world in the future. One could certainly also refer here to Kant's famous pedagogical insight that coercion towards the educated is only justified if it serves their freedom; every violation of this modern pedagogical maxim therefore confirms its validity.

In summary, there is an important difference between the concepts of 'the West and the Rest' (Hall) and 'modernity/coloniality' (Mignolo). While Hall, as seen, distinguishes between the West and the Rest on a first level, and between the good and bad sides of the Rest on a second level, the perspective is reversed in the concept of modernity/coloniality: Although a distinction is also made here on the first level between modernity and coloniality, on a second level it is then made between the good and bad sides of modernity – that is, of the West. By analogy, one could perhaps even say that on this second level a distinction is made between a 'noble West' and a 'ignoble West'.

This difference in perspective reflects, in my opinion, the perspectives behind these concepts: While Hall describes how an understanding of the West has been formed in the West through engagement with non-Western countries, Mignolo shows how an understanding of modernity has developed in former European colonies through engagement with the West. Quite obviously, these two understandings of the West or of modernity, and connected to this, of course, also of the Rest or of coloniality, differ.

5. Civilization and Barbarism

The specific perspective of decolonial theory is already reflected in the discussions mentioned at the beginning, which were held in Argentina in the nineteenth century about the development and civilization of the country. Similar to Alberdi, Domingo Faustino Sarmiento (1811–1888) was also convinced that the young nation state of Argentina could only be civilized through massive immigration. The basic problem of the country was a problem of identity, as Sarmiento explained in his main work, first published in 1845; more precisely, the problem was the division of society between two poles, which Sarmiento called *civilization* on the one hand and *barbarism* on the other. Accordingly, the title of his work is 'Civilisation and Barbarism' (2007).

When Sarmiento speaks of a 'struggle between European civilisation and indigenous barbarism' (Sarmiento 2007: 47) in relation to his homeland, it is hard to overlook the fact that he is following on from and contributing to the discourse described by Hall on the opposition between the West and the Rest. Because the expression 'European civilisation' in Sarmiento's work obviously corresponds to 'the West' in Hall's work and 'indigenous barbarism' to 'the Rest'.

Sarmiento writes his work after Argentina's political independence from Spain and during the subsequent Argentine civil war. This war was also an expression of this struggle between civilization and barbarism and decided the fate of the country, that is, whether the country would orient itself towards civilization, and thus towards Europe and the European Enlightenment, or towards the native barbarism with regard to future developments. Not surprisingly, Sarmiento advocates civilization, calls for the establishment of schools and cities, republican and democratic institutions, the development of infrastructure – and also immigration, especially from Europe, preferably from England, Germany or Scandinavia (cf. Rehrmann 2005: 148).

Even though Sarmiento identifies himself with the upper-class European culture and education, and distances and distinguishes himself just as clearly from the customs and traditions of the simple Argentinean rural population from the remote interior, it would certainly be short-sighted to understand him only as a representative of the European or Eurocentric discourse about 'the West and the Rest'. For compared to Hall's reconstructed way of thinking and speaking about the West and the Rest, in which the Rest is always the very other, the opposite of the West, Sarmiento's way of thinking and speaking differs in that for him the Rest – or as he says: barbarism – is not the very other. On the contrary, Sarmiento consistently follows European or Eurocentric thinking and locates himself, his compatriots and his country outside the West. The Rest or the barbarians are – from Sarmiento's perspective – 'us', while here Europe stands for the other; and this is precisely the problem he is discussing. Sarmiento thus reflects on the relationship between 'the West and the Rest', but not from the perspective of the West, like Hall, but from that of the non-West, or the Rest, or, as we say today, from the Global South.

The special feature of the early Argentine identity discourse can thus be seen in the fact that, on the one hand, people identified with Europe and European culture and education and, on the other hand, explicitly distanced themselves from it. The result was then, in a sense, a double negation. While the independence movement from Spain was fuelled by the idea that Argentines are not Europeans and Spaniards are not Americans, the Creoles who came to power with independence paradoxically demarcated themselves from the Amerindian and Afro-American sections of the population by referring back to their European ancestry. Mignolo (2000) therefore speaks of a double Creole consciousness.

6. Decolonial Border Thinking

The double Creole consciousness – the simultaneous identification with and demarcation from Europe – is also clearly reflected in decolonial theory. For here it is emphasized that the relationship between modernity and coloniality or between the West and the Rest can be thought of in two fundamentally different ways – and should be thought of in both ways if possible. Mignolo (2012) therefore also uses the expression and notation 'modernity/coloniality' and points out that the slash between the two words can be interpreted as both a separating and a connecting element. Border thinking, as he has in mind with reference to Gloria Anzaldua's concept of border thinking, would ideally make it possible to understand modernity and coloniality as phenomena that are both connected and to be separated. This border thinking corresponds to the double Creole consciousness in that, on the one hand, one identifies with modernity (and the West) and criticizes coloniality, and on the other hand, one distances oneself from modernity (and the West) and criticizes it because of its entanglement with coloniality.

The first perspective on the relationship between modernity and coloniality addressed here largely corresponds to the understanding of the West and the Rest outlined by Hall, which primarily corresponds to the modern, Western self-understanding. This understanding of modernity develops in distinction from what is understood in turn as non-modern. The non-modern is evident in space and time, both in the customs and traditions of non-European societies and cultures, but also in the pre-modern and unenlightened traditions of Europeans themselves. Both phenomena – European backwardness and colonial barbarism – then culminate in Spanish colonialism, as outlined retrospectively by Sarmiento and other representatives of the Enlightenment, for example, entirely in line with the so-called *leyendra negra*.

While the first view critically deals with the negative sides or the negative side effects of modernity, such as colonial oppression and violence, the second view of the relationship between modernity and coloniality critically deals with the positive sides of modernity. To be more precise, the first view and the understanding of modernity that is developed here is criticized by pointing out the function of this concept in the colonial matrix of power. For it is precisely by referring to the positive achievements of modernity – from the idea of human rights to the various emancipation movements – that colonial or post- and neocolonial structures of domination and power are legitimized to this day, according to the (decolonial) critique. While the first view corresponds to the modern or Western self-understanding, as Hall also describes it, the second view is characteristic of a way of thinking that is equally critical of power but anti-modern or anti-Western in the sense described.

The term 'anti-modern' is not only problematic with regard to an unintended association with practices that despise human rights but is also misleading insofar as we are dealing here with a decidedly power-critical way of thinking, and the critique of power actually constitutes the core of the modern self-understanding. This reference is important insofar as decolonial theory wants to emphasize and show that not only Europe and the West have produced emancipatory concepts but also – at least to some extent – the 'barbarians' in the (former) colonies. For while the first view of the relationship between modernity and coloniality described above, which is critical of power and colonialism, is primarily based on the experiences of Europeans or colonizers made in the course of European expansion, the second view described here primarily reflects the critical thinking of those who, as Mignolo (2012: 71) puts it, 'were colonised by bourgeoisies who in turn emancipated themselves from monarchies'.

The border thinking idealized by decolonial theory, which is supposed to move along the border 'that separates and connects modernity and coloniality' (Mignolo 2012: 200), is challenged insofar as both anti-colonial and anti-modern critical thinking can inspire emancipatory movements or liberation movements. But both, taken individually, tend to be one-sided in their own way and, due to their blind spots, also go hand in hand with specific forms of oppression and restriction of other ways of living and thinking. It is probably due to Latin American history that it is relatively easy here to identify sometimes with the West and modernity and sometimes with the Rest and coloniality.

7. Teacher Migration and Education at the Border of Modernity and Coloniality

If we look back at the South American discourses on education and migration from the nineteenth century, we can see that, with regard to our current topic

– the recognition, employment or recruitment of refugee or migrant teachers from the Global South – the debates at that time were about state-building and development, with the education of the population being attributed a central role. Priority was therefore given to building a national education system, for which suitable teachers were of course needed.

However, the reflections of Alberdi and Sarmiento indicate that in the discussions about education at that time, the professional and didactic competences of teachers played a subordinate role. Presumably, it was assumed that teachers needed certain qualifications to be able to teach in a qualified manner. Often, it was probably also secondary whether the teachers themselves had immigrated or, in relation to their ancestors, had a migration background. The decisive factor was rather the attitude of the teachers, that is, whether they were on the side of civilization, enlightenment and modernity or on the side of barbarism.

This can at least be said for Sarmiento, who recruited over sixty female teachers from the United States so that they could then train future teachers in Argentina. He apparently considered these North American teachers to be particularly progressive, modern and civilized so that he hoped that these qualities would also be transferred to the culturally backward Argentinean teacher trainees in teacher training. However, it must also be mentioned in this context that these female teachers were defamed by conservative and Catholic circles, since as foreigners and Protestants they seemed unsuitable to advance the formation of a Catholic national identity (cf. Roitenburd 2009; Knobloch 2013: 225).

Given the liberal intellectuals' focus on modernity and civilization, it is not surprising that Alberdi and Sarmiento were not generally in favour of immigration. Rather, they expected an enriching and educational effect only from immigrants from countries of origin that they considered civilized, enlightened and modern. After all, they needed people who were more industrious and mature than those who had lived in Argentina until then.

Accordingly, Alberdi (1915) emphasizes that these must be civilized European immigrants and not people from China, India, Africa or the Ottoman Empire. Argentina, however, faced the problem, Alberdi said at the time, that civilized Europeans – and by this he meant mainly northern Europeans – would migrate to North America:

> Northern Europe will go spontaneously to North America; and as the north in both worlds seems to be the world of liberty and industry, South America must give up the illusion of having immigrations capable of educating it in liberty, peace and industry, if it does not attract them artificially. The only spontaneous

immigration of which South America is capable is that of the populations it has no need: they come of their own accord, like weeds. America can be sure that it will have this population without taking it with it; for European civilisation expels it from its bosom like scoria. (Albderi 1915)

Accordingly, Alberdi then also sharply distinguished between the desired and undesired Europeans, whom he also refers to as 'basura' (rubbish):

> This must not detract from the memory that there are foreigners and foreigners; and that if Europe is the most civilised land in the world, there are in Europe, and in the heart of its brilliant capitals themselves, more millions of savages than in the whole of South America. All that is civilised is European, at least in origin, but not all that is European is civilised; and the hypothesis of a new country populated with Europeans more ignorant of industry and liberty than the hordes of the Pampa or the Chaco is perfectly conceivable. (Alberdi 1915)

Even if one considers Alberdi's choice of words and expressions inappropriate, one will nevertheless have to admit that his reflections are in some respects quite similar to the current discourses on immigration in Europe. For today, too, a distinction is made between desired and undesired immigration, and between immigrants from more progressive societies and those from more backward ones, or, as one can say with Hall, between immigrants from the West and those from the Rest. And just as in the nineteenth century in South America, modern pedagogy today is of course oriented towards a concept of modernity with which it distances itself – albeit usually expressed differently – from backwardness and barbarism, from oppression, exploitation, colonialism, slavery and despotism and so on, and in the course of this distancing contours itself. Can education today be thought of in any other way than as emancipatory?

The idea of modernity, and thus also the traditional idea of the West, is perhaps the most important reference for the pedagogical orientation of teachers and other educators. If one looks at works on the history of pedagogy from the German-speaking sphere, it usually quickly becomes apparent that the non-Western world plays virtually no role here, if it is mentioned at all; thus even America remains to a certain extent undiscovered in many descriptions (cf. Knobloch 2020; an exception: Koerrenz et al. 2017). By concealing, so to speak, the fact that the European, Western and modern self-understanding developed – at least also – in the confrontation with the non-Western and largely colonized world, a narrative is constructed that makes modernity appear as a genuinely European phenomenon to which the Rest of the world contributed nothing. The works thus completely follow the rhetoric of modernity described by Mignolo and are therefore perfectly suited to demonstrate the cultural and intellectual superiority of the West and the backwardness of the Rest.

If we now open up the history of pedagogy in the way Hall did with the history of modernity, the history of European colonialism and the former European colonies first come into view. Although this also brings the dark side of European modernity into focus – not to say central moments of modern European barbarism – it does not deconstruct the thesis of the cultural superiority of the West constructed by the rhetoric of modernity, which is based on the Enlightenment and the emancipation movements of the European bourgeoisie: because it is precisely the critique of colonial barbarism through which the self-understanding of the European Enlightenment and civilization gains contour. It is therefore not enough to follow Hall's deconstruction of the concept of 'the West and the Rest' with regard to the development of contemporary decolonial pedagogical theories and orientations.

According to Mignolo (2012), if one wants to decolonize the history of modernity and modern thought, it is necessary to work out when and where a positive and independent contribution to modernity was made from the dark side of modernity. By this is meant a contribution to *intellectual emancipation*. And Mignolo recognizes this contribution, which has been largely overlooked until now, in the understanding that coloniality is the dark side of modernity. It is about understanding the rhetoric of modernity and the logic of coloniality; or, to put it another way, it is about recognizing that the colonization of thought is a central moment and legacy of modern European colonialism. According to the argumentation of decolonial theory, this can be seen in the relatively uniform understanding of modernity and coloniality or of the (progressive or modern) West and the (backward or colonial) Rest that has prevailed globally until now.

In summary, it can be stated that with regard to the question of whether it plays or should play a role in the recruitment of teachers and in the recognition of qualifications from abroad if they come from so-called non-Western countries, a twofold answer can be given. First: With regard to the rules mentioned in the German federal state used as an example, it can be stated that the migration background does not play a role in the recognition of training. Rather, it is required here that all teacher trainees fulfil certain formal minimum requirements. This concerns subject-specific, didactic and linguistic knowledge and skills. In addition, at least basic knowledge of educational science and pedagogy is required. If one maintains that all teachers should have such knowledge and skills, it seems reasonable and necessary to demand corresponding formal proof from all of them.

Second: While formally it does not and should not matter whether teachers come from Western or non-Western countries, the preceding considerations have also shown that it is quite informative for pedagogy and educational science to deal with historical and current concepts of the West and non-West. For the question arises as to what exactly we mean when we speak of Western and non-Western countries. This seems particularly informative since such demarcations were and are used to come to an understanding about the objectives and effects of modern (and colonial) pedagogy.

In this context, it seems particularly important to note that the debate on the ideas of modern (Western) pedagogy can hardly be conducted reasonably and comprehensively without also addressing colonialism, the phenomenon of coloniality and thus the so-called non-Western history of modern pedagogy. However, the example of Latin America and Argentina also made it clear that such disputes have been going on there – that is, in former European colonies – for a long time. While this is hardly surprising, at least in retrospect, it is all the more surprising that colonialism and the so-called non-Western countries have played almost no role in current German works on the history of pedagogy. Accordingly, there are hardly any elaborated and recognized educational theories that deal with colonialism, coloniality and epistemic decolonization and can provide meaningful orientation for educational practice. This appears to be a major omission, especially at a time when the borders between the West and the non-West are becoming increasingly permeable and unclear.

The phenomenon of migrant and refugee teachers from the Global South can therefore be taken as an occasion to address the long overdue task of directing all efforts towards the development of decolonial pedagogical theories that both connect to our pedagogical traditions and yet broaden horizons. Of course, it would then be worth considering whether substantive discussions of such pedagogical concepts should be made compulsory as part of teacher training and in-service training, not only for teachers from non-Western countries but of course for everyone who wants to become a teacher. Until then, teachers and trainee teachers as well as educational scientists can only be strongly advised to deal as critically and comprehensively as possible with the concepts and theories already available on this complex of topics. That there are some interesting starting points for this should have become clear with the previous considerations.

References

Alberdi, J. B. (1915), *Bases y puntos de partida para la organización política de la República de Argentina*, Buenos Aires. Available online: http://www.cervantesvirtual.com/obra-visor/bases-y-puntos-de-partida-para-la-organizacion-politica-de-la-republica-argentina--0/html/ff3a8800-82b1-11df-acc7-002185ce6064.html (accessed 04 March 2021).

Bezirksregierung Detmold (n.d.), *Anerkennung ausländischer Lehramtsqualifikationen aus Staaten außerhalb der EU*. Available online: https://www.bezreg-detmold.nrw.de/system/files/media/document/file/4.46_merkblatt_anerkennung_2016.pdf (accessed 18 February 2021).

Hall, S. (2019), 'The West and the Rest: Discourse and Power', in S. Hall (ed.), *Essential Essays. Volume 2*, 141–84, Durham and London: Duke University Press.

Knobloch, Ph. D. Th. (2013), *Pädagogik in Argentinien. Eine Untersuchung im Kontext Lateinamerikas mit Methoden der der Vergleichenden Erziehungswissenschaft*, Münster: Waxmann.

Knobloch, Ph. D. Th. (2020), 'On the Epistemic Decolonization of "Western" Education: Reflections on the History of Pedagogy', *Journal for Research and Debate*, 3 (7). doi:10.17899/on_ed.2020.7.5.

Koerrenz, R., K. Kennklies, H. Kauhaus and M. Schwarzkopf (2017), *Geschichte der Pädagogik*, Paderborn: Schöningh.

Mignolo, W. D. (2000), 'La colonialidad a lo largo y a lo ancho: el hemisferio occidental en el horizonte colonial de la modernidad', in E. Lander (ed.), *La colonialidad del saber: eurocentrismo y ciencias sociales. Perspectivas latinoamericanas*, 55–85, Buenos Aires: CLACSO.

Mignolo, W. D. (2009), 'Coloniality: The Darker Side of Modernity', in C. S. Breitwisser (ed.), *Modernologies. Contemporary Artists Researching Modernity and Modernism. Catalog of the Exhibit at the Museum of Modern Art*, 39–49, Barcelona: MACBA.

Mignolo, W. D. (2012), *Epistemischer Ungehorsam. Rhetorik der Moderne, Logik der Kolonialität und Grammatik der Dekolonialität*, Wien: Turia + Kant.

MKFFI NRW (Ministerium für Kinder, Familie, Flüchtlinge und Integration des Landes Nordrhein-Westfalen) (n.d.), *Wegweiser NRW für die Anerkennung von im Ausland erworbenen Befähigungsnachweisen und Qualifikationen für Zuwanderer und Zuwanderinnen*. Available online: https://www.einwanderer.net/fileadmin/downloads/ausbildungsfoerderung/Anerkennung_im_ausland_erworbener_Qualifikationen_NRW.pdf (accessed 18 February 2021).

Quijano, A. (2000), 'Colonialidad del poder, eurocentrismo y América Latina', in E. Lander (ed.), *La colonialidad del saber: eurocentrismo y ciencias sociales. Perspectivas latinoamericanas*, 201–46, Buenos Aires: CLACSO.

Rehrmann, N. (2005), *Lateinamerikanische Geschichte. Kultur, Politik, Wirtschaft im Überblick*, Reinbek: Rowohlt.

Roitenburd, S. N. (2009), 'Sarmiento: entre Juan Manso y las maestras de los EEUU. Recuperando mensajes olvidados', *Antíteses*, 2 (3): 39–66.

Sarmiento, D. F. (2007), *Barbarei und Zivilisation. Das Leben des Facundo Quiroga*, Frankfurt am Main: Eichborn.

Reframing the Teacher in an Age of Migration
Concluding Thoughts

Sabine Krause, Michelle Proyer and Gertraud Kremsner

Introduction

The book's diverse contributions – divided into three sections – have thrown very different shades of light on the situation of teachers. Our aim of bringing together a wide range of contributions on the topic of *The Making of Teachers in an Age of Migration* has brought about a significant change in how the book's title can be read. Thus, rather than focusing on questions of teacher education systems or the teacher's relationship to students and subject matter in a rapidly changing world, the contributions gathered here focused on aspects that are less often considered: Who is both formally and socially recognized as a teacher, and who is not [yet]? What training is expected, and what knowledge is valued? In which relationships do international teachers [not] find themselves in schools? What opportunities to act are granted to them, and which are denied?

These questions have been analysed and discussed in differing ways. While some contributions put teachers in general at centre stage and address migrating teachers only indirectly (e.g. Biesta), others focus solely on – differing terminology intended – migrant, refugee, displaced, international or internationally trained teachers (Obermayr and Sowinetz, Schmidt et al., Tarisayi, Shah, Manik). At least three contributions look at (more or less 'unlabelled') teachers who teach in heterogeneous groups and classes (Yolcu, Thoma, Shah), while others consider students in teacher preparation programs – with a wide range of approaches to what those programs could look like: from 'regular' university training (bachelor's and master's programs: Ress, Marom) to courses dedicated to refugee or migrant teachers (Obermayr and Sowinetz, Schmidt et al.), to career jumpers and lateral entry teachers (Voigt and Engel), to those who only study the very basics of education (Kretchmar). Alongside these considerations is the range of voices that the authors of each chapter directly or indirectly present: we learn not only from policy papers (Biesta, Yolcu, Kretchmar) and historical documents (Knobloch) but also from the voices of African teachers in Brazilian classrooms (Ress), displaced teachers (Obermayr and Sowinetz; Schmidt et al.), teachers teaching refugee students (Thoma, Shah), Zimbabwean migrant teachers in South African classrooms (Tarisayi), Turkish and Jordanian teachers as well as Syrian refugee teachers (Shah), South African migrant teachers in the UK and the United Arab Emirates (Manik) and – as in Marom's chapter – racialized teacher candidates (Indigenous, East Asian Canadian, South Asian Canadian).

There are also other factors worth mentioning because a wide range of approaches is visible among the contributions of this book. This holds true in terms of theoretical considerations, which cover a broad field of theories used in educational science, but – apart from historical framings, such as Knobloch's – regarding empirical strategies from interview studies to discursive analyses of policy texts to secondary qualitative analysis. Besides the groups addressed in the chapters, it can also be noted that the invited authors cover most, albeit not all, continents, although it has to be mentioned that the majority of authors work in Europe (Biesta, Ress, Obermayr and Sowinetz, Thoma, Terhart, McDaid, Proyer, Engel, Voigt, Knobloch), three work in North America (Schmidt, Marom, Kretchmar), two in Africa (Tarisayi, Manik), one in Asia (Yolcu) and one in Oceania (Shah).

In our concluding remarks, we will highlight three lenses through which we choose to read the texts to bring out certain issues: First, the challenge of theoretically and empirically researching this topic. Second, if we are to break through hegemonic knowledge and hegemonic structures, which voices are heard and whose knowledge is valued? Third, we will discuss qualifications, localities and proportionalities of acknowledgements by focusing on the making of a teacher who migrates. We have decided not to dedicate an extra subsection to the use of (a common national) language but to consider this topic in every subsection because the issue holistically permeates the making of a teacher. We are well aware that the selection is non-exhaustive, but it enables initial insights into overarching issues, challenges and blind spots that need further research.

Challenges with Theoretical and Empirical Approaches to (the Making of) Teachers

The book's title already reveals hegemonic practices and understandings when it asks about 'making', which goes back to the idea that teachers are a special 'kind of people' recognizable through certain characteristics or knowledge. All contributions to this book address the question of characteristics or point out gaps in the construction of teachers as a kind of people. The term 'kinds of people' refers to the theoretical work of Ian Hacking and was adopted by Popkewitz et al. (2017), who ask what (cultural, social or political) practices are carried out or strived for that ultimately lead to the 'fabrication' (creation or production) of – in this case – teachers. In their studies, Popkewitz, Diaz and Kirchgasler strive 'to explore how particular qualities and capabilities inscribed in the fabrication of people in schools do not merely render what is there; they introduce historical principles and distinctions that organize who that kind of person is (and is not), and prescribe who that person should (and should not) become' (Popkewitz, Diaz and Kirchgasler 2017: 4). In the search for how these practices come about, that is, towards which shared ideas they are oriented, they draw on Hacking's conception of the 'looping effect'. The idea is that the practices of professionals are influenced not only by scientific (scholarly) ideas and theories but also by the ideas of others in social space:

> Looping directs attention to how people spontaneously come to fit the categories given to them. These kinds of people do not exist until the practices – often those of the social sciences – make possible new objects of reflection and bring them into being (Hacking 1986: 223). The intersections of theories, practices, and technologies – as tools for knowing and governing people – provide new ways to experience oneself as a kind of person that did not previously exist. (Hacking 1992; Popkewitz, Diaz and Kirchgasler 2017: 5)

Teachers' practices emerge through social, ethical and political references to others, and it is thus also these factors that determine the 'kind of people' that teachers are. The contributions to this volume imply the perspective of 'fabrication' through the intersection of theory, practice and technology, when they report on social practices in schools (Manik, Tarisayi) and consider theoretical approaches to teaching and education (Biesta), the (self-) technologies that accompany policies (Yolcu) or (colonial) styles of thinking revealed in the use of language (Knobloch). Looking at the practices that stem from intersections, it is possible to point to the effects of the use of language: 'Language does not transmit ideas from one head to another in any simple way. Instead, language enacts power, misunderstandings, unconscious slips, relation, and performative iterations just as readily as it transmits ideas' (Bingham 2012: 87).

The theoretical background presented in the book's first chapters assumes that pedagogical settings are central to teacher action. The pedagogical

(Schäfer 2012) goes beyond aspects of (classroom) management and asks what education's ultimate goal is? Thus, it confronts normative demands on teaching and learning but is also always concerned with the extent to which it can provide or pretend to provide an answer for learners. Here, the practices and their reflections by teachers come into play. In the words of Sharon Todd (2012: 80):

> I stand up in the class, with my own (often implicit) desires, wanting the students to get something from the course, to change and alter not only *what* they think, but also *how* they think, introducing them to new possibilities that provoke their curiosity and, hopefully, new insights. At the same time, I try – really try – not to impose my ideas.

Todd points to the central problem that teachers must face, namely that they want to achieve a goal that concerns factual knowledge and styles of thinking. It is the teacher's responsibility to convey this and, at the same time, to reflect on the extent to which she can, may and will assert her desires and where these must be constrained by the desires of the learners and the goal of promoting self-action by learners (see Biesta in this volume). The aim of self-action puts the learner at the centre: 'It is not about having knowledge about our students that matters, but listening to them, attending to their presence revealed through the words they speak' (Todd 2012: 83). Here is a connection to the co-construction of knowledge that should take place in teaching and learning settings (a two-way process, as mentioned with reference to Freire in the introduction to this book). This is especially true if we speak *educationally* about teacher education (Phelan 2013) and recognize that teachers assume the responsibility of demonstrating knowledge and performance to others against the backdrop of their own experiences while being critically aware of their doings (Burbules and Berk 1999).

In addition to theoretical discourses and analyses of praxis, the teachers' own experiences ultimately shape their actions and practices. It is never the idea of teaching alone in the classroom but the imaginings of learners, teaching and the (tasks of) school that shape teachers' practices. If, then, teachers' experiences – like those of the teachers included in this book – are shaped by moving between several countries and different systems of thought, practices also differ in a correspondingly diverse way.

Susanne Ress showed in her contribution how the mobility of people is accompanied by the mobility of perceptions and understandings of the world. International teachers must navigate these two forms of mobility: Trained and practised in thinking according to one form of understanding pedagogical processes, they are confronted with different understandings in other countries that cannot always be seamlessly combined. Travelling ideas and/or de-localizing understandings are a major challenge in traditional teacher education. Usually, it enters the stage the other way around: hegemonic understandings of teaching and learning replace local understandings (mainly discussed regarding large-scale assessments like PISA, e.g. Kim 2017). Steps must be taken to *undo* hegemonic thinking because local or regional forms of reasoning and performance have already been replaced.

One of the great challenges in educational science is that in life, as in academic/scientific study, we become accustomed to and actively engage in certain traditions and styles of thinking that shape practices and creative ways of thinking and assembling new things. Ways of reasoning and continuously evolving ideas about human beings, the community/society, solidarity, the world and the future also produce possibilities for the new/other. How, then, is it possible to undo hegemony? While Knobloch's chapter helped to untangle the ways and complexities that styles of reasoning took and still take, Kretchmar and Marom remind us to include those voices that are still unheard. Thus, this book attempts to contour the processes of *rethinking* and *unthinking* as productive processes that still have knowledge and thinking as central elements but outline them anew.

The new also poses methodological challenges for researchers, as does the view of margins or marginalized voices, marked as such during research. Both theoretical explanations and empirical work search for perspectives that only appear marginal from the hegemonic standpoint. In this volume, the authors call for openness in research, a more kaleidoscopic way of reasoning that values the (still) indeterminate feeling of being affected by something, an echo that cannot (yet) be put into words, elaborated or ordered (Fendler 2012; Akbari 2007). This moment of foreboding indeterminacy has the potential to shake seemingly fixed theoretical frames and – sensitized to the power of prior determinations – to ask what prior understandings can be used, are present or could be conceived. Attentiveness to such moments could be used to understand knowledge production as dynamic and contextually shaped.

Critical Reframing the Making of Teachers in an Age of Migration

To question the understanding of the teaching personnel is also to ask for narratives of the teacher. Whose voices are heard when we analyse 'hegemonically-induced hindrances and barriers to the teaching profession', as promised in the first paragraph of this book? Who is allowed to speak, in which contexts and who is not? Who do we think of when we imagine teachers in classrooms or teacher trainees at universities? How do we (re)produce these images? For whom do we prepare teacher trainees?

As shown in the overview of this book, diverse voices are presented in this volume: we learn about teachers and teacher trainees who are either (at the edge of being) marginalized themselves or work with heterogeneous students in different parts of the world. Critical reflection on these questions necessarily leads to the impression that teachers and teacher trainees – just like any other group in our current societies – need to have certain assets to be valued. However, first and foremost, they need to be seen. To make this aspect clear, we narrow down Goodley's (2014: 23) analysis of valued citizens in the following Table 14.1 to apply it to teachers who work in (inter)national contexts:

Considering this list and considering that teachers have to be 'better' citizens if they are to educate future citizens, it could be stated that citizenship is perhaps the most certain asset that teachers have to possess. We might find that teachers must tick many boxes no matter where they come from or where they work. Not being cognitively, socially and emotionally able and competent, biologically and psychologically stable, non-disabled, 'sane', autonomous and so on is considered

Table 14.1 Valued Citizens of the Twenty-First century

The Valued Citizen Is . . .	. . . Produced Through the Practices of . . .
Cognitively, socially and emotionally able and competent	Disabling or ableist societies
Biologically and psychologically stable, genetically and hormonally sound and ontologically responsible	Societies governed by biotechnologies and new potentialities of eugenics (e.g. prenatal screening or the Human Genome Project)
Hearing, mobile, seeing, walking	Cultures that value mobility, hearing, speaking, sight, bodily control and comportment
Normal: sane, autonomous, self-sufficient, self-governing, reasonable, law-abiding and economically viable	Normal societies that value forms of cognitive ability, mental health, meritocracy and entrepreneurship (that are actually deeply neurotic about such achievements)
White, heterosexual, male, adult, breeder, living in towns, global citizen of Western Europe and North America (WENA)	Long histories of colonialism, heteronormativity, patriarchy and class welfare that, to this day, continue to uphold able-bodiedness as a key associated mark of citizenship

Adapted from: Goodley (2014: 23).

a no go and unthinkable, with student safety being placed at the forefront of such reasoning. Nevertheless, there is so much that we do not see when we look at this list (or ask ourselves how we imagine teachers in any other way). For instance:

- If given the opportunity, what would [national] teachers propose as essential for themselves? How would they imagine the 'ideal' teacher? Would it make a difference if they speak of teachers in general or about what they bring or lack? Asking these questions might help analyse [if and] how hegemonic constructions permeate narratives about teachers.
- Similar questions apply to internationally trained teachers: the barriers they face due to their international training may mean that they could 'show' signs of incorporated hegemonic constructions around the predominance of locally 'desirable' criteria. When we take a closer look at this particular group, some of the assets of 'valued citizens' listed above could be rated highly positively on the one hand, for example, in relation to tremendous efforts in terms of mobility. However, studies and chapters in this book suggest that international teachers do not necessarily see the positive aspects of this feature but are somewhat devastated by the hindrances they face when entering local job markets. On the other hand, this group is likely to be attributed with negative characteristics, such as trauma (particularly assigned to refugee teachers), which challenge assumptions of emotional stability and/or economic autonomy. First and foremost, they are likely to be non-White and come from countries outside of WENA, thus challenging Eurocentric expectations and images about teachers.
- Educating teachers also involves creating specific kinds of students. So, what kinds of teachers do we want/need for what kinds of students (future citizens)? How does this change schooling and the idea of school in general? What would students (from which kinds of schools) say if asked to imagine their 'ideal' teacher? How would they imagine the 'ideal' student?

We can see from this list that borders are drawn not only for territories but also for social spaces and groups. These constructions permeate all of us. In concluding a book like this, we have to remain aware that we need to discuss these issues with experts and researchers and with those addressed in our research and our theoretical reflections (see again, Hacking's looping effect). As editors of this book, we have made the voices of (international) teachers heard. Nevertheless, we have to admit that both students' and parents' voices are under-represented here, as are voices from some parts of the world (e.g. South Asia and South America) and certain groups in geographical areas otherwise represented (e.g. Indigenous people, religious groups and other minorities or intersectional aspects, respectively).

Further, we acknowledge major blind spots, for example, due to the requirement of English as an academic or second language or because we simply did not see them. As editors, who were we unable to reach for contributions to this book? Who is left out of our research, or as authors in general? And – just as importantly – who cannot use our considerations, reflections and findings due to the complex use of (a second or even 'foreign' and written) language?

Qualifications, Locations and Their Disruption – the Making of Teachers in Mobility and Its Boundaries

In Part II of this volume, contributions focus on what makes a teacher from an international standpoint, looking at the mobility of teachers and their qualifications. Most of these contributions, but also selected from other parts, can be discussed under the broader conceptual frameworks of dislocations, disproportionalities of acknowledgements, disqualifications and de-qualifications. This refers to the fact that some of the teachers addressed in this book are either from somewhere else or have returned from other places and are therefore dislocated. Some of them have received training in different educational institutions than the ones considered traditional in a specific country or are denied access to a system at all, which implies that only (small) parts, if any, of their earlier training are regarded or acknowledged. Thus, they have to either requalify or surrender to being de-qualified (e.g. Smyth and Kum 2010).

To make a long story short and to put it rather bluntly: Someone who was a teacher in one place is not automatically perceived as one in another place. Or: Someone who has received training in one place might face the fact that their certificate will not, or only partly, be acknowledged. This takes us back to *what makes a teacher* – and we might want to add 'in a specific place' or 'entitled by a specific authority'. Additionally, it is interesting to ask *who decides* that, but this question would require another book (cf. Gorlewski and Tuck 2018). At the same time, we might also return to the issue of language. So, *what is 'in' a name*? A teacher is a teacher is a teacher . . . or not. During the transition from one place to another, a teacher becomes internationally trained, internationally educated and displaced (see Bense 2016 for a detailed literature review).

Interestingly, we know that processes of recognizing internationally acquired qualifications pose challenges created mainly by national policies (Donlevy,

Mejerkord and Rajania 2016). Differing structural contexts, such as the design of teacher training programs and curricula, school systems and subjects, come into play. The latter, especially in relation to languages that are (not) taught as part of the school curriculum in a specific country, often degrades teachers to work as language assistants or prevents access to schools full stop. This also highlights that many countries still employ a hegemonically evolved monolingual orientation in their educational systems. These systems refrain from including languages of (recent) migrant groups into their curricula or limit these to minor efforts to support first-language acquisition or programs to eradicate deficits in majority languages. This affects students and points to discriminatory practices towards non-local teachers, for example, in terms of linguistic practices (Schmidt et al.).

In some cases, even county, district, region or province-specific variations may play a role and complicate things even further. We rarely learn about the interrelatedness of reasons for the limited flexibility around recognition, especially in growing migration movements, student diversity and understaffing crises. This non-immediate appreciation of a teacher from a non-local context holds true in many places of the world. It impacts the possibilities of pursuing a career as a teacher, especially on an equal level with local teachers regarding pay, possibilities and responsibilities. The diverse origins and frames of reference regarding the teaching repertoire of internationally trained teachers make this visible. Here, too, only the other – from an international perspective – makes the self-evident clear and puts it 'to the test'. The internationally trained teacher confronts us with the task of asking what makes a teacher and what hegemonic ideas are woven into the idea of *becoming, being and remaining a teacher*. Complex dynamics come into play in places where national borders not only mark physical territory but also underpin territorial, cultural or localized knowledge. Aspects such as Indigenous knowledge and its teaching (Tetpon et al. 2015) and references to teachers acting as so-called representatives of minorities or minority teachers (García and Weiss 2019) offer an alternative to hegemonic views centred on a particular country and its systems. The principle of actual borderlands or 'borderscapes' (Brambilla 2015) and the reframing of geographical, national and philosophical notions can also affect the idea of what makes a (good) teacher. Teachers from and/or in unknown territories may struggle to do their job due to the personal, interpersonal or structural issues that have been addressed in this volume – bearing in mind that teaching is a highly situated profession and all teachers face 'unknown territories' daily. We have only recently begun to learn about the dynamics and relationships that affect teachers who move from one place to another and re-enter the profession.

Research activities on specific locations are more advanced (e.g. by Manik) than, for example, the situation of recently arrived refugee teachers (Obermayr and Sowinetz). Contributors have provided personal accounts from teachers themselves and pointed to the challenges they face in teaching and with local colleagues (Tarisayi, Shah), but they have also highlighted structural reasons for discrimination (Schmidt et al., Marom, Kretchmar; all in this volume).

This complexity holds true for geographical locations but could also refer to variations in training, an issue that deeply touches the understanding of what makes a teacher. Some of the persons acting as teachers about whom we can read in this book have been trained to do something else, while others need recertification despite long years of practice and high levels of knowledge. This points to elements of *disproportionality* and *disqualification* and the absurdity that education systems, in some cases, enable easier access to untrained individuals than to differently trained ones from other locations. This act of actual and active exclusion also involves de-qualification.

Outlook

With its focus on teachers, this book has touched on the relations that bind teachers and shape the understanding of what it means to be a teacher, the social relations of the profession and the recognition of being a teacher. These aspects call for further in-depth research.

Interestingly, many studies into teacher shortages, qualification schemes and issues related to quality sometimes leave out student perspectives, opinions and needs. If included, they tend to be limited to children and young people from migrant backgrounds who are often assumed to pose a threat to perceived balances in nationally established education systems. Similarly, the focus on migration and the teaching profession is more often than not limited to the image of the teacher as an apparent expert on migration. On the one hand, this is due to his or her own experiences of (forced) migration and potential to act as a role model. On the other hand, it is because similar languages and experiences in similar cultural environments are supposed to create a certain kind of communality, even though teachers might speak different dialects or represent different minority groups. Reducing teachers to their migration backgrounds points to a constricted, one-sided supposed awareness of cultural diversity. These ideas are infused by perceptions present in teachers' environments (colleagues, parents, administration, etc.) and point to a hegemonically induced, and thus reduced, view (Rotter and Timpe 2016; Bressler and Rotter 2017). One of the aims of this book has been to propose globalized embeddedness that might enable a reorientation of such discourses.

Even though many contributions of this book call for unbureaucratic hands-on solutions for already trained and professional teachers in terms of recognition processes, we have to be aware of misguided proposals that tally with neoliberal policies, for example, fast-track programs that reproduce hegemonic structures by placing graduates primarily in low-income schools mostly serving students of colour, a trend that spreads globally.

As Knobloch's chapter of this book shows, historicizing the present helps us understand developments and possibilities in (teacher) education by exploring the nexus of politics, policy and education and its contribution to current discourse. Further contributions, both empirical and theoretical, should consider historicizing their thinking and argument to foster reflexivity.

As suggested by Kretchmar, a new vision for teacher education needs to 'understand the way society outside of the classroom impacts student learning and they need theory and skills that can support them to navigate their context and work relationally with students, communities and families' (Kretchmar in this volume: 213). Teacher preparation, therefore, not only needs to build on democratic structures that have genuine community engagement (including teamwork from teachers and parents) but also needs to learn how to 'merge their own background and experience with the language, culture and history of their school's community/communities' (ibid.). After carefully studying this book's contributions, we have to emphasize and add that if we understand teachers as part of a school's communities (which we do), we also need to learn to value their individual backgrounds. Developing mutual understanding requires strategic support, mentorship and orientation for international teachers and all school members.

References

Akbari, R. (2007), 'Reflections on Reflection: A Critical Appraisal of Reflective Practices in L2 Teacher Education', *System*, 35 (2): 192–207.

Bense, K. (2016), 'International Teacher Mobility and Migration: A Review and Synthesis of the Current em-pirical Research and Literature', *Educational Research Review*, 17: 37–49.

Bingham, C. (2012), 'Two Educational Ideas for 2011 and Beyond', in G. J. J. Biesta (ed.), *Making Sense of Education*, 85–91, Dordrecht: Springer.

Brambilla, C. (2015), 'Exploring the Critical Potential of the Borderscapes Concept', *Geopolitics*, 20 (1): 14–34.

Bressler, C. and C. Rotter (2017), 'The Relevance of a Migration Background to the Professional Identity of Teachers', International Journal of Higher Education, 6 (1): 239–50.

Burbules, N. C. and R. Berk (1999), 'Critical Thinking and Critical Pedagogy: Relations, Differences, and Limits', in T. S. Popkewitz and L. Fendler (eds) *Critical Theories in Education: Changing Terrains of Knowledge and Politics*, 45–65, New York: Routledge.

Donlevy, V., A. Mejerkord and A. Rajania (2016), *Study on the Diversity Within the Teaching Profession With Particular Focus on Migrant and/or Minority Background: Annexes*. Available online: https://www.bvekennis.nl/wp-content/uploads/documents/16-0781.pdf (accessed 8 November 2021).

Fendler, L. (2012), 'Lurking, Distilling, Exceeding, Vibrating', *Studies in Philosophy and Education*, 31 (3): 315–26.

García, E. and E. Weiss (2019), 'The Teacher Shortage is Real, Large and Growing, and Worse Than we Thought. The First Report in "The Perfect Storm in the Teacher Labor Market" Series', Economic Policy Institute, 26 March. Available online: https://www.epi.org/publication/the-teacher-shortage-is-real-large-and-growing-and-worse-than-we-thought-the-first-report-in-the-perfect-storm-in-the-teacher-labor-market-series/ (accessed 31 October 2021).

Goodley, D. (2014), *Dis/Ability Studies. Theorising Disablism and Ableism*, London and New York: Routledge.

Gorlewski, J. and E. Tuck, eds (2018), *Who Decides who Becomes a Teacher?: Schools of Education as Sites of Resistance*, London and New York: Routledge.

Hacking, I. (1986), 'Making up People', in T. C. Heller, M. Sosna and D. E. Wellbery (eds), *Reconstructing Individualism: Autonomy, Individuality, and the Self in Western Thought*, 222–36; 347–8, Stanford: Stanford University Press.

Hacking, I. (1992), 'Statistical Language, Statistical Truth, and Statistical Reason: The Self-authentification of a Style of Scientific Reasoning', in E. McMullan (ed.), *The Social Dimensions of Science*, 130–57, Notre Dame: The University of Notre Dame.

Kim, J. H. (2017), 'The Traveling of PISA: Fabricating the Korean Global Citizen and the Reason of Reforms', in T. A. Popkewitz, J. Diaz and C. Kirchgasler, *A Political Sociology of Educational Knowledge*, 53–68, London and New York: Routledge.

Phelan, A. M. (2013), 'Speaking Educationally About Teacher Education', in G. J. J. Biesta, J. Allan, and R. Edwards (eds), *Making a Difference in Theory*, 179–91, London and New York: Routledge.

Rotter, C. and M. Timpe (2016), 'Role Models and Confidants? Students With and Without Migration Backgrounds and Their Perception of Teachers With Migration Backgrounds', *Teaching and Teacher Education*, 59: 92–100. doi:10.1016/j.tate.2016.05.016.

Schäfer, A. (2012), *Das Pädagogische und die Pädagogik: Annäherungen an Eine Differenz*, Paderborn: Ferdinand Schöningh.

Smyth, G. and H. Kum (2010), 'When They don't use it They Will Lose it': Professionals, Deprofessionalization and Reprofessionalization: The Case of Refugee Teachers in Scotland', *Journal of Refugee Studies*, 23 (4): 503–22. doi:10.1093/jrs/feq041.

Tetpon, B., D. Hirshberg, A. Leary and A. Hill (2015), 'Alaska Native-focused Teacher Preparation Programs: What Have we Learned?', *Growing our own: Indigenous Research, Scholars, and Education. Proceedings From the Alaska Native Studies Conference 2015*, Fairbanks.

Todd, S. (2012), 'Going to the Heart of the Matter', in G. J. J. Biesta (ed.), *Making Sense of Education*, 79–84, Dordrecht: Springer.

Index

acceleration   86–90, 96
Africa   7–8, 10, 50, 54–8, 60, 63, 133–45, 169–81, 233, 240
Afrophobia   133–4
agency   21–2, 26, 113, 149–61, 176–7, 215
Argentina   8, 11, 220, 229–30, 233, 236
artistry of teaching   26–9
Asia   7–8, 172, 174, 188, 190, 193, 240, 245
Austria   7, 9, 50, 67–79, 85–6, 89, 92, 103, 105–10, 114–15

belonging   2, 5–10, 52, 57, 60, 62, 68, 71–2, 79, 85–6, 133, 135–6, 138, 141–2, 145, 172–3, 179, 181–2, 188
border   10–11, 52–3, 61, 67, 135, 153, 181, 204, 212–13, 231–2, 236, 245, 247
Bosnia and Herzegovina   70
Brazil   7, 50, 54–63
bridging programme   102–16

Canada   7–10, 103, 105–6, 108, 112, 114–15, 170, 172, 180, 185–6, 188, 190–1, 194, 196–7, 225
career jumpers   7, 10, 119–29, 239
certification   10, 69, 102, 106, 185, 204–11, 248
charter school   206, 209–11
citizenship   51, 174–5, 190, 244
civilization and barbarism   229–31
classrooms
    diverse-   8, 32–46
    inclusive-   45
    -management   33, 37, 39–40, 102, 116, 242
colleague   3, 16, 21, 49, 73–4, 80, 111–14, 126, 133, 138–45, 175, 179, 248
colleague-outsider conundrum   133–45

colonial   7–9, 49–50, 53–6, 62, 181, 186, 194, 196, 220, 225–36, 241, 244
colonialism   181, 186, 225–8, 231–6, 244
coloniality   97, 226–8, 231–2, 235–6
competence   2–5, 52, 110, 121, 123–9, 233
conflicts   26, 44, 55, 57, 96, 152, 204
construction
    co-   3, 242
    de-   108, 150, 235
    global-   15, 18, 20, 21, 23–4, 29–30, 61, 211–13
    social-   54, 170, 172, 187, 195, 241, 245
control societies   34, 40
cooperation   54–6, 85, 89–90, 94, 124, 134–5
Critical Race Theory   186–7

decolonial   8, 62, 226–7, 229, 231–2, 235–6
decoloniality   62, 226
difference   15, 19, 22, 27, 33–9, 41–5, 49–56, 60–2, 102, 109–10, 121–2, 126, 151–2, 159, 178, 180, 228–9, 245
discourse   14, 16, 21, 33, 35, 38, 46, 49–54, 63, 85, 87, 104, 110, 115, 123–4, 149, 152–6, 161, 185, 188, 190–1, 196–7, 224–6, 230–6, 242, 249
discrimination   5, 9–10, 104, 110, 115, 136, 154, 169–75, 180–1, 192, 248
displaced teachers   68–70, 76–8, 240
diverse   1, 3–4, 8–9, 17, 32–46, 53, 61, 88, 104, 111–12, 185, 190, 193, 195–7, 204–5, 226, 239, 242, 244, 247
diversity   1–4, 6, 8, 10, 17, 32–41, 45–6, 113, 115, 124, 135, 185–93, 196–7, 247–8

education
  authorities   70, 74–5, 91, 114, 144, 159, 176
  policy   4–11, 16–19, 22, 29, 116, 126–7, 152, 155, 174–5, 180–1, 204, 207, 210–12, 249
  politics of   7, 9, 83, 86, 95, 204
  studies   1, 7–8, 69, 73, 87, 103, 106–11, 114, 126, 129, 136–7, 144, 154, 169–77, 180–2, 185, 240–1, 245, 248
  system   49, 55, 70, 113, 115, 128–9, 153, 157–8, 191, 196, 204, 233, 248
educational
  cultures   15–16, 22, 24, 209
  histories   2, 54–6, 119, 172, 181, 188, 204–5, 214, 221, 223, 225, 227, 234–6, 249
  practices   36, 38, 40–6, 86–7, 241–2
  qualifications   221–2, 233, 246
  structures   15–16, 22, 30, 78–9, 86–9, 94, 108, 114, 124, 127, 196, 214, 249
employment   1, 75, 78, 81, 93, 106, 111, 113, 123, 136–7, 153, 176, 233
EPIK model   123, 128–9
equity   160–1, 190, 204, 208, 211
Europe   7–8, 49–55, 61, 67, 106, 109, 134–6, 220–36, 240, 244
exclude   6, 105, 143, 172, 189
experience
  professional-   73, 80, 110, 177, 181

foreigners   133–8, 140–4, 233–4

Germany   7–10, 50, 103, 105–6, 108–11, 114–15, 119–23, 125–7, 129, 136, 221–2, 225, 230
global construction of teachers   211–13
global construction of teaching   18–20, 24
globalisation   105, 204, 213, 215, 249
Global North   10, 103, 105–8, 134
Global South   11, 134, 152, 170, 220, 230, 233, 236
governance   8, 34–5, 40, 43, 45, 69, 203
  being governed   244
governmental   7–8, 33–5, 37, 40, 46, 87

hegemonic   1, 8, 16, 29, 44, 103–4, 108, 160, 240, 243, 245, 247, 249

hierarchies   45, 61, 115

identity   2, 5–6, 8, 11, 50, 55, 58, 62, 68, 72, 111, 135, 149, 151–2, 156, 160, 170, 172, 179, 186, 224–5, 229–30, 233
ideology   51, 55, 105, 113, 115, 187, 211, 224, 226
immigrant   32–4, 37–41, 44, 104, 112, 114, 133–7, 142, 170, 178, 180, 185–8, 190, 192, 195, 220–1, 233–4
immigration   11, 32, 43, 55, 171, 174, 197, 220–1, 229–30, 233–4
inclusion   1, 38, 85, 161, 189, 196
inclusive
  pedagogies   33–6, 44–5
  teacher   41, 43
  teaching   32, 34, 36, 38–40, 43, 45
indigenous   2, 8, 53, 138, 142–5, 188, 191, 194, 220, 230, 240, 246–7
inequality   86, 129
integration   10, 38, 43, 54–61, 77, 86, 92, 124, 133–6, 141–4, 150, 153–6, 160, 169–70, 173, 177, 180–2, 188
international   4–7, 9, 11, 19, 35, 42, 49–61, 102, 106–7, 110, 114, 123, 126, 135, 153–8, 169–73, 175–9, 196–7, 211–15, 239, 242, 245–9
internationalization   2, 4–6, 49–54, 57, 61, 197
Iran   70
Ireland   7, 9, 103, 105–8, 114–15

Jordan   7, 10, 150–3, 156–60, 240

labour market   49–52, 68–9, 81, 108, 114–15, 135
language   4, 9, 21–3, 30, 43–4, 50, 58, 61, 73, 76, 85–6, 96, 102–16, 136, 142–5, 154–6, 169, 173, 187, 192, 196, 222, 224, 226, 240–1, 246–7
  multilingual   50, 86, 102, 104–5, 110–16
  skills   76, 109, 111, 115, 136, 154, 222
lateral entry teachers   136–8, 140–3, 145, 148–51

Latin America 221, 225-8, 232, 236
limitation 6, 11, 45, 68, 102, 123-4, 151, 189, 215

migrants 67, 85, 134-7, 141-2, 170, 221
minority 32, 77, 105, 179, 187, 193-5, 247-8
mobility 6, 8-9, 49-59, 61-2, 102, 114, 171, 180, 242, 244-6
modernity and coloniality 227-32, 235
movement 1-2, 27, 38, 49-54, 59-62, 67, 135, 204, 221, 231-2, 235, 247

nation 1-2, 11, 50, 56, 62-3, 80, 92, 96, 108, 142, 220, 229
national cultures of education 15-16
neoliberal 8-11, 85-8, 95-6, 203-15, 249
neoliberal educational policies 87, 203-6
neoliberalism 9, 87, 203-4
non-Western countries 11, 221-3, 229, 235-6
norm 9, 57-8, 191, 193
North America 54, 193, 233, 240, 244

participation 36, 41, 57, 85, 89, 94, 109, 110, 152
pedagogy 8, 63, 85, 88, 104-5, 113, 115, 206, 234-6
perspectives 6-10, 60-1, 67, 75, 85-9, 94, 123, 190, 213, 229, 243, 248
post-colonial 7, 9, 49, 53, 56
profession 1-5, 9, 17, 68-74, 77-9, 102, 107, 109, 116, 119, 121, 123, 125, 152, 160, 169, 181-2, 185, 189, 210, 213, 222, 247-8
professional
  development 33-5, 39-43, 106, 170, 192, 213
  devices 32, 35, 39-40, 43, 45
  discourse 152, 196
  expériences 73, 80, 110, 177, 181
  identity 68, 72, 149, 161, 171-2, 176, 181
  integration 10, 170, 173, 177, 181-2
professionalism 62, 123-4
professionals 1, 4-6, 17, 21, 86, 89-91, 95-6, 152, 181, 206, 241

qualification 6, 24-6, 69, 77, 79, 106, 114, 119, 121-4, 174, 181, 221-2, 248
  re- 69, 75, 80

racial 10, 53, 55, 58-61, 134, 171, 179, 181, 186-9, 192-3, 196, 204, 213-14
racialized 8, 10-11, 56, 60, 186-97, 240
racialized teacher candidates 10-11, 187, 189, 191, 194, 196-7
recertification 9, 102, 185, 248
recognition 11, 17, 43-4, 68, 72-8, 103, 110, 125, 138, 144-5, 149, 170, 174, 180, 221-2, 235, 248-9
refugee (s) 50, 67-9, 76, 81, 111, 135, 151, 154-60, 221
  students 7, 38, 86, 95, 153-4, 240
  teachers 7, 9, 49-55, 61-2, 150, 160, 236, 240, 245, 248
residency 53-4, 91, 174

self-assessment 34-7, 39, 42-3, 45
social cohesion 33-4, 37-8, 41, 44-5, 135
societies 7, 9, 34, 36, 40, 50, 61, 95-6, 135, 142, 171, 186, 223-5, 231, 234, 244
  migration 9, 95
South Africa 133-9, 142-5, 170-80
South America 232-4, 245
student
  object or subject 24-6
  mobility 52, 57
Syria 151, 159, 161, 221
Syrian refugee 7, 150, 153-60, 240
teacher
  agency 21, 150-2, 160-1
  in Austria 67, 71-8, 115
  becoming a- 18, 40, 65, 74, 211
  being a- 8, 15-29, 62, 71-2, 194, 248
  bridging programmes 102-6, 108, 110, 114-16
  career jumpers 7, 10, 119-29, 239
  displaced 7, 68-70, 76, 78
  education 5-7, 16, 18, 32, 34-8, 40-1, 45, 63, 106, 185-90, 193-7, 203-10, 212, 214, 239, 242, 249

educational personnel 150, 155
fast track 5, 8, 11, 125, 206–11, 249
identity 152
internationally educated 5, 7, 102, 107, 185, 197, 246
internationally trained 9, 239, 245–7
lateral entry- 7, 119–29
making of- 4, 34, 49, 54, 239, 246
migrant- 10, 107, 133, 136–45, 169–82, 185, 233, 239–40
preparation 11, 170, 203–14, 239, 249
professionalism 62, 123–4
recertification 9, 102, 185, 248
remaining 67, 76–7, 174, 247
training 5, 8, 40, 68, 70, 73, 116, 119, 121, 125, 128, 156–7, 172, 221, 233, 236, 239
two-tiered system 203–15
Teach for All 211–12
Teach for America (TFA) 207–12
teaching profession 4, 9, 70–2, 76–7, 102, 107, 119, 121, 123, 125, 222, 248

technicism 20, 29
translingual activism 7, 9, 103–5, 113–15
transnational 9–10, 49, 52, 54, 62, 102, 104, 107–8
Turkey 10, 32, 38, 41, 45, 150–1, 154–6, 160

United Arab Emirates 10, 169, 171, 240
United Kingdom (UK) 8, 10, 169, 171–82, 240
United States 4, 8, 11, 180, 204–6, 211–12, 215, 220, 233

violence 6, 10, 133–7, 154, 157–8, 225, 228, 231

western 11, 123, 179, 186, 188, 191–2, 197, 221–5, 227–36, 244
whiteness 211, 217, 220–5, 228

Zimbabwe 7, 140, 144–5
Zimbabwean migrant teachers 133, 136–45, 240

www.ingramcontent.com/pod-product-compliance
Lightning Source LLC
Chambersburg PA
CBHW062127300426
44115CB00012BA/1838